Grammar Source
Second Edition

RELATED TITLES

Math Source, Second Edition

Word Source, Second Edition

Writing Source, Second Edition

GRAMMAR SOURCE

Second Edition

The Smarter Way to Learn Grammar

Elizabeth Chesla

PUBLISHING

New York • Chicago

Editorial Director: Jennifer Farthing
Senior Editor: Ruth Baygell
Production Editor: Caitlin Ostrow
Production Artist: Maria Warren
Cover Designer: Carly Schnur

© 2006 by Kaplan, Inc.

Published by Kaplan Publishing, a division of Kaplan, Inc.
888 Seventh Ave.
New York, NY 10106

Printed in the United States of America

November 2006
10 9 8 7 6 5 4 3 2 1

ISBN-13: 978-1-4195-5120-8
ISBN-10: 1-4195-5120-5

Kaplan Publishing books are available at special quantity discounts to use for sales promotions, employee premiums, or educational purposes. Please call our Special Sales Department to order or for more information at 800-621-9621, ext. 4444, e-mail kaplanpubsales@kaplan.com, or write to Kaplan Publishing, 30 South Wacker Drive, Suite 2500, Chicago, IL 60606-7481.

Contents

About the Author

Elizabeth Chesla has taught writing and literature courses at colleges and universities for over twelve years. She is the author of several books on test preparation, reading comprehension, and writing. She currently writes from home in Pennsylvania in between diaper changes, ballet lessons, and soccer games for her children.

Introduction

Dear Reader,

Is your writing plagued by runaway commas? Do you find you use fifteen words for a point you could have made in three?

Whatever the reason, you picked up this book, which means you want to improve your grammar—a smart decision. Why? **Because knowing and using good grammar will get you places**. Good grammar can improve your test scores, get you hired or promoted—or simply give you more confidence when interacting with other people.

The problem is, most people have found improving their grammar a tedious process. But it doesn't have to be. Allow us to introduce the **Building Block Method**.

This teacher-approved method was devised by the experts at Kaplan to make learning as painless as possible. You'll begin with basic grammar principles. Then you'll move on to a system for learning and memorization that draws on real-life situations as practice exercises—a convenient way to learn grammar while going about your everyday life.

There's no smarter way to learn. So get started—good grammar is only a few building blocks away!

HOW TO USE THIS BOOK

The eighteen chapters in this book are divided into three sections, beginning with fundamentals, so everything else builds upon a firm foundation.

Section I: The Building Blocks of Smarter Grammar and Sentence Structure

The first nine chapters cover the fundamentals, from the most basic parts of sentences to the rules for sentence boundaries and word order.

Section II: The Building Blocks of Smarter Style and Usage

Once you've mastered sentence structure, this section reviews the fundamentals of clear and effective style, including diction, tone, and concision.

Section III: The Building Blocks of Smarter Punctuation and Mechanics

The final section reviews the rules for punctuation, capitalization, and spelling to make your sentences clear and error-free.

Whether you read this book from start to finish or only want to brush up on certain topics, you can systematically improve your skills. Each chapter contains five key components:

1. Building Block Quiz

Begin each chapter with a short quiz. The first few questions will cover material from earlier lessons; if you get them wrong, go back and review! The next seven questions will test the material to be covered in that chapter. This quiz helps reinforce what you've already learned while targeting the information on which you need to focus in each chapter. Plus, you'll get even more review from the explanations, which tell you why each answer choice is right or wrong.

2. Detailed Lessons

Each chapter explains in detail one specific grammar or style concept, with lots of relevant examples and memory aids. Remember, don't start a new chapter if you haven't mastered the earlier material—or you'll be building on a weak foundation.

3. Plentiful Practice

Repetition is the key to mastery. So be prepared to practice, practice, practice! You'll find everything from simple matching exercises to exercises that ask you to apply the skills you're learning to practical, real-life situations. By "learning from all sides," you're much more likely to retain the information.

4. Summary

Each chapter concludes with a concise review of key points.

5. Chapter Test

At the end of each chapter, you'll take a 20-question diagnostic Chapter Test, covering material in that chapter and key concepts from previous chapters. The Chapter Test will help ensure that you master each chapter before you move on to the next.

THREE BASIC PRINCIPLES

Many people are intimidated by grammar because there are so many rules to remember. But all of those rules are based on just three underlying principles:

Balance   Clarity   Consistency

Subject-verb agreement is about balance. Pronouns and verb tenses need to be consistent. Correct spelling and punctuation make your meaning clear. We'll remind you of these core principles throughout the book. By recalling them, you'll find any rule easier to learn and remember.

With a system as easy as this, good grammar is well within your reach. All you have to do is take the first step. Good luck!

SECTION I

Grammar and Sentence Structure

CHAPTER 1

The Parts of Speech

Start your study of grammar with this 10-question Building Block Quiz.

BUILDING BLOCK QUIZ

Read each sentence below and determine the part of speech of the underlined word.

1. Jack and Jill went up the hill to fetch a pail of <u>water</u>.

    (A) noun   (B) pronoun   (C) verb
    (D) interjection   (E) preposition

2. Jack <u>fell</u> down and broke his crown.

    (A) conjunction   (B) verb   (C) adjective
    (D) adverb   (E) pronoun

3. "<u>Ouch</u>!" he cried.

    (A) preposition   (B) adverb   (C) conjunction
    (D) noun   (E) interjection

4. Jill continued <u>up</u> the hill.

    (A) verb   (B) preposition   (C) adjective
    (D) noun   (E) pronoun

5. She filled the bucket and headed back to where <u>Jack</u> lay.

    (A) pronoun   (B) interjection   (C) noun
    (D) verb   (E) adverb

6. Jill balanced the bucket on <u>her</u> head as she walked.

   (A) verb   (B) conjunction   (C) adjective
   (D) pronoun   (E) preposition

7. "I thought we were a team," she said to Jack, "<u>but</u> I guess not."

   (A) conjunction   (B) adverb   (C) noun
   (D) interjection   (E) verb

8. "It seems that every time we come here, you fall, and I <u>have</u> to do all the work."

   (A) pronoun   (B) adjective   (C) noun
   (D) adverb   (E) verb

9. "Enough is enough!" she said <u>angrily</u>.

   (A) conjunction   (B) adjective   (C) adverb
   (D) preposition   (E) interjection

10. And she dumped the entire pail of <u>ice-cold</u> water on Jack's head.

    (A) noun   (B) adjective   (C) pronoun
    (D) conjunction   (E) adverb

Answers and Explanations

1.   A

A noun is a person, place, or thing. *Water* is a thing.

2.   B

Verbs express action or a state of being. *Fell* is an action.

3.   E

Ouch! expresses pain. An interjection is a short, usually emotional, word or phrase that can stand alone as a sentence.

4.   B

Prepositions express the relationship (often, but not always, in time or space) between two words. *Up* is a preposition showing the spatial relationship between the verb and the hill.

5.   C

Jack is a person, therefore a noun.

6.   D

Pronouns most often replace nouns or other pronouns. *Her* replaces the noun *Jill*.

7.   A

Conjunctions connect words or parts of sentences. *But* connects the independent clauses *I thought we were a team* and *I guess not.* In the first sentence, *and* joins *Jack* and *Jill.*

8.   E

Have is a verb expressing a state of being. *Come* is a verb expressing action.

9.   C

Adverbs modify or describe verbs, adjectives, and other adverbs. *Angrily* modifies the verb *said*, telling us how Jill spoke.

10.   B

Adjectives modify or describe nouns or pronouns. *Ice-cold* describes the noun *water*.

We begin this book with a thorough review of the parts of speech— what they are, how they work, and why they matter. Basic? Yes. Essential? You bet.

In this and every other chapter, if you aced the Building Block Quiz, congratulations—chances are you already know most of the material in the chapter. Make sure you've mastered the material by taking the Chapter 1 Test. If that goes just as well, by all means, move on! If not, find the sections in the lesson that cover your weaknesses. Do the practice exercises to sharpen your skills and then head on to the next chapter.

FORM AND FUNCTION

Words are the building blocks of sentences: we string them together in endless combinations of phrases, clauses, and sentences to express our ideas.

GRAMMAR SPEAK

A **phrase** is a related group of words that *does not* contain both a subject and a verb (though it may contain either).

A **clause** is a related group of words that *does* contain both a subject and a verb. An **independent clause** expresses a complete thought and can stand alone as a sentence. A **subordinate clause** cannot stand by itself; it depends on another clause to complete its meaning.

Each word serves a particular *function* within a phrase, clause, or sentence. A word might describe, name, or connect; it might show the relationship between two ideas or express emotion. A word's function can affect the *form* it will take as well as its placement. So the parts of speech are much more than just another list of things to memorize; they are the foundation of grammar.

Take the word *beauty*, for instance. Its noun form is *beauty,* the thing. If you change its part of speech, you change its form and its function in a sentence:

	Form	Function	Example
Noun	beauty	name a thing	I am overwhelmed by your beauty.
Verb	beautify	express an action	Flowers will beautify this abandoned lot.
Adjective	beautiful	describe a noun or pronoun	You are so beautiful.

However, not all words change form when they change part of speech.

Adjective:	Hermione is a <u>model</u> student.
Noun:	Hermione earns her tuition money by working as a hand <u>model</u>.
Verb:	Hermione will <u>model</u> her roommate's designs in the student fashion show.
Verb:	I am <u>cooking</u> Thanksgiving dinner for the family this year.
Noun:	I enjoy <u>cooking</u>.
Adjective:	The <u>cooking</u> class has been cancelled.

NOUNS

Function

Nouns name a person, place, or thing.

Form

- Nouns can be **singular** (*tree, glass*) or **plural** (*trees, glasses*). Most plurals are formed by adding *–s* or *–es*.
- **Collective** nouns (also called **group** nouns), name a class or a group—a single entity composed of more than one unit (e.g., *team, faculty, series*). They are usually treated as singular (one *team* vs. the plural, two *teams*).
- **Concrete** nouns name tangible things (things you can experience directly with your senses: *spider, motorcycle, contract*) and **abstract** nouns name an idea or quality (things you can't experience with your senses: *love, apathy, peace*).
- **Proper** nouns refer to *specific* people, places, or things: *Albert Einstein, the Milky Way, Middletown Academy*; **common** nouns refer to *general* people, places, or things: *scientist, galaxy, high school*.

MEMORY TIP

To remember what a noun is, try this mnemonic: *noun* rhymes with *Johnstown*. *John* is a person, *Johnstown* is a place, and *town* is a thing.

Practice 1

In the paragraph below, determine whether each underlined word is or is not a noun.

One of the most well-known fairy tales is "Little Red <u>Riding Hood</u>."
yes / no

There are hundreds of <u>versions</u> of this story throughout the <u>world</u>.
yes / no yes / no

In the <u>most</u> popular version in <u>America</u>, Little <u>Red</u> Riding Hood is
yes / no yes / no yes / no

saved by a woodsman, who <u>cuts</u> her out of the wolf's <u>belly</u>. In other
yes / no yes / no

versions, Little Red Riding Hood <u>tricks</u> the wolf into letting her out.
yes / no

I find these versions <u>more</u> satisfying, because <u>Little Red Riding Hood</u>
yes / no yes / no

saves herself through her own <u>ingenuity</u> rather than being <u>rescued</u>
yes / no yes / no

by someone else.

PRONOUNS

Function

Pronouns take the place of or refer to one or more nouns (and sometimes whole phrases or clauses, which we'll cover later in this chapter).

Form

There are six main types of pronouns:

Personal pronouns refer to specific people or things: *I love you.*	*Singular*: I, me, you, she, her, he, him, it *Plural*: we, us, you, they, them
Possessive pronouns indicate ownership: *This is my house.*	*Singular*: my, mine, your, yours, her, hers, his, its *Plural*: our, ours, your, yours, their, theirs
Reflexive pronouns indicate that the person or thing that performs the action also receives the action: *I hurt myself.*	*Singular*: myself, yourself, himself, herself, itself *Plural*: ourselves, yourselves, themselves
Relative pronouns introduce subordinate clauses that modify a noun or pronoun in the sentence: *Annette is the one who came up with the idea.*	who, whom, whose, which, that
Demonstrative pronouns identify or point to specific nouns: *This is my house.*	this, that, these, those
Indefinite pronouns refer to non-specific people or things: *Has anybody seen my keys?*	all, another, any, anybody, anyone, anything, both, each, either, everybody, everyone, everything, few, many, neither, none, nobody, no one, nothing, one, several, some, somebody, someone, something
Interrogative pronouns introduce questions: *What is going on here?*	who, whom, whose, which, what

Rachel let me borrow her old wig so no one will recognize me at the party. Now this is more like it!

The words *this, that, these, those* and some of the indefinite pronouns can also be adjectives. The test is whether they are alone (and therefore replacing a noun) or precede a noun (and therefore modify that noun).

Adjective: This soup is delicious! (*This* modifies *soup*.)

Pronoun: This is delicious! (*This* replaces the noun *soup*.)

Adjective: All dogs go to heaven. (*All* modifies *dogs*.)

Pronouns: Justice for all. (*All* replaces *the people*.)

Practice 2

Find and underline the nine words functioning as pronouns in the paragraph below.

One of the most well-known fairy tales is "Little Red Riding Hood." There are hundreds of versions of this story throughout the world. In the most popular version in America, Little Red Riding Hood is saved by a woodsman, who cuts her out of the wolf's belly. In other versions, Little Red Riding Hood tricks the wolf into letting her out. I find these more satisfying, because Little Red Riding Hood saves herself through her own ingenuity rather than being rescued by someone else.

VERBS

Function

Verbs express an action or state of being.

Form

Verb forms change depending upon the **person(s)** performing the action and the **tense** (when the action takes/took/will take place). You'll review verb forms and tenses in chapters 3 and 4.

In all tenses except the present and past, the **verb** consists of several words, the base, which expresses the main action or state of being, and one or more **helping verbs,** which help indicate the tense (as well as voice or mood, which we'll see in chapters 3 and 4).

In the following examples, helping verbs are underlined once, the form of the base verb twice:

> I <u>am</u> exhausted!
> I <u>am</u> <u>having</u> a great time.
> You <u>should have</u> <u>been</u> more careful.
> We <u>did</u> not <u>know</u> that you <u>were</u> <u>coming</u>.
> The evidence <u>does</u> not <u>support</u> your accusations.
> We <u>will</u> <u>certify</u> that these documents <u>are</u> real.

Note that *am* is the base verb in the first sentence and a helping verb in the second. Forms of *be*, *do*, and *have* can be either helping verbs or base verbs. In the meantime, consider the function: is it describing the action of the sentence, or is it helping to indicate the tense—when the action takes place?

Practice 3

Underline the verbs in the following sentences, putting one line under <u>helping verbs</u> and two under <u>base verbs</u>. Only underline verbs that are functioning as verbs.

1. Look before you leap.
2. Don't count your chickens before they hatch.
3. Those who live in glass houses should not throw stones.
4. The early bird catches the worm.
5. You will reap what you sow.
6. Good things come to those who wait.
7. Do unto others as you would have done unto you.
8. Sticks and stones will break my bones, but words will never hurt me.
9. A watched pot never boils.
10. Rome was not built in a day.

ADJECTIVES

Function

Adjectives describe or modify nouns and pronouns. They tell us which one, what kind, or how many.

> Talk is <u>cheap</u>. (*Cheap* describes the noun *talk*.)
>
> What an <u>outrageous</u> accusation! (*Outrageous* describes the noun *accusation*.)
>
> There are <u>several</u> problems with this proposal. (*Several* describes the noun *problems*.)
>
> You are so <u>patient</u> with your children. (*Patient* describes the pronoun *you*.)

Form

Adjectives don't take a specific form because just about any kind of word can function as an adjective:

> He is a <u>book</u> aficionado. (What kind of aficionado? *Book*. Here, *book* is not a thing but a modifier.)
>
> Follow <u>that</u> car! (Which car? *That* one. *That* doesn't replace a noun; it describes one.)
>
> Please grab the <u>baking</u> powder from the pantry. (What kind of powder? *Baking* powder. *Baking* isn't an action but a description.)

Practice 4

In each sentence that follows, determine which word, if any, is an adjective.

1. Meet me at the farmers' market.
2. Gala apples are in season.
3. I'll buy two dozen of them.
4. Who is that woman?
5. That smarts!
6. Elena is very smart.
7. She's also a very likeable person.
8. I am a musician.
9. Pigs are rather docile animals.
10. I've never seen a more egregious error.

ADVERBS

Function

Adverbs describe or modify verbs, adjectives, and other adverbs. They tell us when, where, how, and why; under what conditions; and to what degree.

Notice the difference between adjectives and adverbs, which are commonly confused:

Adjective: I am very <u>patient</u>. (*Patient* modifies the pronoun *I*.)

Adverb: I am waiting <u>patiently</u>. (*Patiently* tells us how I am *waiting*.)

Here are more examples of adverbs:

You will feel <u>better</u> <u>soon</u>. (*Better* modifies the verb *feel* and tells us how. *Soon* modifies *feel better* and tells us when.)

He talks <u>so</u> <u>rapidly</u> that I can <u>hardly</u> understand him. (*Rapidly* modifies the verb *talks* and tells us how. *So* modifies the adverb *rapidly* and also tells us how. *Hardly* modifies the verb *understand* and tells us to what degree.)

Form

Adverbs come in different shapes and sizes: *yesterday, very, clearly, never*. Many adverbs are formed by adding *–ly* to adjectives (e.g., *happy → happily, slow → slowly*).

MEMORY TIP

To remember the difference between adjectives and adverbs, note that adjectives modify nouns or pronouns, while **ad**verbs modify verbs as well as **ad**jectives and other **ad**verbs.

Practice 5

Find and underline the adverbs in the following sentences.

1. Speak softly and carry a big stick.
2. Never say never.
3. Love your children unconditionally.
4. Treat yourself well and be happy.
5. You are what you eat, so choose your foods wisely.
6. Don't be so modest!
7. History often repeats itself.
8. Your spot has already been taken.
9. Just yesterday I finished the second novel in the trilogy.
10. We are desperately trying to get an answer.

PREPOSITIONS

Function

Prepositions express the relationship (often in time or space) between two words in a sentence. Prepositions include:

about	before	in	out	under
above	behind	inside	outside	underneath
across	below	into	over	unlike
after	beside	like	past	until
against	between	near	since	unto
along	by	next	through	up
among	despite	of	throughout	upon
around	during	off	till	with
as	for	on	to	within
at	from	onto	toward	without

Form

Prepositions always come in **prepositional phrases** beginning with the preposition and ending with a noun or pronoun. Prepositional phrases usually modify the first word (a noun or verb) in the relationship:

> Please put the book _on the table_.

On is the preposition; *on the table* is the prepositional phrase showing the relationship between the verb *put* (the first word in the relationship) and *table* (the second). It answers the question *where*, so it functions as an adverb.

> We were lost _in the woods_ for hours.

In is the preposition; *in the woods* is the prepositional phrase. The preposition here shows the relationship between *lost* and *woods* and also tells us where. Here are more examples:

> _During_ the show, I fell asleep _in_ my chair.
>
> Bring your registration form _with_ you.
>
> Go _through_ the tunnel, then turn left _at_ the light.

Practice 6

Underline the ten prepositional phrases in the following sentences.

In the bottom of the ninth inning, Moses Jones hit a line drive into left field. Ollie Wilkins raced to third and Javier Mercado scored, sliding into home just before the tag. Behind his glove, pitcher Dennis Delaney spit on the ball. It spun wildly over home plate, but Willie Thomas sent the ball sailing out of the park.

CONJUNCTIONS

Function

Conjunctions join two or more parts of sentences—words, phrases, or clauses—and express the relationship between those parts.

Form

There are four kinds of conjunctions, each with a very specific function:

Coordinating Conjunctions

Coordinating conjunctions connect grammatically equivalent elements (words, phrases, or clauses). There are only seven coordinating conjunctions: *and, or, nor, for, but, so,* and *yet.* The grammatically equivalent elements are bracketed in the sample sentences below.

> We are [ready] <u>and</u> [willing] to go.
>
> Hang your coat [in the closet] <u>or</u> [on the door].
>
> [I would like to go], <u>but</u> [I can't].
>
> [Sam is working today], <u>so</u> [he can't go either].

Remember, coordinating conjunctions work with *equivalent* parts; they can connect two words, phrases, or independent words, phrases, or clauses, but not an independent clause and a dependent clause.

MEMORY TIP

Coordinating conjunctions connect grammatically equivalent elements. You can remember it this way: a *coordinated* outfit has *matching* clothes; a *coordinating conjunction* connects *matching* grammatical elements.

Correlative Conjunctions

Correlative conjunctions are the *either/or, not only/but also* pairs. They also connect grammatically equivalent elements and include the following:

both…and	neither…nor
not only…but also	whether…or
not…but	as…as
either…or	

You will <u>either</u> wash the dishes <u>or</u> dry them and put them away.

Not <u>only</u> is he handsome, <u>but</u> he's <u>also</u> brilliant.

<u>Whether</u> you like it <u>or</u> not, I'm coming with you!

Subordinating Conjunctions

Subordinating conjunctions are adverbs that introduce subordinate clauses. They're distinct from "regular" adverbs because they connect subordinate and independent clauses, showing the relationship between the two:

[We'll go outside] [<u>when</u> it stops raining].

[Independent clause][subordinate clause]

When connects the two clauses and shows the relationship between them (one action will take place after the other).

Subordinating conjunctions include the following:

after	even if	now that	that	where
although	even though	once	though	wherever
as	how	rather than	unless	whether
as if	if	since	until	while
because	if only	so that	when	
before	in order that	than	whenever	

In the examples below, the subordinating conjunctions are underlined and the subordinate clauses are bracketed. Notice that the subordinate clauses cannot stand alone because they do not express a complete thought.

[<u>Because</u> the proposal is due tomorrow], we need to finish it as soon as possible.

I'll cancel my meeting [<u>so that</u> we can have lunch together.]

We'll work on the proposal [<u>while</u> we eat.]

After lunch, we can return to my office, [<u>where</u> we'll try to finish up.]

[<u>After</u> we've submitted the proposal,] we'll go out to celebrate.

Notice that in the second to last example, *after* is simply a preposition, not a subordinating conjunction; *after lunch* is a prepositional phrase, not a subordinate clause. In the last sentence, however, *after* does introduce a subordinate clause, so it functions as a subordinating conjunction.

Conjunctive Adverbs

Conjunctive adverbs introduce independent clauses. They're distinct from "regular" adverbs because they connect clauses and show the relationship between them:

> I mixed the colors over and over; <u>finally</u>, I got the exact shade I was looking for.

Finally introduces the second independent clause and shows its relationship to the first.

The most common conjunctive adverbs are:

as a result	furthermore	nevertheless	thus
consequently	however	similarly	
finally	moreover	therefore	

> You cheated; <u>therefore</u>, you are disqualified from the race. (*Therefore* introduces an independent clause and shows its relationship to the previous clause.)

Notice how this is different from a subordinating conjunction introducing a subordinate clause:

> <u>Because</u> you cheated, you are disqualified from the race.

The independent clause *therefore, you are disqualified from the race* can stand alone, but the dependent (subordinate) clause *because you cheated* cannot.

Here are more examples of sentences with conjunctive adverbs:

> It may seem as if you have no choice; <u>however</u>, there are actually many options.
> Although hybrid cars are more expensive, they are more cost effective in the long run. <u>Moreover</u>, they are much better for the environment. (Notice the subordinating conjunction *although* introducing the initial subordinating clause.)

You'll need to know these four kinds of clauses because they have specific functions; you can't use a conjunctive adverb when you need a coordinating conjunction. Still, the bottom line is this: these words *connect* and show the relationship between words, phrases, or clauses.

Here are the four conjunctions and their functions in a nutshell:

Type	Function	Examples
coordinating	connects equal parts	*and, or, for*
correlative	connects equal parts	*either/or*
subordinating	connects a subordinate clause to an independent clause	*although, if, because*
adverb	connects an independent clause to the preceding clause	*however, thus*

Practice 7

Underline the conjunctions in the following sentences (some have more than one). Underneath each, write which type of conjunction it is: coord (coordinating), corr (correlative), sub (subordinating), or conj (conjunctive adverb).

Example: The game is tied, <u>so</u> it'll go into overtime.
coord

1. I'll say yes, even though I should know better than to listen to you.

2. I want to believe you, but I can't.

3. Children are neither as naïve nor as innocent as we like to think.

4. The battle was over, and the general was soundly defeated, yet he still believed the attack was a victory.

5. I will come along for moral support; however, I'm warning you, if you try to get me involved, I will leave.

6. We've had bad experiences the last two times we ate at Café Café; therefore, we've decided to move our weekly brunch to Kate's Kitchen.

INTERJECTIONS

Function

Interjections are sudden, usually emotional words or phrases that can stand alone as sentences.

Form

Interjections can be a single word or a short phrase. They are almost always followed by an exclamation point.

Hey! Look out! Egads! Holy cow! Unbelievable!

Practice 8

Write three sentences with interjections.

SUMMARY

When it comes to parts of speech, the key is to look at *what the word is doing* in the sentence.

Part of Speech	Function	Examples	Notes
Noun	Name a person, place, or thing.	book, Ali, infatuation	Nouns can be **singular** or **plural**, **concrete** (tangible) or **abstract** (intangible), **proper** (a specific person, place or thing) or **common** (general), and **collective** (a group functioning as a unit, such as *team*).
Pronoun	Replace or point to a noun.	me, you, them, that	There are **personal** (*I, me, them*), **possessive** (*mine, ours*), **reflexive** (*yourself, ourselves*), **relative** (*that, which, who*), **demonstrative** (*this, that*), and **indefinite** (*anybody, no one*) pronouns.

Verb	Express action or state of being.	believe, juggle, float	**Base verbs** express the main action of the sentence. **Helping verbs** help indicate the tense of the base verb.
Adjective	Modify a noun or pronoun.	thoughtful, noisy, inquisitive	
Adverb	Modify a verb, adjective, or other adverb.	hardly, boldly, very, never	
Preposition	Express a relationship (often in time or space) between two words	in, under, over, around, through	
Conjunction	Join parts of sentences and express the relationship between those parts.	and, for, yet; either/or; because, since; however, therefore	Four types: **coordinating** and **correlative conjunctions** (connect equal parts), **subordinating conjunctions** (introduce subordinate clauses) and **conjunctive adverbs** (introduce independent clauses).
Interjection	Express surprise or emotion.	Hey! Ouch! Oh no!	

Practice: On Your Own

Choose an article in your favorite newspaper or magazine, a page in the book you're reading, or even a letter you receive in the mail. Spend some time reading it carefully and looking for the eight parts of speech you reviewed in this chapter. Do you see all four types of conjunctions? Do you see helping verbs and base verbs working together?

Practice Answers and Explanations

Practice 1

Hood, versions, world, America, belly, Little Red Riding Hood, and *ingenuity* are nouns. *America* and *Little Red Riding Hood* are proper nouns. All of these nouns are concrete except *ingenuity,* which is abstract.

Riding is an adjective describing *Hood.* (As a complete phrase, *Little Red Riding Hood* is a noun; otherwise, *little, red* and *riding* all describe *hood.*) *Most* is an adverb modifying *well-known. Red* is an adjective modifying *Hood. Cuts* and *tricks* are both verbs in this paragraph. *More* is an adverb modifying *satisfying. Rescued* is a verb.

Practice 2

<u>One</u> of the most well-known fairy tales is "Little Red Riding Hood." There are hundreds of versions of this story throughout the world. In the most popular version in America, Little Red Riding Hood is saved by a woodsman, <u>who</u> cuts <u>her</u> out of the wolf's belly. In other versions, Little Red Riding Hood tricks the wolf into letting <u>her</u> out. I find <u>these</u> more satisfying, because Little Red Riding Hood saves <u>herself</u> through <u>her</u> own ingenuity rather than being rescued by <u>someone</u> else.

This functions as an adjective because it immediately precedes and points to the noun *story. These* replaces *versions in which Red saves herself,* so it functions as a pronoun.

Practice 3

1. <u>Look</u> before you <u>leap</u>.
2. <u>Don</u>'t <u>count</u> your chickens before they <u>hatch</u>.
3. Those who <u>live</u> in glass houses <u>should</u> not <u>throw</u> stones.
4. The early bird <u>catches</u> the worm.
5. You <u>will</u> <u>reap</u> what you <u>sow</u>.
6. Good things <u>come</u> to those who <u>wait</u>.
7. <u>Do</u> unto others as you <u>would have</u> <u>done</u> unto you. (*Do* can be a helping verb, but here it is the main action of the sentence.)
8. Sticks and stones <u>will</u> <u>break</u> my bones, but words <u>will</u> never <u>hurt</u> me.
9. A watched pot never <u>boils</u>. (*Watched* is functioning as an adjective; it describes the kind of pot rather than an action.)
10. Rome <u>was</u> not <u>built</u> in a day.

Practice 4

1. *Farmers'* describes *market*.
2. *Gala* describes *apples*.
3. *Two* modifies *dozen*.
4. *That* modifies *woman*.
5. No adjective. Here, *that* is a relative pronoun replacing an unspecified noun.
6. *Smart* describes *Elena*. (Notice that *smarts* in sentence 5 is a verb.)
7. *Likeable* describes *she*.
8. No adjective. Even though *musician* tells us something about *I*, it is still a noun naming a thing.
9. *Docile* modifies *animals*. Even if you don't know what *docile* means, you should see that it functions as an adjective, telling what kind of animals they are.
10. *Egregious* modifies *error*. If you don't know what *egregious* means, you should still see that it describes *error*.

Practice 5

1. *Softly* modifies the verb *speak*. (*Big* is an adjective modifying *stick*.)
2. *Never* is an adverb telling us when.
3. *Unconditionally* modifies the verb *love*.
4. *Well* modifies the verb *treat*. (*Happy* is an adjective modifying the unstated subject of the sentence, *you*.)
5. *Wisely* is an adverb modifying the verb *choose*.
6. *So* modifies the adjective *modest*.
7. *Often* modifies the verb *repeats* and tells us when.
8. *Already* modifies the verb *taken*.
9. *Just* modifies the adverb *yesterday*. Both tell us when.
10. *Desperately* modifies the verb *trying*.

Practice 6

<u>In the bottom</u> of the ninth inning, Moses Jones hit a line drive <u>into left field</u>. Ollie Wilkins raced <u>to third</u> and Javier Mercado scored, sliding <u>into home</u> just <u>before the tag</u>. <u>Behind his glove,</u> pitcher Dennis Delaney spit <u>on the ball</u>. It spun wildly <u>over home plate,</u> but Willie Thomas sent the ball sailing <u>out of the park</u>.

Practice 7

1. *Even though* is a subordinating conjunction introducing a subordinate clause.
2. *But* is a coordinating conjunction connecting two independent clauses.
3. *Neither...nor* is a correlative conjunction.
4. *And* and *yet* are both coordinating conjunctions connecting independent clauses.
5. *However* is a conjunctive adverb introducing an independent clause. *If* is a subordinating conjunction introducing a subordinate clause.
6. *Therefore* is a conjunctive adverb introducing an independent clause.

Practice 8

Answers will vary. Some possibilities are: *Hurry! Yo! What! Uh-oh! Wow! Yikes!*

CHAPTER 1 TEST

Old Mother Hubbard <u>went</u> to the cupboard to fetch her <u>poor</u> doggie
                  1   2

a <u>bone</u>. <u>When</u> she got there, the cupboard was <u>completely</u> <u>bare</u>. "<u>Drat!</u>"
   3   4   5   6   7

said Old Mother Hubbard. "<u>This</u> won't <u>do</u>!" "No, it won't," said the dog,
                                 8   9

who then had Mother Hubbard <u>for</u> dinner.
                           10

<u>Little</u> Miss Muffet sat <u>on</u> a tuffet, eating her <u>curds</u> and whey. Along
 11   12   13

came a spider <u>who</u> sat down <u>beside her</u> and said, "<u>Boo!</u>" "Sorry, Spidey.
           14   15   16

<u>Your</u> scaring days are over," Miss Muffet replied <u>calmly</u>, <u>and</u> <u>dumped</u>
 17   18 19 20

her curds and whey on the spider.

Directions: Each underlined word or phrase in the foregoing paragraphs is one of the following. Write the correct choice under the word, using the most specific choice available (subcategories are indented).

(A) adjective
(B) adverb
(C) conjunction
  (D) coordinating
      conjunction
  (E) correlative
      conjunction
  (F) subordinating
      conjunction
  (G) conjunctive adverb
(H) interjection
(I) noun
  (J) collective noun
  (K) proper noun

(L) preposition
(M) prepositional phrase
(N) pronoun
  (O) demonstrative
      pronoun
  (P) indefinite pronoun
  (Q) possessive pronoun
  (R) relative pronoun
(S) verb
  (T) helping verb

Answers and Explanations

1. S

Went is a verb expressing action.

2. A

Poor is an adjective describing *doggie*.

3. I

Bone is a noun—a thing.

4. F

When is a subordinating conjunction introducing the subordinate clause *when she got there*.

5. B

Completely is an adverb describing the adjective *bare*.

6. A

Bare is an adjective modifying *cupboard*.

7. H

Drat! is an interjection expressing emotion.

8. O

This is a demonstrative pronoun. It replaces the noun phrase *bare cupboard*.

9. S

Do is the verb expressing the main action of the clause.

10. L

For is a preposition showing the relationship between *Mother Hubbard* and *dinner*.

11. A

Little is an adjective modifying *Miss Muffet*.

12. L

On is a preposition showing the relationship between the verb *sat* and *tuffet*.

13. I

Curds is a noun, a thing.

14. R

Who is a relative pronoun referring to *spider*.

15. M

Beside her is a prepositional phrase showing the spatial relationship between the verb *sat* and *her*.

16. H

Boo! is an interjection.

17. Q

Your is a possessive pronoun.

18. B

Calmly is an adverb modifying the verb *replied*.

19. D

And is a coordinating conjunction connecting the verbs *replied* and *dumped*.

20. S

Dumped is a verb expressing action.

CHAPTER 2

Sentence Parts and Patterns

Start with this 10-question Building Block Quiz. The first few questions test material you've already seen.

BUILDING BLOCK QUIZ

Read the sentence below carefully, paying particular attention to sentence parts and structure. Then answer the questions that follow.

> Money will buy a pretty good dog, but it will not buy the wag of its tail. —*Josh Billings*

1. The word <u>pretty</u> is a/an

   (A) noun   (B) pronoun   (C) adjective

   (D) adverb   (E) conjunction

2. The words <u>of its tail</u> constitute a/an

   (A) prepositional phrase

   (B) independent clause

   (C) subordinate clause

   (D) correlative conjunction

   (E) verb phrase

3. The word <u>but</u> is a/an

   (A) preposition

   (B) adverb

   (C) coordinating conjunction

   (D) conjunctive adverb

   (E) subordinating conjunction

4. Which of the following is the subject of its clause?
   (A) money   (B) dog   (C) but   (D) wag   (E) tail

5. Which of the following is a base verb of this sentence?
   (A) will   (B) buy   (C) not   (D) wag   (E) tail

6. The words <u>will buy a pretty good dog</u> constitute a/an
   (A) prepositional phrase   (B) subject   (C) predicate
   (D) subordinate clause   (E) subject complement

7. The word <u>buy</u> is a/an
   (A) linking verb
   (B) helping verb
   (C) intransitive verb
   (D) direct object
   (E) transitive verb

8. The word <u>dog</u> is a/an
   (A) direct object   (B) indirect object   (C) subject
   (D) complement   (E) predicate

9. <u>Money will buy a pretty good dog</u> is a/an
   (A) prepositional phrase
   (B) predicate
   (C) subject complement
   (D) independent clause
   (E) subordinate clause

10. This is which type of sentence?
   (A) simple   (B) compound   (C) complex
   (D) compound-complex   (E) imperative

Answers and Explanations

1.   D

Pretty is an adverb modifying the adjective *good* and telling *how* good. It's also an example of informal language (see chapter 11).

2.   A

Of its tail is a prepositional phrase; *of* is the preposition.

3.   C

But is a coordinating conjunction connecting the two independent clauses *Money will buy a pretty good dog* and *it will not buy the wag of its tail.*

4.   A

Money is the subject of the first clause. (*It* is the subject of the second; *it* replaces the noun *money*.)

5.   B

Buy is the base verb, and *will* is a helping verb, in each of the clauses that constitute this sentence.

6.   C

Will buy a pretty good dog is the predicate of the first clause. The predicate is the verb and any complements, modifiers, or phrases that follow.

7.   E

Buy is a transitive verb; it takes an object. Here the object is *a pretty good dog*.

8.   A

Dog is the direct object of the sentence; it is what is bought.

9.   D

Money will buy a pretty good dog has a subject and a verb and can stand alone, so it's an independent clause.

10.   B

This is a compound sentence consisting of two independent clauses and no subordinate clauses.

Imagine a house in which the front door opens into a closet. To get to the kitchen, you have to go through the attic; the windows are all in the corners. It might have all the right elements, but they're not in the right place.

Now imagine a house that has its kitchen without any floor—or a house with a proper foyer and hallway but without doors. The pieces may be where they belong, but essential pieces are missing.

To be functional, a house—whatever its size or style—must have certain basic elements joined in a logical way. The same goes for sentences; they may come in different sizes and styles, but they must contain the same basic elements and follow certain patterns. This chapter will review sentence types and structure. First, a definition:

> A **sentence** is a series of words that (1) contains a **subject** and a **predicate** and (2) expresses a **complete thought**.

DISCLAIMER

Just about every rule you read in this book can and will be broken. English grammar is *full* of exceptions. So when we say that every sentence has a subject and a verb, we mean it—mostly. An interjection like *Wow!*, for example, is a special kind of sentence.

WHAT IT'S ALL ABOUT: THE SUBJECT

The **subject** of a sentence is *who* or *what* the sentence is about. You can usually find the subject by asking who or what carries out the action of the sentence:

<u>I</u> love to paint.	*Who* loves to paint? *I.*
On Wednesdays and Fridays, <u>Pearl</u> and <u>Jasmine</u> attend karate class.	*Who* attends karate class? *Pearl* and *Jasmine.*
<u>Absolute power</u> corrupts absolutely.	*What* corrupts absolutely? *Absolute power.*
<u>Remaining silent</u> can be just as destructive as telling a lie.	*What* can be just as destructive? *Remaining silent.*

As you can see, the subject usually comes before the verb (what the subject is or does or has done to it). Subject-verb is the word order we expect in the English sentence, the rhythm of our language. Most of the time. There are three exceptions:

- when writers invert the order for effect
- when sentences begin with *there is/are, it is/they are* or *was/were*
- questions

Sorry are <u>we</u> who pretend to be what we are not.	Who or what is sorry? *We* are.
There is <u>no excuse</u> for your behavior.	Who or what is there? *No excuse.*
Do <u>you</u> really believe in UFOs?	Who believes? *You.*
No <u>applications</u> will be accepted after July 15.	What will not be accepted? *Applications.*

Understood Subjects

Do your homework!

Who or what does the homework? The subject is *understood* to be *you*. This is an **imperative** sentence—it gives advice or issues a command:

Please feed the dog.

Try the delicious fried calamari!

FLASHBACK

A **phrase** is a related group of words that *does not* contain both a subject and a verb. A **clause** is a related group of words that *does* contain both a subject and a verb. An **independent clause** expresses a complete thought and can stand alone as a sentence. A **subordinate clause** depends on another clause to complete its meaning.

Practice 1

Underline the subject in each of the following sentences.

1. A watched pot never boils.
2. Every evening, the sun sets over these hills.
3. There are strange goings-on around here these days.
4. What are you doing?
5. Ever since childhood, Lukas has been very artistic.
6. Choose your friends carefully!

Kinds of Subjects

The **simple** subject is the subject minus any modifiers or articles (*a/an, the*). The **complete** subject is the subject with its modifiers and articles:

> **Simple:** The old yellow <u>house</u> on Turner Road is being demolished tomorrow.

> **Complete:** <u>The old yellow house on Turner Road</u> is being demolished tomorrow.

The simple subject can be a single word, a phrase (a group of words without a subject and verb), or a clause (a group of words containing both a subject and verb):

> **One word:** There's a <u>rabbit</u> in your hat.

> **Phrase:** <u>The phrase "once in a blue moon"</u> means every two and a half years.

> **Clause:** <u>What you just said</u> was the best thing anyone has ever said to me.

These subjects are still simple (even though there's more than one word).

Single and Compound Subjects

Subjects can be **single** (one person or thing) or **compound** (two or more people or things).

> **Single subject:** <u>Donovan</u> has entered the contest.

> **Compound subject:** <u>Donovan</u>, <u>Ivan</u> and <u>Melissa</u> have entered the contest.

Single subject: <u>Chimpanzees</u> have highly complex social structures.

Compound subject: <u>Chimpanzees</u> or <u>gorillas</u> have highly complex social structures.

When a compound subject is joined by "and" the subject is plural; when it is joined by "or" it is singular if the last item is singular and plural if the last item is plural.

GRAMMAR SPEAK

Don't confuse *singular* with *single*: a single subject is **one** subject performing the action, but that subject can be plural: *The <u>cats</u> were chased up the tree.*

Practice 2

Underline the complete subject in the sentences below. Is the subject single or compound?

1. Unfortunately, Carlos and Jude did not get along well.
2. Thinking of you is my favorite pastime.
3. Unlike Lucinda, I do believe in miracles.
4. There are many false claims and exaggerated truths during a political campaign.
5. No termites or carpenter ants were found by the inspector.

Where the Subject Is—and Isn't

Because most subjects come before the verb, we usually find them towards the beginning of a sentence. But sometimes one or more words or phrases precede the subject:

Honestly, <u>I</u> did not lie to you.

In the middle of the hottest day of the hottest summer on record, <u>Kiku</u> was born.

If you're having trouble identifying the subject, look for the verb. Then, see who or what performs that action. Who didn't lie? *I* didn't. Who was born? *Kiku*.

Sometimes words or phrases—especially those that come between subjects and verbs—impede your search for the subject. Here's a helpful rule:

REMEMBER THIS!
Subjects are never in prepositional phrases.

Prepositional phrases—like adverbial and adjectival phrases—are not part of the core sentence. You can eliminate them and still have a completely coherent thought:

Memories, like diamonds, are imperfect.

Both *memories* and *diamonds are imperfect*, but *memories* is the subject. *Diamonds* is part of the prepositional phrase *like diamonds;* we can take that phrase out and still have our core sentence. Without *memories*, on the other hand, the sentence wouldn't make sense:

Memories are imperfect.   Like diamonds are imperfect.

In the following sentences, we've bracketed and crossed out prepositional phrases to eliminate other candidates for the subject:

Honestly, I did not lie [to you.]

[In the middle] [of the hottest day] [of the hottest summer] [on record], Kiku was born.

Practice 3
Underline the subject(s) in the following sentences.

1. With my costume on, I won't be recognizable.
2. The boys on the baseball team planned a surprise party for their coach.
3. Raj, terrified of making a mistake, would not raise his hand in class.
4. The gym in the school is in serious disrepair.
5. The color of these walls is quite soothing.

MEET THE PREDICATES

The **predicate** of a sentence is the verb and anything that logically belongs with it—the objects, modifiers, or complements (we'll define these shortly). The predicate usually ends the English sentence. In the sentences below, complete subjects are underlined and predicates are in brackets:

I [love to paint.]

Pearl and Jasmine [attend karate class on Wednesdays and Fridays.]

Remaining silent [can be just as destructive as telling a lie.]

> **GRAMMAR SPEAK**
>
> The **subject** is who or what the sentence is about (who or what performs or receives the action). The **predicate** is the verb and any objects, complements, or modifiers.

Predicates can be single or compound. A compound predicate has the same subject for two or more different verbs:

Single predicate:

A good neighbor [helps when asked].

Compound predicate:

A good neighbor [helps when asked] and [asks for help].

Practice 4

Put a slash (/) between the subject and predicate in each sentence.

Example: The Willow River / floods every spring.

1. For many years, the Republic of Congo was a colony of Belgium.
2. Contrary to popular belief, most species of snakes are not poisonous.
3. The most popular fruit worldwide is the mango.
4. The African continent is full of rich natural resources, including diamonds and oil.
5. Have you heard the news?

Predicates and Sentence Patterns

As you've seen, the basic English sentence pattern is subject-predicate. Predicates come in different shapes and sizes, forming four main sentence patterns:

s-v:	subject - verb
s-lv-c:	subject - linking verb - complement
s-v-o:	subject - verb - direct object
s-v-io-o:	subject - verb - indirect object - object

Linking Verbs and Complements

In some sentences, the base verb is a **linking verb (lv)**—a verb that links a subject **(s)** to its **complement (c)**.

GRAMMAR SPEAK

A **complement** is the part of a predicate that describes or renames the subject. To *complement* means to make perfect or complete; a complement completes the subject. Complements are connected to the subject by a **linking verb**.

I / am / a painter.
s / lv / c

"Once in a blue moon" / means / about once every two and a half years.
s   lv   c

The complement *a painter* describes the subject *I*. The phrase *about once every two and a half years* defines *once in a blue moon*.

Forms of the verb *to be* (*am, is, are, was, were, being,* and *been*) often serve as helping verbs, but when *to be* is the base verb (as in the first example) it is a linking verb. Descriptive verbs, such as *become, feel, appear, look, seem, taste, sound,* and *smell*, are often linking verbs as well.

To test for a linking verb, remove the verb and insert an equal sign; does it make sense?

I = painter

Once in a blue moon = about once every two and a half years

This *doesn't* work for predicates that do *not* have subject complements:

Absolute power *corrupts* absolutely.   I *understand* your message.

Absolute power ≠ absolutely.   I ≠ your message.

> **MEMORY TIP**
> A verb is a **linking verb** if you can replace it with an =.

Practice 5

Here are the sentences from Practice 4. Does each follow the **s-lv-c** pattern?

1. For many years, the Republic of Congo was a colony of Belgium.
2. Contrary to popular belief, most species of snakes are not poisonous.
3. The most popular fruit worldwide is the mango.
4. The African continent is full of rich natural resources, including diamonds and oil.
5. Have you heard the news?

Receiving the Action: Direct Objects

While linking verbs connect a subject and complement, **transitive verbs (tv)** take their action out on a **direct object (o)**: a person or thing in the predicate. There are a number of types of object; when we simply say "object" we mean the direct object.

I / understand / your message.

  s   tv   o

In this sentence, *message* receives the action of the verb; it is what is being understood.

I / will pick up / some milk on the way home from work.

  s   tv   o   [prepositional phrases]

Like subjects, direct objects are never in prepositional phrases.

Practice 6

Circle the direct objects in the following sentences.

1. For some reason, Peter Pumpkin Eater put his wife in a pumpkin shell.
2. The alarm startled me.
3. The general found shelter for his troops.
4. The bus drops Tyler off at his front door.

Who It's For: Indirect Objects

The direct object *directly* receives the action of the verb. The **indirect object (io)** *receives the direct object*.

My boss / will give / me / a raise.

    s   hv tv   io   o

A raise is what will be given, so it is the direct object. But who will receive that raise? *Me*—the indirect object.

Here's one more example:

> The police / questioned / Anna about the accident.
>
>   s   tv   o   [prepositional phrase]
>
> The police / asked / Anna / many questions about the accident.
>
>   s   tv   io   o   [prepositional phrase]

In the first sentence, there is no indirect object; Anna directly receives the action of the verb *questioned*. In the second sentence, *questions* is the direct object and *Anna* the indirect object.

Practice 7

In the following sentences, put a slash (/) between subject and predicate, underline the verb, and use arrows to indicate the movement of the action from subject to verb, from verb to direct object, and from direct object to indirect object.

1. Between you and me, Sanford should offer Anne that position.

2. Please give Elliot my best.

3. I am offering you a second chance.

4. Minsun is sending me mixed signals about our relationship.

Intransitive Verbs

In the most basic sentence pattern, **s-v,** the verb is **intransitive (iv)**; no object receives the action. That doesn't mean nothing follows the verb:

> Geese / fly south in the winter.
>
>   s   iv [adverb]   [prepositional phrase]

Some verbs are only transitive, some only intransitive, and others, like *fly*, can be either. In the sentence above, it's intrasitive, but in the following sentence, it's transitive:

> I / fly / a private jet / for a government official.
>
> s / tv /   o   [prepositional phrase]

Practice 8

Mark each verb **lv** for linking verb, **tv** for transitive verb, or **iv** for intransitive verb. Circle the direct object, if any.

1. I love chocolate chip cookies.

2. You are my true love.

3. I offer you my unconditional love.

4. I live for love.

5. Only love can save me now.

Pattern Variations

As you've seen, the four basic sentence patterns—**s-v**, **s-lv-c**, **s-v-o**, and **s-v-io-o**—can vary (1) when writers invert order for effect, (2) in questions, and (3) in *there is/are* constructions:

> [Why] did / you / give / Michaela / credit [for my work]?
> [adv] hv / s / v / io   / o [prepositional phrase]

TYPES OF SENTENCES

Sentence type is determined by the number and type of clauses a sentence contains. Before attacking them, quickly review what a subordinate clause is. A subordinate clause cannot stand alone. It is *subordinate* to an independent clause, without which it doesn't express a complete thought.

As you saw in chapter 1, subordinate clauses usually begin with a **subordinating conjunction** or a **relative pronoun**. In the following examples each clause is bracketed with a slash between subject and predicate, and the subordinate clause indicator (the conjunction or relative pronoun) is in bold.

[You / act] [**as if** you / don't care].
[independent clause] [subordinate clause]

[[**Whoever** / finds my wallet] / will get a reward.]
[[subordinate clause within] independent clause]

Note that in the second example, the subordinate clause is the subject of the sentence.

> **MEMORY TIP**
>
> **Subordinate** means *inferior to or subject to the control of*. At work, you are *subordinate* to your boss. A subordinate clause is inferior to an independent clause.

Type 1: The Simple Sentence

A simple sentence contains one independent clause and no subordinate clauses. The subject and predicate can be single or compound, but the sentence contains only *one* subject-predicate pair.

I / must be true to myself.   Then I / can be true to others.
s   v   s   v

Type 2: The Compound Sentence

A compound sentence contains two or more independent clauses and no subordinate clauses. The two independent clauses are connected by a **coordinating conjunction** or by a semicolon with or without a **conjunctive adverb** (see chapter 1):

[You / must be true to yourself]; otherwise, [you / cannot be true to others.]

[independent clause] ; conjunctive adverb [independent clause]

Type 3: The Complex Sentence

A complex sentence contains one independent clause with one or more subordinate clauses.

[Before you can be true to [those you / love]], [you / must be true to yourself.]

[subordinate clause [subordinate clause]], [independent clause]

Type 4: The Compound-Complex Sentence

A compound-complex sentence consists of two or more independent clauses and one or more subordinate clauses.

[I / know that [if I / am not true to myself]], [I / cannot be true to others.]
[independent clause [subordinate clause]], [independent clause]

Practice 9

Identify subject-predicate pairs in each proverb below. Bracket each clause; determine whether it is independent or subordinate and how the clauses relate to each other. Mark each sentence S for simple, C for compound, X for complex, or CC for compound-complex.

Example: [The believer is happy]; [the doubter is wise]. —*Hungarian*
       (s)   (p)   (s)   (p)   = C

1. A stumble may prevent a fall. —*English*

2. Never trouble trouble until trouble troubles you. —*Chinese*

3. Deceive the rich and powerful if you will, but don't insult them. —*Japanese*

4. Speak the truth, but leave immediately after. —*Slovenian*

5. A handful of patience is worth a bushel of brains. —*Dutch*

6. Be happy while you're living, for you're a long time dead. —*Scottish*

SUMMARY

A **sentence** is a group of words containing both a **subject** and a **predicate** and expressing a **complete thought**. The **subject** is who or what the sentence is about. In **imperative sentences**, the subject is understood to be *you*. Subjects are never in prepositional phrases. The **predicate** is the verb with its objects, modifiers, and complements.

Both subjects and predicates can be **single** (one singular or plural subject or predicate) or **compound** (two or more singular or plural subjects or predicates).

The basic order for English sentences is subject-predicate, but that order is reversed in questions, *there is/are* statements, and sentences that are inverted for effect. There are four common subject-predicate patterns: **s-lv-c**, **s-v-o**, **s-v-io-o**, and **s-v**.

A **clause** is a group of words containing a subject and predicate. Clauses may be **subordinate** or **independent**. There are four types of sentences: **simple** (one independent clause), **compound** (two independent clauses), **complex** (one independent clause and one or more subordinate clauses), and **compound-complex** (two or more independent clauses and one or more subordinate clauses).

Practice: On Your Own

Choose a page in a newspaper, magazine, a memo from work or school, or a book you've been reading. Identify sentence parts and patterns—subjects and predicates, complements and objects. Find all four sentence patterns and all four types of sentences.

Practice Answers and Explanations

Practice 1

1. <u>A watched pot</u> never boils. The simple subject is <u>pot</u>.
2. Every evening, <u>the sun</u> sets over these hills.
3. There are <u>strange goings-on</u> around here these days.
4. What are <u>you</u> doing?
5. Ever since childhood, <u>Lukas</u> has been very artistic.
6. [<u>You</u>] choose your friends carefully. (The subject is understood.)

Practice 2

1. Unfortunately, <u>Carlos</u> and <u>Jude</u> did not get along well. *compound*
2. <u>Thinking of you</u> is my favorite pastime. *single*
3. Unlike Lucinda, <u>I</u> do believe in miracles. *single*
4. There are <u>many false claims</u> and <u>exaggerated truths</u> during a political campaign. *compound*
5. No <u>termites</u> or <u>carpenter ants</u> were found by the inspector. *compound.* Note that the verb is passive (see chapter 4).

Practice 3

1. *I* is the subject; it is who won't be recognizable.
2. *Boys*. *Team* is part of the prepositional phrase *on the baseball team*.
3. *Raj* is the subject; he is the one who *would not raise*.
4. The *gym is* in disrepair. *School* is part of a prepositional phrase.
5. *Color* is the subject, so the verb is the singular *is*, not the plural *are*. *Walls* is part of the prepositional phrase *of these walls*.

Practice 4

1. For many years, the Republic of Congo / was a colony of Belgium.
2. Contrary to popular belief,/ most species of snakes / are not poisonous. (Note that *species* is the subject, not *snakes*, which is in a prepositional phrase. Also note that "contrary to popular belief" is actually part of the predicate, not the subject.)
3. The most popular fruit in the world / is the mango. (Here *fruit* is the subject; *world* is in a prepositional phrase.)
4. The African continent / is full of rich natural resources, including diamonds and oil.
5. Have /you /heard the news? (Here, *have* is a helping verb and part of the predicate, but because of the question structure, it is separated from the rest of the predicate.)

Practice 5

1. Yes. *Was* is a linking verb. *A colony of Belgium* describes *the Republic of Congo*.
2. Yes. *Are* is a linking verb. *Not poisonous* describes *species*.
3. Yes. *Is* is a linking verb. *Mango* renames *most popular fruit*.
4. Yes. *Is* is once again a linking verb. *Full of rich natural resources* describes *African continent*.
5. No. *The news* does not describe *you*, and *have heard* is not a linking verb; you cannot replace it with = and have a coherent sentence.

Practice 6

1. *Wife* directly receives the action of the verb; she is *put*.
2. *Me* directly receives the action of *startled*.
3. *Shelter* directly receives the action; it is what the general *found*.
4. *Tyler* directly receives the action of *drops*.

Practice 7

1. Between you and me, Sanford / should offer Anne that position.
2. [You] /Please give Elliot my best.
3. I / am offering you a second chance.
4. Minsun / is sending me mixed signals about our relationship.

Practice 8

1. TV. *Love* acts on the direct object *chocolate chip cookies*.
2. LV. *Are* links the subject *you* to the complement *true love*.
3. TV. *Offer* acts on the direct object *unconditional love*. *You* is the indirect object.
4. IV. *Live* does not take an object. (*For love* is a prepositional phrase; notice that *love* cannot be an object because it does not receive the action of the verb.)
5. TV. *Save* acts on the direct object *me*.

Practice 9

1. Simple. [A stumble / may prevent a fall.]
2. Complex. [(You) never / trouble trouble] [until trouble / troubles you.]
3. Compound-complex. [(You) / deceive the rich and powerful [if you / will]], [but (you) / don't insult them.]
4. Compound. [(You) / speak the truth] [but (you) / leave immediately after.]
5. Simple. The subject is *handful*; the linking verb *is*; and the complement *worth a bushel of brains*.
6. Compound-complex. [(You) / be happy [while you're living], [for you're a long time dead.]

CHAPTER 2 TEST

Part A: Questions 1–6 refer to the following sentence:

Reading gives me pleasure, but writing gives me peace.

1. <u>Reading</u> is a/an

   (A) subject   (B) predicate   (C) direct object
   (D) indirect object   (E) intransitive verb

2. [<u>G</u>]<u>ives</u> is a/an
   (A) linking verb   (B) transitive verb   (C) intransitive verb
   (D) helping verb   (E)   predicate

3. [<u>M</u>]<u>e</u> is a/an
   (A) subject   (B) predicate   (C) direct object
   (D) indirect object   (E) complement

4. [<u>P</u>]<u>leasure</u> is a/an
   (A) subject   (B) predicate   (C) direct object
   (D) indirect object   (E) complement

5. The sentence pattern is
   (A) s-v, s-v   (B) s-v-o, s-v-o   (C) s-v-io-o, s-v-io-o
   (D) s-lv-c, s-lv-c   (E)   s-v-o, s-v-io-o

6. The sentence type is
   (A) simple   (B) compound   (C) complex
   (D) compound-complex   (E) inverted

Part B: Questions 7–13 refer to the following sentence:

> A professional writer is an amateur who didn't quit.
> —*Richard Boch*

7. The subject of this sentence is
   (A) professional   (B) writer   (C) amateur
   (D) who   (E) quit

8. The complete predicate of this sentence is
   (A) a professional writer is an amateur who didn't quit
   (B) didn't quit
   (C) who didn't quit
   (D) an amateur who didn't quit
   (E) is an amateur who didn't quit

9. The verb <u>is</u> is a/an
   (A) linking verb   (B) helping verb   (C) transitive verb
   (D) intransitive verb   (E) predicate

10. [A]mateur is a/an
    (A) subject   (B) predicate   (C) direct object
    (D) indirect object   (E) complement

11. [W]ho didn't quit is a/an
    (A) prepositional phrase   (B) independent clause
    (C) subordinate clause   (D) predicate   (E) all of the above

12. The sentence pattern is
    (A) [s-lv-c [s-v]]   (B) [s-lv-c]   (C) [s-v-o][s-v]
    (D) [s-v-io-o]   (E) [s-v [s-lv-c]]

13. The sentence type is
    (A) simple   (B) compound   (C) complex
    (D) compound-complex   (E) inverted

Part C: Questions 14–20 refer to the following sentence:

If you wish to be a writer, write! —*Epictetus*

14. [Y]ou is a/an
    (A) subject (B) predicate (C) direct object
    (D) indirect object (E) complement

15. [W]ish is a/an
    (A) linking verb (B) helping verb (C) transitive verb
    (D) intransitive verb (E) predicate

16. The direct object of this sentence is
    (A) wish (B) writer (C) you
    (D) to be a writer (E) no object

17. If you wish to be a writer is
    (A) prepositional phrase (B) independent clause
    (C) subordinate clause (D) predicate (E) all of the above

18. [W]rite! is a/an
    (A) predicate
    (B) independent clause
    (C) imperative statement
    (D) base verb
    (E) all of the above

19. The sentence pattern is
    (A) [s-v] (B) [s-v-o] (C) [s-v-o][s-v]
    (D) [s-v-io-o] (E) [s-lv-c][s-v]

20. The sentence type is
    (A) simple (B) compound (C) complex
    (D) compound-complex (E) inverted

Answers and Explanations

1. A

The gerund *reading* is the subject of the first independent clause *Reading gives me pleasure*.

2. B

Gives is a transitive verb, taking the direct object *pleasure*.

3. D

Me is the indirect object of *gives*; *me* receives the *pleasure*.

4. C

Pleasure is the direct object of the verb *gives*; it is what is given.

5. C

There are two independent clauses here joined by the coordinating conjunction *but*. Both clauses follow the s-v-io-o pattern.

6. B

This is a compound sentence—two independent clauses, no subordinate clauses.

7. B

Writer is the subject; the writer *is*.

8. E

The predicate is the verb and any complement, modifiers, and phrases that follow: *is an amateur who didn't quit.*

9. A

Is links the subject (*writer*) to its complement (*an amateur who didn't quit*).

10. E

Amateur describes *writer*; it is the subject complement.

11. C

This clause cannot stand alone; the relative pronoun *who* sets it off as a subordinate clause.

12. A

The complement includes a subordinate clause *who didn't quit*, so the pattern is [s-lv-c[s-v]].

13. C

An independent and subordinate clause together create a complex sentence.

14. A

You is the subject—who or what *wishes*.

15. C

In this sentence, *wish* is transitive—it takes the object *to be a writer*.

16. D

The complete object is *to be a writer*—it is what receives the action of *wish*.

17. C

If is a subordinating conjunction introducing a subordinate clause that cannot stand alone.

18. E

Write! is an imperative sentence—the understood but unstated subject is *you*. Thus it is also the predicate and base verb. It is an independent clause—it can stand alone.

19. C

The subordinate clause follows the s-v-o pattern (the object is *to be a writer*); the imperative clause s-v, although the subject is unstated.

20. C

The sentence contains an independent and subordinate clause, so it is complex.

CHAPTER 3

Verb Forms and Tenses

Start with this 10-question Building Block Quiz. The first few questions test material you've already seen.

BUILDING BLOCK QUIZ

Questions 1–4 refer to the following sentence:

> I don't know the key to success, but the key to failure is trying to please everybody. —*Bill Cosby*

1. Which of the following is a base verb in this sentence?
   (A) do   (B) not   (C) know   (D) success   (E) please

2. This sentence is
   (A) simple   (B) compound   (C) complex
   (D) compound-complex   (E) passive

3. The subject of <u>the key to failure is trying to please everybody</u> is
   (A) key   (B) failure   (C) trying
   (D) you (unstated)   (E) everybody

4. In this sentence, <u>is</u> is a/an
   (A) helping verb   (B) object   (C) intransitive verb
   (D) transitive verb   (E) linking verb

5. The simple past tense of <u>know</u> is
   (A) know   (B) knew   (C) known
   (D) knowed   (E) knowing

6. Which of the following is the base form of <u>know</u>?
   (A) know   (B) knew   (C) known
   (D) knowed   (E) knowing

7. Which of the following is the present participle of <u>know</u>?
   (A) know   (B) knew   (C) known
   (D) knowed   (E) knowing

8. Which verb correctly completes the following sentence:
   I have always ___ the truth.
   (A) know   (B) knew   (C) known
   (D) knowed   (E) knowing

9. Which verb correctly completes the first blank in the following
   sentence: *If I ___ what really happened, I ___ what to do.*
   (A) know   (B) knew   (C) had known
   (D) would know   (E) would have known

10. Which verb correctly completes the second blank in the
    following sentence: *If I ___ what happened, I ___ what to do.*
    (A) know   (B) knew   (C) had known
    (D) would know   (E) would have known

Answers and Explanations

1. C

In the clause *I don't know the key to success*, the base verb is *know*. *Do* (in *don't*) is a helping verb. In the clause *but the key to failure is trying to please everybody* the base verb is the linking verb *is*.

2. B

The coordinating conjunction *but* joins two independent clauses: *I don't know the key to success* and *the key to failure is trying to please everybody* (*trying to please everybody* is not a clause because there is no subject).

3. A

The *key* is what *is*, so it is the subject.

4. E

Is links the subject (*key*) to its complement (*trying to please everybody*).

5. B

Know takes the irregular past tense form *knew*.

6. A

Know is the base form of the verb (*I know*).

7. E

The present participle is the base form + *-ing*: *knowing*.

8. C

This sentence requires the past participle *known* for the present perfect tense, used for actions that began in the past and are still occurring in the present.

9. C

This conditional statement speculates about something that didn't happen in the past, so use the past perfect. *Had known* is the past perfect of *know*.

10. E

Again, for speculation about something that didn't happen in the past, use *could have, would have,* or *might have* + past participle: *would have known*.

Some—perhaps most—of this will be old hat for you. You don't need to be told that the past tense of *do* is *did,* but maybe you need to be reminded of irregular past participle forms or what the subjunctive is. And though you already know many of the rules, it's probably been years since you've seen them clearly articulated.

VERBS

As you've seen, verbs express an **action** or **state of being**. All verbs include a form of the **base verb**, which expresses the main action or state of being. **Helping verbs,** such as *will, would,* and *should*, help express some tenses (when the action occurred).

A **linking verb** connects a subject to its complement (see chapter 2). When *be* is not a helping verb, it is usually a linking verb.

A **transitive verb** takes a direct object (a person or thing that directly receives the action). It may have an indirect object as well (a person or thing receiving the direct object). **Intransitive verbs** do not have complements or direct objects (nothing receives the action of the verb).

BASIC VERB FORMS

English verbs have three basic forms from which the various tenses are fashioned.

Base Form

The base form of a verb is the first-person singular, present-tense: the form you'd use in the sentence *I* _____ or after *to:*

> I *want, think, see, feel, create, destroy*

> To *want, think, see, feel, create, destroy*

The exception is the verb *be*, which uses **be** as its base form, not *am* (I *am*).

Present Participle Form

For regular verbs, the present participle is formed by adding *–ing* to the base form.

wanting, thinking, seeing, feeling, creating, destroying

The present participle is used with different helping verbs to form specific tenses:

am thinking   was thinking   had been thinking

Past Participle Form

Irregular verbs take a variety of past participle forms: *thought, seen, felt.* You'll cover these in detail in a moment. For regular verbs, the past participle is formed by adding *–ed* to the base form. If the verb ends in *e*, add *d*; if it ends in *y*, change the *y* to *i* and add *–ed*.

wanted   created   destroyed   hurried

The past participle is used with different helping verbs to form specific tenses:

have created   had created   should have created

Practice 1

Write the base, present participle, and past participle forms for the verbs listed below. Some may already be in their base form.

Verb	Base	Present Participle	Past Participle
1. fades			
2. snores			
3. dry			
4. complains			
5. dances			

TENSES

Simple Tenses

The simple tenses are derived from the base form of the verb. The simple present and past do not use helping verbs.

Simple Present

For regular verbs, all persons and numbers *except* third-person singular use the **base form** of the verb. The third-person singular (he, she, and it) uses the **base form** + *s/-es*. (For most verbs ending in *-y*, change the *-y* to an *i* and add *es*.)

	Singular		Plural	
first person	I	*talk, smile*	we	*talk, smile*
second person	you	*talk, smile*	you	*talk, smile*
third person	he/she/it	*talks, smiles*	they	*talk, smile*

Some verbs are irregular. The big present-tense irregulars are *be, do,* and *have.* *Have's* third person singular form, of course, is *has*, not *haves*, and *do's* third person singular is *does*. But *be* is irregular all around:

	Singular		Plural	
first person	I	*am*	we	*are*
second person	you	*are*	you	*are*
third person	he/she/it	*is*	they	*are*

Use the simple present for:

1. habitual actions: Henderson's dog always <u>follows</u> me down the block.

2. actions occurring at the moment : I <u>think</u> I <u>see</u> someone I <u>know</u> over there.

3. facts or general truths: The first Tuesday in November <u>is</u> Election Day.
Absolute power <u>corrupts</u> absolutely.

Simple Past

For regular verbs, form the past tense by **adding -ed to the verb base**. (Add -d if verb ends in e; if verb ends in -y, change -y to -i and add -ed).

cried   insisted   reviewed   surprised

Use the simple past for actions completed entirely in the past:

I <u>cried</u> tears of joy when I heard the news.

Irregular Past Tense and Past Participle

Over 100 English verbs are irregular: they take different forms for the past tense and/or past participle. The following pages list the most common irregular verbs and their base, past, and past participle forms. Take a few minutes to review the list. Highlight any verbs whose irregular forms you haven't mastered.

The most irregular verb—be—has past and past participle forms that change in person and number:

Person	Present	Past	Past Participle
I	*am*	*was*	*have been*
you	*are*	*were*	*have been*
he, she, it	*is*	*was*	*has been*
we	*are*	*were*	*have been*
they	*are*	*were*	*have been*

Base Form	Simple Past	Past Participle

These past and past participle forms are the same:

have	had	had
bite	bit	bit
dig	dug	dug
bleed	bled	bled
hear	heard	heard
hold	held	held
light	lit	lit

Base Form	Simple Past	Past Participle
meet	met	met
lay	laid	laid
pay	paid	paid
say	said	said
sell	sold	sold
tell	told	told
shine	shone	shone
shoot	shot	shot
sit	sat	sat
spit	spat	spat
spin	spun	spun
creep	crept	crept
keep	kept	kept
deal	dealt	dealt
kneel	knelt	knelt
leave	left	left
mean	meant	meant
send	sent	sent
spend	spent	spent
sleep	slept	slept
bring	brought	brought
buy	bought	bought
catch	caught	caught
fight	fought	fought
teach	taught	taught
think	thought	thought
feed	fed	fed
flee	fled	fled
find	found	found
grind	ground	ground

These have different past and past participle forms:

Base Form	Simple Past	Past Participle
begin	began	begun
ring	rang	rung
sing	sang	sung
spring	sprang	sprung
do	did	done
go	went	gone
see	saw	seen
lie	lay	lain
drink	drank	drunk
shrink	shrank	shrunk
sink	sank	sunk
stink	stank	stunk
swear	swore	sworn
tear	tore	torn
wear	wore	worn
blow	blew	blown
draw	drew	drawn
fly	flew	flown
grow	grew	grown
know	knew	known
throw	threw	thrown
drive	drove	driven
strive	strove	striven
choose	chose	chosen
rise	rose	risen
break	broke	broken
speak	spoke	spoken
fall	fell	fallen

Base Form	Simple Past	Past Participle
shake	shook	shaken
take	took	taken
forget	forgot	forgotten
get	got	gotten
give	gave	given
forgive	forgave	forgiven
forsake	forsook	forsaken
hide	hid	hidden
ride	rode	ridden
write	wrote	written
freeze	froze	frozen
steal	stole	stolen

These past participles are the same form as the base:

come	came	come
overcome	overcame	overcome
run	ran	run

Simple Future

Form the simple future with the helping verb *will* + base form:

will debate   will be   will announce

Use the simple future for:

1. actions that will take place in the future

   The judges <u>will</u> <u>announce</u> the winner tomorrow.

2. actions that are predictable given certain circumstances

   Your property taxes <u>will</u> <u>increase</u> significantly if you move closer to the city.

As you'll see later, the future can also be expressed by the present progressive tense.

Practice 2

In each sentence below, put the base form of the base verb in the proper form and simple tense.

Example: Yesterday we ___paid___ (pay) off our mortgage.

1. Next week, I _____ (share) our ideas with the town council.

2. Last month, I _____ (go) to the museum six times.

3. Meena _____ (buy) her produce from an organic farmer.

4. I _____ (live) on Main Street for fifteen years before I _____ (find) this house.

Perfect Tenses

The perfect tenses are used to indicate actions that are, have been, or will be completed before another stated time.

> **MEMORY TIP**
>
> One meaning of *perfect* is *completed;* the perfect tenses describe actions that are, have been, or will be completed.

Present Perfect

To form the present perfect, add *have* or *has* + past participle:

has asked   have been   has helped

Use the present perfect for:

1. actions that began in the past and are still occurring in the present

I have been a volunteer at the hospital for the last fifteen years.

2. actions that began in the past and have been completed at an unspecified time

We have explored several alternatives but have not found a viable solution.

Past Perfect

This tense is formed with *had* + past participle:

had asked   had been   had suggested

Use the past perfect for actions already completed before another past time or action

I <u>had</u> <u>been</u> a hospital volunteer for years before I accepted a paid position.

Before my eighth birthday, I <u>had</u> already <u>moved</u> ten times.

He had been digging for over an hour before he asked for a larger shovel.

Future Perfect

Form this tense by adding *will* + *have* + past participle:

will have decided   will have found   will have forgotten

Use it for actions that will be completed before or by a specific future time:

By the time the renovations are completed, I <u>will</u> <u>have</u> <u>gone</u> 10% over budget.

Before our vacation is over, we <u>will</u> <u>have</u> <u>seen</u> all seven wonders of the world.

Practice 3

Use the context of the sentences below to determine which tense belongs in each blank.

> **Example:** I <u> have eaten </u> (eat) at Nellie's Diner every Wednesday for over a year now.

1. I _____ (miss) the bus three times already this week.
2. By the time you get back home, you _____ (forget) me.
3. I give up; Cecile's incessant badgering _____ (wear) me down.
4. I _____ (intend) to say something completely different from what actually came out of my mouth.

Progressive Tenses

The aptly named progressive tenses describe actions *in progress* at a particular time. The six progressive tenses follow. Notice how each tense's name describes its form: the *present progressive* is formed with the *present* tense of *be* and the *progressive* form (the present participle).

> ### MEMORY TIP
> Tense names are descriptive. The *perfect* tenses describe actions that are, were, or will be completed. The *progressive* tenses describe actions that are, were, or will be *in progress*.

Present Progressive

To form this tense, use the **present tense of** *be* **(*am, is, are*) + present participle (*-ing*)**

    is buying   are talking   am thinking

Use the present progressive for:

1. actions currently in progress

    We <u>are</u> <u>thinking</u> of throwing a surprise party for Ted's birthday.

2. future actions that will occur at a specific time

    We <u>are</u> <u>going</u> to win back our title next year.

Past Progressive

The past progressive uses the **past tense of** *be* **(*was, were*) + present participle (*-ing*)**:

    was counting   were looking   were sleeping

Use the past progressive for actions that were in progress in the past:

    They <u>were</u> <u>looking</u> for you everywhere!

Future Progressive

Form the future progressive by using *will* + *be* + present participle (*-ing*):

will be waiting   will be fighting   will be trying

Use the future progressive for actions that will be in progress in the future:

I <u>will</u> <u>be</u> <u>fighting</u> an uphill battle to get this motion approved.

Present Perfect Progressive

The present perfect progressive uses *have/has* + *been* + present participle:

have been thinking   has been waiting   have been fighting

Use the present perfect progressive to express an action that has been in progress for a length of time:

We <u>have</u> <u>been</u> <u>thinking</u> for months about throwing Ted a surprise birthday party.

Past Perfect Progressive

Form the past perfect progressive with *had* + *been* + present participle:

had been thinking   had been expecting   had been feeling

Use the past perfect progressive to express that an action had been in progress for a length of time:

We <u>had</u> <u>been</u> <u>thinking</u> of throwing Ted a surprise birthday party until he told us how much he hated surprises.

Future Perfect Progressive

For the future perfect progressive, use *will* + *have* + *been* + present participle:

will have been serving   will have been studying

Use the future perfect progressive to express how long an action will be in progress:

> By the time I finish my degree, I <u>will</u> <u>have</u> <u>been</u> <u>studying</u> ants for two decades.

Practice 4

Use the context to determine the correct progressive form of the verb to insert in the blank.

> **Example:** You _have been going_ (go) on for hours now.

1. I _____ (think) about you constantly since the day we met.
2. I _____ (think) about you constantly—until I met Horace.
3. I _____ (think) about you when you called.
4. I _____ (think) about you while you are gone.

Conditional Tenses

The conditional tenses are generally used to express what we *would* do or things that *would* happen. Conditional statements have two parts: a subordinating "if" clause (the condition) and an independent "then" clause (the result):

> [If I take one extra course each semester,] [I should graduate a semester early.]

> [subordinating "if" clause] [independent "then" clause]

The verb forms in each clause vary depending upon the kind of conditional statement (see the table on the following page).

If your sentence:	Use this in the "if" clause:	Use this in the "then" clause:	Example:
states a conditional fact	simple present	simple present	When the car <u>hits</u> 65 miles per hour, it <u>starts</u> to shimmy.
makes a prediction	simple present	*will, can, may, should* or *might* + base form of base verb	If I <u>take</u> one extra course each semester, I <u>should</u> graduate a semester early.
speculates about something unlikely to happen	past tense	*could, might,* or *would* + base form of base verb	If I <u>won</u> the lottery, I <u>would</u> <u>quit</u> my job and <u>travel</u> the world.
speculates about something that didn't happen in the past	past perfect	*could have, might have,* or *would have* + past participle	If I <u>had won</u> the lottery, I <u>would have quit</u> my job and <u>traveled</u> the world.
speculates about something that's contrary to fact	*were* (the subjunctive; see below)	*could, might,* or *would* + base form of base verb	If I <u>were</u> rich, I <u>would quit</u> my job and <u>travel</u> the world.

Practice 5

Circle the correct verb form in each of the sentences below.

1. If I (leave / left) now, I (should get / would get) there on time.
2. If I (could have / had) ten arms, I (could get / could have gotten) a lot more done.
3. If I (was / were) famous, I (would have / will have) no trouble getting a reservation.
4. If I (had gone / went) with you to the party, I (would have been / would be) the only one without a costume.
5. When water (freezes / is frozen), it (will expand / expands).

Subjunctive Mood

Moods are different from tenses in that they are used for certain kinds of statements rather than to indicate when actions take place (see chapter 4).

The present subjunctive expresses something wished for, requested, or contrary to fact. The subjunctive **mood** uses the **base form** for all verbs in the present tense except, as usual, *be*, which uses *were* for the subjunctive.

> Dentists recommend that you floss your teeth daily.
>
> If I <u>were</u> a little older, I might be a little wiser.

Practice 6

Circle the correct verb form in the parentheses.

1. If only I (was / were) more successful.
2. I ask that you please (refrain / refraining) from applause until the end of the speech.
3. I only wish I (was / were) there for you when you needed me.
4. Connie recommends that Elijah (does / do) some research before he plants his garden.

GETTING YOUR TENSES RIGHT

Knowing which tense to use probably comes naturally for the most part—unless, of course, English is not your native language. In that case: practice, practice, practice! Here are a few guidelines for those tenses that tend to get you tangled:

Memorize those irregular forms. If you don't yet know the past tense and past participles of irregular verbs, commit them to memory.

Don't confuse the past tense with the past perfect. The past perfect indicates that an action *has already been completed* by a certain time in the past:

> By the time we reached the store, it <u>had</u> <u>closed</u>. (past perfect)

Don't overuse past perfect. Don't use the past perect to describe two past actions that occurred almost *simultaneously;* use the past tense for both actions:

Incorrect: As soon as the boat <u>had left</u> the dock, Damon <u>began</u> to feel sick.

Correct: As soon as the boat <u>left</u> the dock, Damon <u>began</u> to feel sick.

Don't forget the subjunctive. The subjunctive is slipping out of everyday usage, but it should be used to express what is wished for, requested, or contrary to fact.

Practice: On Your Own

Look through a magazine or newspaper article to identify the tenses covered in this lesson. See if you can find examples of each tense and each conditional construction as well as the subjunctive.

SUMMARY

Basic Verb Forms

Base form: Use the first-person, singular, present-tense form—the form that fills in the blank in the sentence *I* _____. The base form of *be* is *be.*

Present participle: Add *–ing* to the base form

Past participle: For regular verbs, add *–ed* to the base form.

Main Tenses

Tense	Use for
Simple present	Habitual actions, actions occurring at the moment, and facts or general truths
Simple past	Actions completed entirely in the past

Tense	Use for
Simple future	Actions that will take place in the future; actions that are predictable given certain circumstances
Present perfect	Actions that began in the past and are still occurring in the present; actions that began in the past and have been completed
Past perfect	Actions already completed at the time of another past action; actions already completed by a specific past time
Future perfect	Actions that will be completed before or by a specific future time
Present progressive	Actions currently in progress; future actions that will occur at a specific time
Past progressive	Actions that were in progress in the past
Future progressive	Actions that will be in progress in the future
Present perfect progressive	Actions that have been in progress for a length of time
Past perfect progressive	Actions that had been in progress for a length of time
Future perfect progressive	Actions that will be in progress

Conditional & Subjunctive

Conditional statements have two parts: the "if" clause and the "then" clause. The tenses you use depend upon the kind of conditional statement you're making.

The **subjunctive** expresses things that are wished for, requested, or contrary to fact. Because you don't often use the subjunctive in speech, it may sound awkward or incorrect.

Practice Answers and Explanations

Practice 1

1. fade, fading, faded
2. snore, snoring, snored
3. dry, drying, dried
4. complain, complaining, complained
5. dance, dancing, danced

Practice 2

1. *will share.* The action will take place in the future, so use the simple future.
2. *went.* The action was completed entirely in the past, so use the simple past.
3. *buys.* This is a habitual action, so use the simple present.
4. *lived, found.* The first action was completed entirely in the past; this should be clear because there is a second action taking place *afterwards* that has already been completed. The past perfect tense isn't needed because the word "before" establishes the sequence of events. Thus both verbs are in the simple past.

Practice 3

1. *have missed.* The context suggests that this action occurred in the past and may still be occurring.
2. *will have forgotten.* The action will be completed by a specific time.
3. *has worn.* The action began in the past and has been completed at some unspecified time.
4. *had intended.* The action had already been completed by the time of another past action (saying something).

Practice 4

1. *have been thinking.* The present perfect progressive expresses actions that have been in progress for a length of time.
2. *had been thinking.* The past perfect progressive is used for actions that had been in progress for a length of time.
3. *was thinking.* The past progressive indicates that actions were in progress in the past (*when you called*).
4. *will be thinking.* The future progressive expresses actions that will be in progress in the future.

Practice 5

1. *leave, should get.* This sentence makes a prediction, so it needs the simple tense in the "if" clause and *should* + base form in the "then" clause.
2. *had, could get.* This sentence speculates about something unlikely to happen, so it requires the past tense in the "if" clause and *could* + base form in the "then" clause.
3. *were, would have.* This sentence speculates about something that's contrary to fact, so the "if" verb should be *were* and the "then" verb *would* + base form.
4. *had gone, would have been.* This sentence speculates about something that didn't happen in the past, so the "if" verb should be in the past perfect and the "then" verb *would* + *have* + past participle.
5. *freezes, expands.* This sentence status a conditional fact, so both verbs should be in the simple present.

Practice 6

1. *were.* The present tense subjunctive of *be* is *were.*
2. *refrain.* This verb expresses a request, so it is subjunctive.
3. *were.* This verb expresses a wish, so it is subjunctive.
4. *do.* This verb uses the subjunctive to express recommendation or request.
5. *choose.* This verb expresses a wish.

CHAPTER 3 TEST

Choose the verb or verbs that correctly complete each sentence.

1. The dream I had last night is one I __ for many years now.
   (A) have   (B) have had   (C) am having
   (D) have been having   (E) had

2. Cheyenne __ she would never lie to me again.
   (A) swears   (B) swored   (C) sworn
   (D) did swear   (E) swore

3. By the time the troops __, the city __ deserted.
   (A) arrived, had been   (B) arrived, was
   (C) had arrived, had been   (D) arrive, is   (E) did arrive, was

4. The boat had __ less than a quarter mile offshore.
   (A) sank   (B) sunk   (C) sinked
   (D) sanked   (E) been sinking

5. LuAnne __ five classes this semester.
   (A) took   (B) did take   (C) takes
   (D) is taking   (E) will have taken

6. If you __ the truth, you wouldn't be in this position now.
   (A) know   (B) knew   (C) had known
   (D) did know   (E) known

7. We __ there on time.
   (A) had been   (B) was   (C) were
   (D) having been   (E) were being

8. Today more people __ by email than ever before.

    (A) communicates

    (B) have communicated

    (C) communicate

    (D) are communicating

    (E) have been communicating

9. The foreman has asked that Tyson __ an anger management class.

    (A) would attend   (B) will attend   (C) does attend

    (D) attends   (E) attend

10. The number of families living in poverty __ by another five percent by the time Maya leaves office.

    (A) will have dropped   (B) will drop   (C) will be dropping

    (D) dropped   (E) is dropping

11. I __ devastated if you go.

    (A) am   (B) will be   (C) have been

    (D) will have been   (E) were

12. Studies show that most voters __ their leaders based on personality rather than issues.

    (A) will choose   (B) have chosen   (C) are choosing

    (D) choose   (E) chose

13. If you have numbness in your arms, it __ a sign of carpel tunnel syndrome.

    (A) is   (B) were   (C) might be

    (D) could have been   (E) was

14. Immediately after he uttered the words, Rashaad __ what he said.
    (A) regretted   (B) did regret   (C) had regretted
    (D) would have regretted   (E) was regretting

15. We have been __.
    (A) forsaked   (B) forsaken   (C) forsook
    (D) forsoken   (E) forsake

16. It took me 20 years, but I have finally __ my fear of heights.
    (A) overcame   (B) overcomed   (C) overcoming
    (D) overcomed   (E) overcome

17. Contrary to what they previously believed, scientists __ that
    spinal chord cells *can* regenerate.
    (A) discovered   (B) did discover   (C) have discovered
    (D) discover   (E) had discovered

18. Complaints about customer service __ steadily since Julianna
    took over.
    (A) have been declining   (B) declined   (C) are declining
    (D) were declining   (E) had declined

19. Rudy __ getting rid of his television, but he is not sure he can
    live without it.
    (A) considered   (B) is considering   (C) was considering
    (D) had considered   (E) considers

20. At least once a week, Jelena __ her house top to bottom.
    (A) is cleaning   (B) has cleaned   (C) will clean
    (D) will be cleaning   (E) cleans

Answers and Explanations

1.   B

The present perfect is used for actions that began in the past and are still occurring.

2.   E

The irregular past tense form of *swear* is *swore*.

3.   A

The second action was completed by the time of the first, so it is in the past perfect.

4.   B

Sunk is the irregular past participle form of *sink*. Choice (E) could be correct if you had a context that made it likely the sinking had been ongoing at some time in the past.

5.   D

The present progressive expresses actions that are currently in progress (*this semester*).

6.   C

The past perfect is used for actions already completed in the past.

7.   C

The simple past expresses that an action has been completed entirely in the past.

8.   D

The present progressive expresses actions currently in progress (*today*).

9.   E

This sentence expresses a request and requires the subjunctive.

10.   A

The future perfect expresses actions that will be completed by a specific future time.

11. B

The simple future expresses actions that will take place in the future and actions that are predictable given certain circumstances (*if you go*).

12. D

The simple present tense is used for stating general facts or truths as well as habitual actions.

13. C

This conditional statement makes a prediction and needs the present tense *might* + base in the "then" clause.

14. A

These actions both occurred at the same time in the past, so both should be in the simple past.

15. B

The irregular past participle form of *forsake* is *forsaken*.

16. E

The irregular past tense form of *overcome* is *overcame*.

17. C

The present perfect expresses actions that began in the past and have been completed.

18. A

The present perfect progressive expresses actions that have been in progress for some time (*since Julianna took over*).

19. B

The present progressive is for actions currently in progress.

20. E

The simple present expresses habitual actions.

CHAPTER 4

Helping Verbs and Other Tricky Matters

Start with this 10-question Building Block Quiz. The first few questions test material you've already seen.

BUILDING BLOCK QUIZ

1. In the following sentence

    The <u>waiting</u> room is crowded with patients.

    the word <u>waiting</u> is a/an

    (A) noun   (B) verb   (C) adjective   (D) adverb   (E) pronoun

2. Circle the subject(s) and underline the predicate(s):

    DNA evidence has exonerated thousands of people who had been wrongly convicted.

For questions 3–10, which verb correctly completes the sentence?

3. At the end of the ceremony yesterday, the couple ___ candles to symbolize their union.

    (A) lighted   (B) light   (C) had lighted

    (D) lightened   (E) lit

4. I ___ drive a manual but don't know how to drive a stick shift.

    (A) can   (B) might   (C) should

    (D) would   (E) must

5. Collette believes the document ___ forged.
   (A) may been   (B) might was been   (C) could been
   (D) might have been   (E) might had been

6. Can you imagine ___ that much money?
   (A) having   (B) have   (C) to have   (D) had   (E) has

7. The committee has decided ___ the deadline by another two weeks.
   (A) extend   (B) extending   (C) for extending
   (D) extends   (E) to extend

8. When he returned to his office, Dr. Morgan ___ the fossil carefully on the table.
   (A) lay   (B) lie   (C) laid   (D) lain   (E) lied

9. The cost of living has ___ by another two percent.
   (A) rose   (B) risen   (C) rised   (D) rosed   (E) raised

10. The door that I had locked was open, so I ___ back to my car and called 911.
    (A) run   (B) ran   (C) runs   (D) had run   (E) am running

Answers and Explanations

1.   C

Waiting is an adjective describing *room*.

2.

DNA evidence has exonerated thousands of people who had been wrongly convicted. The first clause is independent, and its simple subject is *evidence*; *who* is the simple subject of the subordinate clause.

3.   E

The past tense of the irregular verb *light* is *lit*.

4.   B

The context of the sentence suggests ability, so *can* is the correct helping verb.

5.   D

(A), (B) and (C) leave out the helping verb *have*. (E) incorrectly uses the past tense *had*.

6.   A

The verb *imagine* is followed by a gerund (a word ending in *–ing* that acts as a noun).

7.   E

Idiomatically, the verb *decide* must be followed by an infinitive: *to + base form*.

8.   C

Use *lay* when something is placed or set somewhere; use *lie* when someone or something rests or reclines. Here, something being placed or set down. The past tense of *lay* is *laid*.

9.   B

Raise means to move something up; *rise* means to go up, and is correct. There is no object to be moved up (it's intransitive). The past participle of *rise* is *risen*.

10.   B

The verb must be in the simple past. The past tense of the irregular verb *run* is *ran*.

Another chapter about verbs. Once again, you probably already know most of what you'll cover. And you've got a solid foundation from the first three chapters.

HELPING VERBS

Helping verbs can indicate the tense of the base verb; only two tenses (the simple past and simple present) don't require them. Helping verbs also have specific meanings—so it's important to use the right one.

Kinds of Helping Verbs

There are two kinds of helping verbs. The first kind are forms of **have**, **do**, and **be** that indicate different tenses. The second kind, called **modals**, do not change.

	Modals:
Have: have, has, had	can, could
Do: do, does, did	may, might
Be: be, am, is, are, was, were, being, been	must, ought, need, should
	shall, should
	will, would

Some of these are always helping verbs—*must* and *should*, for example. (Even in a sentence like *I must*, the action verb is unstated but understood from the context: *I must go* or *I must try.*) But some helping verbs also function as base verbs. *Have* can be a transitive verb meaning *to possess* (I *have* a dog); *been* can be a linking verb indicating a state of being (I have *been* lonely).

Forms to Use with Helping Verbs

Idiomatically, only certain verb forms can follow a helping verb and some helping verbs must work in specific combinations. Even if it's old hat to you, these rules are worth a thorough review:

- Use the **base form** after modal helping verbs:
  I <u>must</u> <u>talk</u> to you right away.
- Use the **base form** after forms of *do:*
  Judges <u>do</u> not <u>make</u> laws; they interpret them.
- Use the **present participle** after forms of *be:*
  I had <u>been</u> <u>expecting</u> such a reply.

Notice that this is true only when *be* is a helping verb, not a linking verb:

Helping verb: They have <u>been</u> thwarting our efforts to pass this measure. (*Have* and *been* are helping verbs; *thwarting* is the base verb.)

Linking verb: Our efforts to pass this measure have <u>been</u> thwarted. (*Have* is a helping verb, *been* is the base verb linking the subject [*efforts*] to the complement [*thwarted*].)

> ### FLASHBACK
> A word's *function* determines its part of speech. *Thwarted* could be the past tense verb or an adjective.

- Use the **past participle** after forms of *have*:
  I <u>had</u> <u>given</u> up on finding them.
- *Be* should be preceded by a modal, unless it is used as an imperative.
  This <u>could</u> <u>be</u> very interesting.
  <u>Be</u> good for grandma. [imperative]
- *Been* must be preceded by *have, has,* or *had:*
  I <u>had</u> <u>been</u> expecting such a reply.

Practice 1
How would you correct the following verb errors?

1. I would have help you if you had asked.
2. I been waiting for hours!
3. The air conditioner does not working anymore.
4. The package should arrived today.
5. Their predictions are always been correct.

What Helping Verbs Mean

As this chart shows, the modal helping verbs suggest very specific meanings.

Helping Verb	Meaning	Examples
will/would, shall	intention, obligation	We *shall* do our best. I *would* like to come along.
can/could	ability	I *can* say the alphabet backwards. We *could* help you paint that room.
may/might, can/could	permission	*May* I join you? We *could* have come along if we'd wanted to.
may/might	possibility	I *may* join you later. The bill *might* pass by a slim margin.
should	recommendation, obligation	You *should* join us! You should do your homework.
should	expectation	We *should* win by a large margin.
must, have (to), ought (to), need (to)	necessity	You *must* join us. We *have to* win.

Note that some have more than one meaning. *I may come* can mean I have permission to come OR that it's possible that I will come. *I can come* means I'm *able* to come.

Practice 2

Insert the helping verb that conveys the correct meaning for the context.

1. Helene said we _____ attend the meeting if we want.
2. We _____ do our best to make you comfortable during your stay.
3. Applications _____ be received by January 1.
4. I think Col. Jenkins _____ openly challenge you at the meeting tonight.

INFINITIVES AND GERUNDS

Which is correct: *I like to cook* or *I like cooking*?

Both are correct. Idiomatically, the verb *like* can be followed by either an **infinitive** (*to* + base form) or a gerund (base form + *-ing*). But not all verbs are so flexible.

Gerunds

A gerund is a base verb form + *-ing* that functions as a noun. Don't confuse it with a present participle, which may be part of the verb or may function as an adjective:

Part of the **verb** (present participle):   I am cooking.

        Gerund (noun; direct object):   I love cooking.

        Adjective (present participle):   I've signed up for a cooking class.

Gerunds can be subjects, complements, or objects (direct objects, indirect objects, or objects of a preposition):

        Subject: Painting is my passion.

        Complement: My passion is painting.

Practice 3

Determine whether the underlined words are gerunds or part of the verb. For each gerund, identify whether it is a subject, complement, or object.

1. <u>Helping</u> others is my main goal.
2. I love <u>helping</u> others.
3. My goal is <u>helping</u> others.
4. Lulu has been <u>helping</u> me all day.

Use a gerund:

- after a preposition:
  I am *sorry* for <u>asking</u> such a silly question.
- after certain verbs, including:

admit	deny	imagine	quit
appreciate	discuss	keep	recall
avoid	dislike	miss	resist
can't help	enjoy	postpone	risk
consider	escape	practice	suggest
delay	finish	put off	tolerate

Please *keep* <u>working</u> while I take this call.

Infinitives

Unlike gerunds, which share a form with present participles, infinitives have a form unto themselves: *to + base form*. Infinitives are often part of a verb phrase:

I plan <u>to submit</u> my letter of resignation tomorrow.

GRAMMAR SPEAK

A **gerund** is a verb form ending in *-ing* functioning as a noun.
An **infinitive** is the base form of a verb preceded by *to*.

To can also be a preposition, of course, as in *to the moon*. If it is followed by a verb, it's part of an infinitive; if it is followed by a noun or pronoun, it is a preposition.

Infinitive: to bar an action, to screen applicants

Preposition: to the bar, to the screen

Use an infinitive

- after certain verbs, including:

agree	decide	need	refuse
ask	expect	offer	venture
beg	fail	plan	want
choose	hope	pretend	wish
claim	manage	promise	

We have *agreed* <u>to amend</u> the original contract.

- after the following verbs, when they are directly followed by a noun or pronoun:

advise	convince	order	urge
allow	encourage	persuade	want
ask	expect	remind	warn
cause	force	require	
command	need	tell	

I *warned* <u>you</u> not <u>to touch</u> that snake!

MEMORY TIP

If you're a native English speaker, you've heard these idioms all your life and know *"I have asked Wilma coming to the meeting"* is wrong. If English is your second language, memorize these guidelines and then *read, read, read*—to develop that inner ear.

Practice 4

In each sentence below, a verb in base form follows a blank. Indicate whether the gerund (G) or infinitive (I) correctly completes the sentence.

1. The commission hopes ___ (stabilize) the wolf population within two years.

2. I have been thinking of ___ (buy) a new car.

3. Nothing you say can convince me ___ (change) my mind.

4. Lately, I've gotten into the habit of ___ (talk) outloud to myself.

5. We will not tolerate ___ (cheat) of any kind.

6. I miss ___ (talk) to you every day.

7. We will manage ___ (clean) up this mess somehow.

TROUBLESOME VERBS

Pop quiz: Which of the following sentences is correct?

　a. I will <u>lie</u> down for a nap.　**b.** I will <u>lay</u> down for a nap.

The correct answer is **a.**—but even people with PhDs have trouble with this one! In fact, three sets of English verbs tend to give *everyone* trouble:

　lie / lay　　　　**sit / set**　　　　**rise / raise**

The words in each pair mean similar things, but not *exactly* the same thing. That's because one verb in each set takes an object—the action is performed *on* someone or something—and the other verb doesn't (the subject performs the action on itself):

No object (intransitive)	**Takes an object (transitive)**
lie: to rest or recline	**lay:** to put or place
I will lie down.	*Lay your body down.*
rise: to go up	**raise:** to move (something) up
[You] Rise and shine!	*Raise your hand.*
sit: to rest	**set:** to put or place (something)
Please, Henrietta, sit down.	*Set your bags down.*

Note: The verb *set* can also mean *to go down*: *The sun <u>sets</u> in the west.* When *set* has this meaning, it does not take an object.

These troublesome verbs are also irregular in their past tense and past participle forms. The chart on the following page gives their present participle, past, and past participle forms (see chapter 3).

Present	Present Participle (with *am, is, are*)	Past	Past Participle (with *have, has, had*)
lie	lying	lay	lain
lay	laylng	laid	laid
rise	rising	rose	risen
raise	raising	raised	raised
sit	sitting	sat	sat
set	setting	set	set

Practice 5

Choose the verb that will correctly complete each sentence. If the verb is transitive, circle the direct object.

1. It's been a long day; I'm going to (lay / lie) down for a while.
2. Please (raise / rise) for the National Anthem.
3. That's Glen, (setting / sitting) over there in the corner.
4. The stakes have (raised / risen); it's more important now than ever.
5. After you (sit / set) your things down, come in the kitchen for some coffee.

CONSISTENCY

Remember the three core principles that underlie the rules for grammar and style: **balance**, **clarity**, and **consistency**. Consistency in verb tense, mood, and voice is essential for correctness and clarity.

Consistent Tense

A common grammar mistake, especially in narrative writing, is an unnecessary shift in verb tense. We do this in speech all the time: When describing a past event, we may get involved in the story and switch to the present tense (and back again):

> The storm intensified, and soon it starts raining so hard I can't see more than a few feet in front of me. I had to stop, praying that no one will hit me from behind.

You know that the action took place in the past—it starts in the past tense, and the context makes the present tense wrong. But the shifts between tenses are still disconcerting.

You may wish to tell the story in the present; it's a convention writers often use to make the story feel more immediate. But the verb tenses should be consistent:

> **Past:** The storm <u>intensified</u>, and soon it <u>started</u> raining so hard I <u>couldn't</u> see more than a few feet in front of me. I <u>had</u> to stop, praying that no one <u>would</u> hit me from behind.

> **Present:** The storm <u>intensifies</u>, and soon it <u>starts</u> raining so hard I <u>can't</u> see more than a few feet in front of me. I <u>have</u> to stop, praying that no one <u>will</u> hit me from behind.

Remember that consistency is a matter of avoiding *unnecessary* shifts. The shift is *necessary* if it indicates that the actions occurred at two different times:

> Here we <u>are</u>: Telford, the town where I <u>was</u> born.

Practice 6

Correct any unnecessary shifts in tense in the following paragraph.

I'd always wanted to go to the Grand Canyon, so I was thrilled when my dad announced we will be going there for our family vacation. Then he tells us we're going to drive instead of fly—a four-day journey with three kids crammed into a small car. I tell

him he's off his rocker. That's when he told us we weren't going in

our car—we're renting a Winnebago, and we're going to stay at

camp sites along the way. That was the kind of vacation I have

always dreamed of. I am sure it wasn't easy for them to plan that

trip, but I will always remember it as the best vacation of my life.

Consistent Mood

Grammatical **mood** refers to the kind of statement you are making. Moods are not tenses; they indicate the nature of the statement—whether it is a fact, wish, or command. You already know the **subjunctive**, the least common of the three moods in English (see chapter 3), and the **imperative** (see chapter 2). The mood in which most sentences are written is the **indicative**.

Indicative

The indicative mood expresses facts, opinions, and questions. Conjugate verbs normally—that is, use the tense that will accurately express when the action occurs.

George Washington <u>was</u> the first president of the United States.

What <u>did</u> you <u>say</u>?

Imperative

The imperative is used for commands or expressions of advice. The imperative takes the base form of the verb and often omits the subject (usually an understood *you*).

Always <u>proofread</u> your resume before sending it.

Subjunctive

Use the subjunctive for things wished for, requested, or contrary to fact (see chapter 3).

> We ask that Kyle <u>keep</u> his dog in a cage while we visit with the baby.
>
> If I <u>were</u> you, I'd accept Josh's offer.

Shifting Mood

An unnecessary mood shift, like an unnecessary tense shift, can be disconcerting or confusing. The following paragraph shifts from the indicative to the imperative midway through. To be consistent, it should be entirely in the imperative or the indicative mood:

Shifting: Applicants must fill out all forms completely. All forms should be typed or filled out in black or blue ink. Staple and clearly label each supporting document. Submit your application no later than January 12.

Indicative: Applicants must fill out all forms completely. All forms should be typed or filled out in black or blue ink. Each supporting document must be stapled and clearly labelled. Applications must be received no later than January 12.

Imperative: Fill out all forms completely. Type your application or use black or blue ink. Staple and clearly label each supporting document. Submit your application no later than January 12.

Again, remember that sometimes a shift is not unnecessary:

> As Mary Heaton Vosse wrote, "The art of writing is the art of applying the seat of the pants to the seat of the chair." So, if you want to be a writer, sit down and write!

Practice 7

How would you rewrite the following to make it consistent in mood?

Smoke detector batteries should be replaced twice a year. A good time to do this is at daylight savings time each spring and fall. Also, make sure your carbon monoxide detector is functioning properly.

Consistent Voice

There are two voices: **active** and **passive**. Active sentences have a clear agent of action: the subject. Passive sentences remove or displace the agent of action—it is demoted to a prepositional clause or lost entirely:

> Active: <u>Someone</u> stole my purse.
>
> Passive: <u>My purse</u> was stolen [by someone].

The active voice is more direct and more engaging than the passive, and in general it is preferred. But the passive is correct: (1) when you want to minimize the significance of the agent of action, (2) when you want to emphasize the receiver of the action, or (3) when the agent is unknown.

Unnecessary shifts between the active and passive voices make for awkward and potentially confusing writing:

> Shifting: James Joyce absorbed the details and ethos of Dublin, his native city, and these are what are portrayed in his short stories.

This sentence shifts to the passive for no reason—the same subject performed both actions (see chapter 9).

> Consistent: James Joyce absorbed the details and ethos of Dublin, his native city, and portrayed them in his short stories.

Practice 8

How would you rewrite the following paragraph consistently in the active voice?

Mark your calendar: It's time for our five-year reunion! Included in the cost of $40 per couple is dinner. Music for the evening will be provided by a live band, so please plan to dance. If you wish to be included in the class directory, please fill out the attached form. It should be returned no later than April 15.

SUMMARY

There are two kinds of **helping verbs**: forms of *have, do,* and *be* and modals: *can/could, will/would, shall/should, may/might,* and *must.* Specific verb forms must precede or follow certain helping verbs.

Helping verb	Should be preceded by	Should be followed by
be	modal	present participle
been	have, has, had	---
do	---	base
have	---	past participle
modal	---	base

Helping verbs also have specific meanings:

Helping Verb	Meaning
will/would, shall	Intention
can/could	Ability
may/might, can/could	Permission
may/might	Possibility
should	Recommendation
should	Expectation
must, have/had (to)	Necessity

Gerunds are a verb form ending in *–ing* that acts as a noun. **Infinitives** are *to + verb base.*

- Always use gerunds after prepositions.
- Always use gerunds after certain verbs, including *admit, enjoy,* and *resist.*
- Always use infinitives after certain verbs, including *agree, need,* and *want.*
- Always use infinitives after certain verbs when the verb is followed by a noun or pronoun, including *advise* and *tell.*

The verbs *lie/lay, sit/set,* and *rise/raise* are often confused because they have similar meanings. Remember that *lie, sit,* and *rise* do not take objects. *Lay, set,* and *raise,* on the other hand, have different meanings because an object receives the action.

Avoid unnecessary shifts in verb tense, mood, or voice. The three moods (or types of statements) are the **indicative** (for facts, opinions, and questions), the **imperative** (for commands or advice), and the **subjunctive** (for things that are wished for or contrary to fact). The two voices are the **active** and the **passive.**

Practice Answers and Explanations

Practice 1

1. *Help* needs to be in the past participle form, *helped*, since it follows *have*.
2. *Have* needs to be inserted before *been*: *I have been waiting*.
3. *Working* needs to be changed to *work*; the base form follows forms of *do*.
4. *Arrived* needs to be changed to the base form *arrive* since it follows a modal. Or, you could insert *have*: *should have arrived*, because *arrived* is the past participle, and the past participle should follow the modal *have*.
5. *Are* needs to be changed to *have* since it precedes *been*.

Practice 2

1. *May* or *can*. The context suggests permission, so either of these verbs will do.
2. *Will*. The context suggests intention.
3. *Must*. The context suggests necessity.
4. *May*. The context suggests possibility.

Practice 3

1. *Helping* is a gerund and the subject of the sentence (the complete subject is *helping others*).
2. Here *helping* is also a gerund and the direct object of *love*.
3. Again, *helping* is a gerund, and part of the complement
4. Here *helping* is part of the verb of the sentence.

Practice 4

1. *to stabilize*. An infinitive should follow the verb *hope*.
2. *buying*. A gerund should always follow a preposition.
3. *to change*. An infinitive should follow the verb *convince* when *convince* is followed by a noun or pronoun (in this case, *me*).
4. *talking*. A gerund should always follow a preposition.
5. *cheating*. A gerund should follow the verb *tolerate*.

6. *talking*. A gerund should follow the verb *miss*.

7. *to clean*. An infinitive should follow the verb *manage*.

Practice 5

1. *lie*.

2. *rise*.

3. *sitting*.

4. *risen*.

5. *set*. The direct object is *things*.

Practice 6

I'd always wanted to go to the Grand Canyon, so I was thrilled when my dad announced we would be going there for our family vacation. Then he <u>told</u> us we <u>were</u> going to drive instead of fly—a four-day journey with three kids crammed into a small car. I <u>told</u> him he <u>was</u> off his rocker. That <u>was</u> when he told us we weren't going in *our* car—we <u>were</u> renting a Winnebago, and we <u>were</u> going to stay at campsites along the way. That was the kind of vacation I <u>had</u> always dreamed of. I am sure it wasn't easy for them to plan that trip, but I will always remember it as the best vacation of my life. (Remember, some tense shifts are correct.)

Practice 7

<u>Imperative</u>: Replace smoke detector batteries twice a year. A good time to do this is at daylight savings time each spring and fall. Also, make sure your carbon monoxide detector is functioning properly.

<u>Indicative</u>: Smoke detector batteries should be replaced twice a year. A good time to do this is at daylight savings time each spring and fall. Also, carbon monoxide detectors should be checked to ensure they are functioning properly.

Practice 8

Mark your calendar: It's time for our five-year reunion! Dinner is included in the cost of $40 per couple. A live band will provide music for the evening, so please plan to dance. If you wish to be included in the class directory, please fill out the attached form and return it no later than April 15.

CHAPTER 4 TEST

Part A: For questions 1-13, choose the verb or verb phrase that correctly completes the sentence.

1. From its premiere in August of 1981, MTV (Music Television) ___ a phenomenal force in American pop culture.

   (A) is   (B) has been   (C) is been   (D) has be   (E) have been

2. No one ___ the extent to which MTV has influenced American society.

   (A) predicted   (B) could have predict   (C) could have predicted

   (D) could predict   (E) could have predicting

3. Some ___ say such claims about the impact of MTV are grossly exaggerated.

   (A) must   (B) have   (C) could   (D) may   (E) should

4. Perhaps. But here's something you might want ___: the flashing images of music videos have permanently altered the way commercials and even television shows and movies are made.

   (A) to consider   (B) considering   (C) considered

   (D) consider   (E) have considered

5. MTV can also be credited with ___ the reality show craze with its premiere of "The Real World" in 1992.

   (A) jumpstart   (B) jumpstarted   (C) having jumpstart

   (D) to jumpstart   (E) jumpstarting

6. In addition, artists such as Madonna ___ such phenomenal successes if it weren't for MTV.

   (A) could not be   (B) might not have been   (C) might not being

   (D) should not have been   (E) would not have been

7. If you have never watched MTV, you ___, if only to see a reflection of our nation's youth.

   (A) could   (B) would   (C) should   (D) might   (E) must

8. From the beginning, MTV decided it wanted ___ to young viewers (ages 13–34) rather than to "grow old" with its original audience.

   (A) appealing   (B) to appeal   (C) appeal
   (D) appealed   (E) appeals

9. Over the years, many stars have ___ in the MTV universe, including Madonna, Michael Jackson, and Duran Duran.

   (A) rised   (B) rose   (C) rosed   (D) risen   (E) raised

10. Some argue, however, that the sun ____ on MTV—that the music has been lost amid all the game shows and reality programming.

    (A) is setting   (B) is sitting   (C) sat   (D) sit   (E) setted

11. Who knows what ___ ahead for MTV?

    (A) lay   (B) lie   (C) lays   (D) lain   (E) lies

12. MTV has certainly not ___ all of its eggs in one basket—so most analysts contend that its future remains bright.

    (A) lain   (B) laid   (C) lied   (D) lay   (E) layed

13. But it would be wise for MTV to address concerns viewers have ___ about its programming.

    (A) rose   (B) risen   (C) raised   (D) rosed   (E) rosen

Part B. For questions, 14–20, choose the answer that will make the sentence consistent in tense, mood, and/or voice.

14. When it started over twenty years ago, for example, MTV showed only music videos—there ___ any commercials.

    (A) aren't   (B) haven't been   (C) will not be

    (D) weren't   (E) were not being

15. Now MTV has not only commercials, but also cartoons, reality shows, and game shows ___.

    (A) are seen by viewers as well.

    (B) are part of MTV's regular line-up.

    (C) are aired by the network.

    (D) are scattered throughout the daily schedule.

    (E) can be seen throughout the day.

16. Over the years, the irreverence of shows pioneered by MTV, such as the infamous "Beavis and Butthead," has often shocked and sometimes ___ viewers.

    (A) offending   (B) having offended   (C) offends

    (D) offended   (E) will offend

17. But ___; older generations have always been appalled by the tastes of the teen generation.

    (A) admit it   (B) listen   (C) don't be surprised

    (D) face the facts   (E) this shouldn't be surprising

18. Remember how offended so many parents were by Elvis—yet ___?

    (A) how adored he was by the younger generation?

    (B) how the younger generation loved him?

    (C) how he was so popular with teenagers?

    (D) how much teens adored him?

    (E) how successful he was?

19. Of course, MTV has changed dramatically over the years. ___
    (A) Take a look and see for yourself.
    (B) Check it out.
    (C) You can watch it and see for yourself.
    (D) Find out for yourself.
    (E) Watch it and see.

20. If you grew up with MTV in the 1980s or even the '90s, ___.
    (A) a channel that is very different today is what you will see.
    (B) you will see a channel that's very different today.
    (C) many changes over the years will be found.
    (D) many differences will be clear.
    (E) a very different channel will be seen.

Answers and Explanations

1. B

The present perfect *has been* is needed here to indicate that the action began in the past and is still occurring in the present.

2. C

The helping verb *could* means *ability* and is therefore needed here. In addition, the past participle (*predicted*) must follow the helping verb *have*.

3. D

The helping verb *may* means *possibility*. This is the only helping verb that fits in the context of the sentence.

4. A

An infinitive should follow the verb *want*.

5. E

A gerund should always follow a preposition (in this case, *with*).

6.   B

The context suggests possibility, so *might* is the correct helping verb (not *could, should,* or *would*). The helping verb *have* must be followed by the past participle (*been*).

7.   C

The helping verb *should* is needed as the context of the sentence suggests recommendation.

8.   B

The verb *want* should be followed by an infinitive.

9.   D

There is no object, so the verb should be *rise*, not *raise*. *Rise* means to go up; *raise* means to move something up. The past participle of *rise* is *risen*.

10.   A

To be consistent and logical in tense, the verb should be in the present progressive form. Because the subject is *sun*, *set* means *to go down*.

11.   E

There is no object, so the intransitive verb *lie* is the correct verb. Its third-person singular present-tense form is *lies*.

12.   B

There is an object here (*all*), so the sentence needs the verb *lay*, meaning to put or place something. The past participle of *lay* is *laid*.

13.   C

The verb *raise* is needed here for the object *concerns*; *raise* means to move *something* up, while *rise* means to go up. *Raise* should also be in the past participle form *raised*.

14.   D

To be consistent in tense and fit the context of the sentence, the verb should be the simple past tense *were*.

15.   B

To be consistent in voice, the second clause should also be active. Only (B) uses the active voice.

16. D

To be consistent in tense, the verb needs to be in its past participle form.

17. E

To be consistent in mood, the opening clause should be in the indicative mood. All other choices are in the imperative.

18. A

To be consistent in voice, both clauses should be passive. All other choices use the active voice.

19. C

To be consistent in mood, the second sentence should also be in the indicative mood. All other choices are in the imperative.

20. B

To be consistent in voice, the second clause should be in the active voice. All other choices use the passive voice.

CHAPTER 5

Subject-Verb Agreement

Start with this 10-question Building Block Quiz. The first few questions test material you've already seen.

BUILDING BLOCK QUIZ

Choose the letter that identifies the grammatical error in each sentence below. If there is no error, choose (E).

1. If <u>you're</u> not <u>feeling</u> well, you <u>should</u> go <u>lay</u> down. <u>No error</u>
   (A)   (B)   (C)   (D)   (E)

2. I <u>have</u> <u>asked</u> you here <u>reviewing</u> the policies that <u>will go</u> into
   (A) (B)   (C)   (D)
   effect next week. <u>No error</u>
              (E)

3. Ever since LeeAnne <u>has started</u> <u>working</u> at Bubba's, she <u>has</u> <u>been</u>
             (A)   (B)   (C) (D)
   more cheerful and self-confident. <u>No error</u>
                          (E)

4. In *Star Wars*, Anakin and R2-D2 accidentally <u>flies</u> into the
                                    (A)
   Death Star and <u>blow</u> it up, <u>saving</u> the Naboo from the <u>attack</u> by
            (B)   (C)   (D)
   Empire droids. <u>No error</u>
           (E)

5. <u>It's</u> clear that Janel, who <u>have</u> <u>been</u> one of Cole's most loyal
   (A)   (B) (C)
   supporters, <u>will</u> get a position on his Cabinet. <u>No error</u>
          (D)   (E)

6. <u>Have</u> anybody <u>seen</u> where I <u>set</u> the book I <u>borrowed</u> from
     (A)   (B)   (C)   (D)
   Adele? <u>No error</u>
         (E)

7. There <u>are</u> no reason why Jackson <u>would</u> <u>refuse</u> the
         (A)   (B)   (C)
   promotion—it <u>will give</u> him everything he's asked for. <u>No error</u>
             (D)   (E)

8. <u>It's</u> Harley's attitude <u>toward</u> authority figures that <u>keeps</u>
   (A)   (B)   (C)
   <u>getting</u> him into trouble. <u>No error</u>
    (D)   (E)

9. <u>No one</u> in the family <u>want to admit</u> that they <u>could</u> all <u>benefit</u>
     (A)   (B)   (C)   (D)
   from family therapy. <u>No error</u>
                (E)

10. <u>Like</u> his novel *The Snapper*, Roddy Doyle's <u>comedy</u>
     (A)   (B)
    The Commitments <u>were</u> also <u>made</u> into a hit movie. <u>No error</u>
               (C)   (D)   (E)

Answers and Explanations

1. D

Lay always acts on an object (we lay something else down). The correct verb is the intransitive *lie*.

2. C

If the verb *ask* is followed by a noun or pronoun, use the infinitive *to review*, not the gerund.

3. A

Use the simple past tense (*started*) to indicate action completed at a definite time in the past.

4.   A

Because there is a compound subject (*Anakin* and R2D2), the verb must be the third-person plural *fly*, not *flies*. The present tense is consistently used and is appropriate.

5.   B

The subject *who* is a relative pronoun referring to *Janel*, a singular subject. Thus the verb must be the third-person singular *has been*.

6.   A

Anybody is an indefinite pronoun that functions as a singular subject; it requires the third-person singular verb *has seen*.

7.   A

The subject is the singular *reason*; the verb should be the third-person singular *is*.

8.   E

There is no error.

9.   B

The subject of this sentence is the indefinite singular pronoun *no one*. (*Family* cannot be the subject because it is part of a prepositional phrase.) The verb should be the third-person singular *wants*.

10.   C

The subject, the singular *The Commitments*, requires the third-person singular verb *was made*.

Remember the three principles: **balance, clarity,** and **consistency.** Subject-verb agreement is all about balance. Subjects and verbs **agree** (that is, are equal) in number and person. If the subject is the first-person singular *I*, the verb must be the first-person singular: _am_. Simple enough, right?

But there are reasons to devote a chapter to subject-verb agreement. For one thing, it isn't always easy to find the subject. For another, certain subjects (like indefinite pronouns and collective nouns) confuse the best of us.

BASIC SUBJECT-VERB AGREEMENT

Fortunately, subject-verb agreement is an issue only in the present tense, including the present perfect tense (with the usual exception, *be*).

	Singular		Plural	
First Person	I	*pretend*	we	*pretend*
Second Person	you	*pretend*	you	*pretend*
Third Person	he, she, it	*pretend<u>s</u>*	they	*pretend*

All use the **base** form *except* the third person singular, which adds *–s* (or *–es*) to the base form.

The verb *be* is irregular in form and must agree in both the present and past tenses:

	Singular		Plural	
First Person	I	*am, was*	we	*are, were*
Second Person	you	*are, were*	you	*are, were*
Third Person	he, she, it	*is, was*	they	*are, were*

> ### REMEMBER THIS!
> Only the third-person singular (he, she, it) takes the *–s* ending.
> All other subjects use the base form (except for the verb *be*).

Practice 1
Circle the correct verb in each pair in parentheses below.

1. Devon (is / are) babysitting for the Smiths this afternoon.
2. If we (concedes / concede), that (do / does) not mean we (agree /agrees) with your position.
3. So then Julia (tell / tells) Wanda, and Wanda (tell / tells) Annette—and the next thing you (know / knows), the whole town (know / knows) about my problem.

IDENTIFYING THE SUBJECT

You learned to find the subject in chapter 2 (go back and review if you've forgotten any of the earlier Building Blocks). Here we offer more detail about "interrupters," inverted sentences, and other things that can befuddle that process.

General Review

The subject can be **single** (one subject) or **compound** (two or more subjects), and each subject can be either singular or plural. Sometimes, especially in imperatives, the subject is unstated (usually an understood *you).* Each clause in a sentence contains a subject and a verb.

[After Ted / **changes** the oil,] [I / **will** rotate the tires.]

Agreement with Single and Compound Subjects

For a single subject, the rule is simple: match the verb to the subject, whether it's singular or plural.

The oil **needs** to be changed. (third-person singular subject and verb)

The tires **need** to be rotated. (third-person plural subject and verb)

Compound subjects are a bit more complicated. There are two rules:

1. If the subjects (whether singular or plural) are joined by *and,* the verb is plural:

The president and his cabinet members **are** on vacation this week.

There are two exceptions:

- If the parts refer to the same person or thing, or work as a single unit, then the verb should be singular:
  Spaghetti and meatballs is the special this evening.

  If the compound subject is preceded by *each* or *every* (thus refering to each subject individually), then the verb should be singular:
  Every freshman and transfer student **is** required to take Student Life.

2. If the subjects are joined by *or* or *nor*, the verb should agree with the subject that's closest to the verb:

Neither the <u>president</u> nor <u>his cabinet members</u> **are** in Washington this week.

Neither the <u>cabinet members</u> nor the <u>president</u> **is** in Washington this week.

Practice 2

Underline the subject(s) and circle the correct verb in each of the following sentences.

1. Neither Bob nor Rob (admit / admits) to starting the rumor.
2. Republicans and Democrats alike (share / shares) a belief in the separation of church and state.
3. Either Santa or his elves (check / checks) the list twice.
4. Either the elves or Santa (check / checks) the list twice.
5. The scouts and their leader (was / were) lost in the woods for hours.
6. Every problem and setback (is / are) an opportunity.

Eliminating Interrupters

The basic order for sentences is *subject-verb,* but that doesn't mean the verb immediately follows the subject. Many "interrupters" can come between subject and verb, including **prepositional phrases** and **modifiers** of all sorts.

Carlos, <u>in fact,</u> will be the best man at my wedding. (prepositional phrase)

Carlos, <u>who is my favorite cousin,</u> will be the best man at my wedding. (clause modifying *Carlos*)

In each example, the subject *Carlos* is separated from the verb by an underlined phrase or clause. The subject of a sentence will not be in one of these interrupters. You can eliminate them to make sure your subject and verb agree:

"The Scream," [~~to the surprise~~] [~~of millions~~], **was** stolen in broad daylight from a museum in Norway.

"The Scream," [~~which is [by far] the most famous painting~~] [~~by Edward Munch~~], **was** stolen in broad daylight from a museum in Norway.

Practice 3

Cross out interrupters, underline the subject(s), and circle the correct verb.

1. A house without a good foundation (is / are) sure to crumble.
2. My sister Meena, the only one of us who doesn't love animals, (have / has) fallen in love with a farmer.
3. A true democracy, it turns out, (is / are) a true challenge.
4. All good things, the saying goes, (come / comes) to an end.
5. The concert, featuring the Oak City Banjo Kings, (begin / begins) at 7:00.

Inverted Sentences

The typical subject-verb sentence pattern may be reversed (1) in questions, (2) in *there is/are* statements, and (3) for effect:

> There is no doubt in our minds.
>
> Long are the dog days of summer.

If you're unsure of the subject, locate the verb. The helping verb may be separated from the main verb, as in the example below. Once you've identified the verb(s), determine who or what performs the action (eliminate prepositional phrases and other interrupters.)

> Where **has/have** the cartons of milk gone?

What *has/have gone*? The cartons. The verb should be the plural *have*.

Practice 4

Underline the subject and circle the correct verb.

1. How many times (have / has) I asked you to stop?
2. There (is / are) strength in numbers.
3. Wise (is / are) the quiet tongue and open heart.
4. When (do / does) the Admissions Office close?
5. In the supply closet, there (is / are) probably dozens of boxes of envelopes.

TRICKY SUBJECTS

Let's say you've identified the subject of a clause: *someone* or *who*. Now what? Here are the rules for titles or phrases, indefinite or relative pronouns, or collective nouns.

Collective Nouns

A **collective** or **group** noun identifies a single entity that is composed of more than one unit: *class, team, faculty, majority, family, series, committee, audience, crowd.* Collective nouns are singular when they act as one unit.

> The <u>committee</u> **meets** Friday at noon.
>
> A <u>majority</u> **is** needed to pass the bill.

But *if* the context of the sentence emphasizes the individual members of the group, collective nouns are plural:

> The <u>committees</u> **meet** each Friday at noon.
>
> A <u>majority</u> of students **feel** unsafe on school grounds.

Titles, Phrases, and Singular Plurals

If the subject is a title, a specified phrase, or a gerund phrase, it is singular:

> **Title:** <u>*Cats*</u> **is** my favorite musical.
>
> **Specified phrase:** "<u>Once upon a time</u>" **is** the standard introduction to a fairy tale.
>
> **Gerund phrase:** <u>Delivering pizzas</u> **is** not a glamorous job, but it pays my bills.

Some words are plural in form but function as singular entities. These include names of academic subjects or bodies of knowledge, such as *mathematics, statistics, economics,* and *physics*, as well as a handful of other words, including *athletics, measles, mumps,* and *news*. Foreign words and medical terms may also appear to be plural because they end in *-s* (e.g., *diagnosis;* the plural is *diagnoses*). Consult a dictionary if you are unsure.

> <u>Physics</u> **is** my favorite subject.   No <u>news</u> **is** good news.

However, when one of these words describes individual items rather than a collective entity, the verb should be plural:

These <u>statistics</u> **show** a strong correlation between goal setting and achievement.

Practice 5

Circle the correct verb in each sentence below.

1. The audience (is / are) in for a real surprise in the second act.
2. Many classes (is / are) overcrowded this semester.
3. *In the Lake of the Woods* by Tim O'Brien (is / are) my favorite novel.
4. Economics (is / are) much more interesting than I'd imagined.
5. *Psychosis* (is / are) a widely misunderstood term.
6. The news (has / have) come from many different sources, which explains why the accounts vary so widely.
7. Treating patients still (takes / take) up most of my day.

Indefinite Pronouns

As you saw in chapter 1, **indefinite pronouns** are those that don't refer to or replace a specific person, place, or thing. The following indefinite pronouns should always be treated as third-person singular subjects:

anybody	everything	someone
anyone	nobody	something
anything	no one	each
everybody	nothing	either
everyone	somebody	neither

Has <u>anyone</u> seen my cat?

"<u>Nothing</u> **is** more real than nothing." —*Samuel Beckett*

If <u>somebody</u> **has** something to say, now is the time to say it.

> **MEMORY TIP**
>
> Most of the singular indefinite pronouns are **-body/-one/-thing** words. Remember that **one** is a single item, so all of these -body/-one/-thing words are singular.

The indefinite pronouns **both, few, many,** and **several** are always plural:

Many of us **agree** with the proposal.

Several pipes **have** burst from the cold.

Remember, sometimes *many* acts as an adjective, though:

Many a day **has** gone by since you promised you'd return.

Finally, a handful of indefinite pronouns—**all, any, none,** and **some**—can be either singular or plural, depending upon their **antecedent**: the noun or pronoun they refer to or replace. Often that **antecedent** is in a prepositional phrase following the pronoun:

None of the money **is** left. (*None* refers to *money*.)

None of the jewels **are** real. (*None* refers to *jewels*.)

Note: The word *plenty* isn't usually an indefinite pronoun, but it can function like one and take a singular or plural verb depending upon what it refers to:

There **are** plenty of napkins on the table.

There **is** plenty of gas in the car.

Practice 6

Circle the correct verb in each sentence.

1. I have a feeling something good (is / are) about to happen.
2. Unfortunately, nothing (have / has) changed since you were last here.
3. Each of the band members (has / have) a solo in this song.
4. Everything (seem / seems) under control now.
5. If anyone (find / finds) out, we're in big trouble.

6. None of his excuses (is / are) legitimate, but all of them (is / are) creative.
7. All of the cookies (has / have) been eaten, but there (is / are) still plenty of cake.
8. I don't think any of these stamps (is / are) valuable.

Relative Pronouns

The **relative pronouns** *who*, *that* and *which* often introduce subordinate clauses (see chapter 2), which means they are often the subject of those clauses. To determine whether the verb should be singular or plural, identify the pronoun's antecedent. In the examples below, the relative pronouns are <u>underlined</u> and verbs are in **bold**. The antecedents are italicized.

This is a *story* <u>that</u> **gets** wilder every time he tells is.

These are *stories* <u>that</u> **get** wilder every time he tells them.

Practice 7

Underline the antecedent for each relative pronoun in the sentences below, then circle the correct verb.

1. Freud's case studies, which often (read / reads) more like novels than medical tracts, are fascinating.
2. The film sparked a lively discussion that (was / were) continued in the hallway after class.
3. *Frankenstein*, which most critics agree (is / are) the first science-fiction novel, was written by Mary Shelley, who (was / were) just 19 years old when it was published.
4. His taste in music is one of the things about him that (drive / drives) me crazy.
5. His taste in music is one thing about him that (drive / drives) me crazy.

SUMMARY

Subject-verb agreement means that subjects and verbs are the same in number (singular or plural) and person (first, second, or third). The third-person singular (he, she, it) adds *–s* to the base form: *I eat, he eats*. Except for the verb *be*, subject-verb agreement is an issue only for present tense verbs.

To correctly identify the subject, eliminate interrupters such as prepositional phrases and modifying clauses.

Here are the **ten rules** regarding subject-verb agreement:

1. When you have a single subject, the verb must match that subject (singular or plural).

2. When you have a compound subject (two or more subjects) connected by *and*, the verb must be plural.

3. When you have a compound subject connected by *or* or *nor*, the verb must match the closest subject. If the subject closest to the verb is plural, the verb should be plural; if the subject closest to the verb is singular, the verb should be singular.

4. For *there is/are* sentences, determine first what *is*—for this is the true subject. Then check for subject-verb agreement.

5. For questions and other inverted sentences, identify the verb (remember, helping verbs will often be separated from main verbs in these constructions). Then determine who or what performs that action—this is the subject. Now check for subject-verb agreement.

6. When the subject is a collective noun (e.g., *team*), it should be followed by a singular verb—unless the collective noun is plural (*teams*) or the context of the sentence emphasizes each individual in the group.

7. When the subject is a title, a specified word or phrase, or a gerund phrase, treat it as a single unit and follow it with a singular verb.

8. A handful of plural words are actually singular most of the time (e.g., *economics* and *news*). Follow these words with a singular verb unless they describe individual entities.

9. Most indefinite pronouns are singular subjects (remember the *one/body/thing* word groups). The indefinite pronouns *all, any, none* and *some* can be singular or plural depending upon their antecedents. What noun or pronoun are they referring to?

10. The relative pronouns *who, that,* and *which* can be singular or plural, depending upon their antecedent. Identify the antecedent to determine correct subject-verb agreement.

Subject-verb agreement is all about **balance**; sentences need harmony between subjects and verbs.

Practice: On Your Own

Write your own sample sentences for each of the subject-verb agreement rules in the Chapter Summary.

Practice Answers and Explanations

Practice 1

1. *is. Devon* is a third-person singular subject.

2. *concede, does, agree.* Only *that* is a third-person singular subject, so it is the only one that takes the *–s* form.

3. *tells, tells, know, knows.* Julia, Wanda, Annette, and *town* are third-person singular subjects and take the *–s* form. *You* is the second-person singular and takes the base form.

Practice 2

1. Subjects: <u>Bob</u> and <u>Rob</u>. Correct verb: *admits.* The verb needs to be singular because the compound subject is joined by *nor*, and the closest subject is third-person singular.

2. Subjects: <u>Republicans</u> and <u>Democrats</u>. Correct verb: *share.* The compound subject is joined by *and* and thus requires a plural verb.

3. Subjects: <u>Santa</u> and his <u>elves</u>. Correct verb: *check.* The compound subject is joined by *or*, so the verb must agree with the closest subject, *elves*, which is plural.

4. Subjects: <u>Santa</u> and his <u>elves</u>. Correct verb: *checks.* The compound

subject is joined by *or*, so the verb must agree with the closest subject, *Santa*, which is the third-person singular.

5. Subjects: <u>scouts</u> and their <u>leader</u>. Correct verb: *were*. The compound subject is joined by *and*, so the verb must be plural.

6. Subjects: <u>problem</u> and <u>setback</u>. Correct verb: *is*. The compound subject is joined by *and*, but it is preceded by *every*, so the verb should be third-person singular.

Practice 3

1. A <u>house</u> ~~without a good foundation~~ (**is**) sure to crumble.
2. <u>My sister Meena</u>, ~~the only one of us who doesn't love animals~~, (**has**) fallen in love with a farmer.
3. A <u>true democracy</u>, ~~it turns out~~, (**is**) a true challenge.
4. <u>All good things</u>, ~~the saying goes~~, (**come**) to an end.
5. The <u>concert</u>, ~~featuring the Oak City Banjo Kings~~, (**begins**) at 7:00.

Practice 4

1. How many times (**have**) <u>I</u> asked you to stop?
2. There (**is**) <u>strength</u> in numbers.
3. Wise (**are**) the <u>quiet tongue</u> and <u>open heart</u>.
4. When (**does**) the <u>Admissions Office</u> close?
5. In the supply closet, there (**are**) probably <u>dozens</u> of boxes of envelopes.

Practice 5

1. *is*. *Audience* is a singular collective noun.
2. *are*. *Classes* is a plural collective noun.
3. *is*. *In the Lake of the Woods* is a singular title.
4. *is*. *Economics* here refers to the academic discipline and is singular.
5. *is*. *Psychosis* is a specified term and is singular.
6. *have*. It may sound awkward, but here the context emphasizes the individual items, so the verb should be plural.
7. *takes*. The gerund phrase *treating patients* should be treated as a singular subject.

Practice 6

1. *is. Something* is a singular indefinite pronoun.
2. *has. Nothing* is a singular indefinite pronoun.
3. *has. Each* is a singular indefinite pronoun. (Note that *each* is the subject, not *band members*, which is part of a prepositional phrase.)
4. *seems. Everything* is a singular indefinite pronoun.
5. *finds. Anyone* is a singular indefinite pronoun.
6. *are, are.* Both *none* and *all* refer to the plural noun *excuses.*
7. *have, is. All* refers to *cookies*; *plenty* refers to *cake.*
8. *are. Any* refers to the plural noun *stamps.*

Practice 7

1. Freud's <u>case studies</u>, which often (**read**) more like novels than medical tracts, are fascinating.
2. The film sparked a lively <u>discussion</u> that (**was**) continued in the hallway after class.
3. <u>*Frankenstein*</u>, which most critics agree (**is**) the first science-fiction novel, was written by <u>Mary Shelley</u>, who (**was**) just 19 years old when it was published.
4. His taste in music is one of the <u>things</u> about him that (**drive**) me crazy.
5. His taste in music is the one <u>thing</u> about him that (**drives**) me crazy.

CHAPTER 5 TEST

Choose the letter that identifies the subject-verb agreement error in each sentence below. If there is no error, choose (E).

1. A jury <u>consist</u> of twelve randomly <u>selected</u> men and women
       (A)   (B)
   whose duty it <u>is</u> to <u>decide</u> the fate of the defendant. <u>No error</u>
            (C)   (D)   (E)

2. I <u>promise</u> that neither fame nor fortune <u>are</u> going to <u>change</u>
     (A)   (B)   (C)
   the way I <u>feel</u> about you. <u>No error</u>
         (D)   (E)

3. I <u>can't</u> <u>believe</u> that no one <u>have</u> taken you up on your <u>offer</u>.
    (A)   (B)   (C)   (D)
   <u>No error</u>
     (E)

4. I <u>know</u> that patience <u>is</u> a virtue, but I <u>seem</u> to <u>have</u> so little of
     (A)   (B)   (C)   (D)
   it. <u>No error</u>
      (E)

5. <u>Did</u> you <u>know</u> that "Les Demoiselles d'Avignon," one of Picasso's
    (A)   (B)
   most famous <u>works,</u> <u>hang</u> in the Museum of Modern Art in
            (C)   (D)
   New York City? <u>No error</u>
              (E)

6. I <u>am</u> not a <u>morning</u> person, so it <u>is</u> my bad luck that statistics,
     (A)   (B)   (C)
   one of my most difficult classes, <u>meets</u> at 8:00 AM. <u>No error</u>
                             (D)   (E)

7. <u>Can</u> you <u>tell</u> me who else besides you <u>have</u> <u>seen</u> these results?
    (A)   (B)   (C) (D)
   <u>No error</u>
     (E)

8. Kathy <u>confesses</u> that "Trading Spaces" <u>has</u> <u>become</u> her favorite
      (A)   (B)   (C)
television show and she <u>watches</u> it religiously. <u>No error</u>
                   (D)   (E)

9. I <u>believe</u> either Carlos or his children <u>is</u> going to pick up
   (A)   (B)
the cake and <u>bring</u> it to the party, so we don't <u>have</u> to worry
          (C)   (D)
about it. <u>No error</u>
      (E)

10. I <u>was</u> surprised to <u>hear</u> that the Senate <u>has</u> repealed the
   (A)   (B)   (C)
amendment we <u>had</u> fought so hard for. <u>No error</u>
        (D)   (E)

11. These dreams of mine that <u>keeps</u> me <u>awake</u> always <u>have</u> the
                   (A)   (B)   (C)
same ending: I <u>am</u> falling into a dark, bottomless pit. <u>No error</u>
        (D)   (E)

12. We <u>have</u> discovered a wonderful new restaurant which <u>feature</u>
     (A)   (B)
fresh seafood—and we <u>are</u> happy to say it <u>is</u> only a few blocks
             (C)   (D)
away. <u>No error</u>
    (E)

13. I <u>want</u> to <u>believe</u> you, but there <u>aren't</u> any question in my
   (A)   (B)   (C)
mind about what <u>happened</u>. <u>No error</u>
         (D)   (E)

14. I <u>am</u> concerned about these statistics, which <u>suggests</u> our
   (A)   (B)
customer base <u>has</u> shrunken considerably since we <u>switched</u>
         (C)   (D)
suppliers. <u>No error</u>
      (E)

15. I <u>have</u> checked with Denise, and she <u>do</u> not know what
  (A)   (B)
 happened to the printer that <u>was</u> supposed to <u>go</u> in your
          (C)   (D)
 office. <u>No error</u>
    (E)

16. As Rebecca <u>smiles</u> and <u>places</u> the wrapped gift on the table,
      (A)   (B)
 Thayer <u>slip</u> the letter from Anna into his pocket before
    (C)
 Rebecca <u>sees</u> it. <u>No error</u>
    (D)   (E)

17. I <u>have</u> asked all of the teachers, and none of them <u>has</u> <u>seen</u>
  (A)   (B) (C)
 the painting that <u>was</u> stolen from the lounge. <u>No error</u>
      (D)   (E)

18. <u>Leading</u> the list of household <u>dangers</u> to children <u>is</u> cleaners
  (A)   (B)   (C)
 that <u>contain</u> poisonous chemicals. <u>No error</u>
   (D)   (E)

19. Everyone in the class <u>is</u> <u>looking</u> forward to spring, when
         (A) (B)
 the days <u>will</u> be longer and recess <u>will</u> once again be outdoors.
    (C)   (D)
 <u>No error</u>
  (E)

20. <u>Are</u> Joline or Aiden <u>coming</u> to help, or <u>do</u> we <u>have</u> to do all
  (A)   (B)   (C) (D)
 the work ourselves? <u>No error</u>
       (E)

Answers and Explanations

1.   A

Jury is a singular collective noun, so it requires the third-person singular verb *consists*.

2.   B

The compound subjects *fame* and *fortune* are connected by *neither...nor*, so the verb should be the singular *is*.

3.   C

The indefinite pronoun *no one* is singular, so the verb should be the third-person singular *has*.

4.   E

No error.

5.   D

The subject of the verb *hang* is *"Les Demoiselles d'Avignon,"* a title that should be treated as a singular subject. Thus the verb should be the third-person singular *hangs*.

6.   E

Statistics here is both the academic discipline and the title of a class, both of which should be treated as singular. *Classes* is part of a prepositional phrase.

7.   C

The subject of the verb *have seen* is *who*, which should be treated as a singular subject. Thus the verb should be *has*.

8.   E

Note that *"Trading Spaces"* is a title that requires a singular verb.

9.   B

The compound subjects *Carlos* and *his children* are connected by *or*, so the verb must agree with the closest subject, *children*. Thus the verb should be the plural *are*.

10.   E

Senate is a collective noun and requires a singular verb.

11. A

The subject of the verb *keeps* is the plural *dreams*, not *mine*, which is part of a prepositional phrase. Thus the verb should also be plural: *keep*.

12. B

The antecedent *which* refers to *restaurant,* which is singular and requires the third-person singular verb *features.*

13. C

The subject of the verb *aren't* is *question*, so the verb should be the singular *isn't.*

14. B

In this case, *statistics* refers not to the academic discipline but to individual numbers. Thus the verb should be the plural *suggest.*

15. B

The subject *she* requires the third-person singular *does.*

16. C

The subject *Thayer* requires the third-person singular *slips.*

17. B

Here the subject *none* refers to the antecedent *teachers,* so the verb should be the plural *have.*

18. C

In this inverted sentence, *cleaners* are *leading the list,* so the verb must be plural.

19. E

Everyone is one of the indefinite pronouns that requires a singular verb.

20. A

The compound subject *Joline* and *Aiden* is connected by *or*, so the verb should be the singular *is.*

CHAPTER 6

Pronoun Agreement, Reference, and Case

Start with this 10-question Building Block Quiz. The first few questions test material you've already seen.

BUILDING BLOCK QUIZ

Choose the word or phrase that correctly fills in the blank. (We've tinkered with quotations to create the error.)

1. After the game, the king and pawn ____ into the same box. —*Italian proverb*

   (A) goes   (B) go   (C) going   (D) gone   (E) had went

2. Under a ragged coat ____ wisdom. —*Romanian proverb*

   (A) lay   (B) lie   (C) lies   (D) lays   (E) lying

3. Don't speak unless you ____ improve the silence —*Spanish proverb*

   (A) can   (B) must   (C) should   (D) may   (E) have to

4. Examine what is said, not ____ who speaks. —*Arab proverb*

   (A) he   (B) they   (C) them   (D) him   (E) we

5. Everyone thinks ____ own burden heavy. —*French proverb*

   (A) his   (B) her   (C) his or her   (D) our   (E) their

6. He is rich ____ owes nothing. —*French proverb*

   (A) whom   (B) who   (C) whose
   (D) whoever   (E) whomever

7. He ____ wants a rose must respect the thorn. —*Persian proverb*

   (A) which   (B) that   (C) who   (D) whom   (E) himself

8. Young pigs grunt as loudly as old pigs grunted before ____.
   —*Danish proverb*

   (A) them   (B) they   (C) us   (D) we   (E) themselves

9. If you see no reason for giving thanks, the fault lies in ____.
   —*Native American proverb*

   (A) yourself   (B) you   (C) us   (D) it   (E) itself

10. A good painter need not give a name to ____ picture, a bad
    one must. —*Polish proverb*

    (A) his   (B) her   (C) its   (D) their   (E) his or her

Answers and Explanations

1. B

The compound subject (*king* and *pawn*) connected by *and* needs the plural verb, *go*. The sentence states a general truth, so the simple present is correct.

2. C

The subject is *wisdom*. There is no object to receive the action (*coat* is the object of the preposition *under*), so the verb is intransitive and in the third-person singular.

3. A

The best choice is *can*, expressing ability. The other helping verbs don't make sense.

4. A

The pronoun here must be in the subjective case, since it is the subject in the clause *he who speaks*.

5.   C

The indefinite pronoun *everyone* is a singular antecedent; because it includes both genders, it needs both third-person singular pronouns.

6.   B

Who is the subject of the verb *owes,* so it must be in the subjective case (*who*, not *whom*).

7.   C

Who is the subject of the verb *wants*. Thus it too must be in the subjective case.

8.   A

The pronoun here is the object of the preposition *before*, so it must be in the objective case. It refers to *young pigs*, so it must be third-person plural.

9.   B

The final pronoun should be consistent with the first, so it should be some form of *you*. The reflexive *yourself* is not logical because *you* isn't performing the action; the subject of the second clause is *fault*.

10.   E

A generic noun such as *painter* can refer to males and females, so the pronoun must include both.

Pronouns replace nouns, other pronouns, phrases, or clauses. Without pronouns, we'd have to keep repeating those antecedents:

| **Without pronouns:** | Kendall says Kendall's mom fixed Kendall's mom's flat tire before Kendall got there to help. |
| **With pronouns:** | Kendall says his mom fixed her flat tire before he got there to help. |

But as handy as pronouns are, they can be problematic. So this chapter is devoted to three issues: agreement, unclear reference, and pronoun case.

KINDS OF PRONOUNS

Pronouns come in six types: personal, possessive, reflexive, relative, demonstrative, indefinite, and interrogative (see chapter 1). Possessive pronouns function as adjectives:

Adjective: <u>My</u> dog is a fantastic swimmer. (*My* modifies *dog*.)

Pronoun: That dog is <u>mine</u>.

Adjective: <u>Several</u> children have the chicken pox. (*Several* modifies *children*.)

Pronoun: There are <u>several</u> left.

Pronouns should *agree* with the words they replace, it must be *clear* to which words they refer, and you must use the proper *case*.

PRONOUN AGREEMENT

Pronouns must agree in number, person, and gender with their **antecedents**.

> **GRAMMAR SPEAK**
> An **antecedent** is what a pronoun replaces or refers to.

A third-person, singular, male antecedent (for example, *Joe*) needs a third-person, singular, male pronoun (*he, his, him, himself*):

Joe parked <u>his</u> car on the curb.

Practice 1

Circle the antecedent for each underlined pronoun below.

Example: (I) love <u>my</u> dog.

1. Mia was the first vegetarian in <u>her</u> family.
2. I thought I'd left my keys here, but now I can't find <u>them</u>.
3. Pass me the folder <u>that</u> has a big coffee stain on the cover.
4. Are <u>all</u> of the children asleep?
5. I think <u>these</u> are the most interesting photographs.

Practice 2

Circle the correct pronoun in parenthesis in each sentence below.

1. Ice skaters practice (its / their) routines for hours each day.
2. As Americans, (you / we) celebrate July 4th as the birth of (your / our) nation.
3. I am impressed by LuAnne's ability to control (her / my) temper.
4. The male peacock displays (their / its) feathers to attract a mate.
5. The photos in this album are losing (their / its) color.

Compound Antecedents

Like subjects, antecedents can be single or compound.

>   **Single:** I love <u>my</u> dog.

>   **Compound:** Toby and I love <u>our</u> dog.

The rules for agreement with compound antecedents are:

1. If a compound antecedent is connected by *and*, the pronoun should be plural. (Notice the plural verbs.)

>   LJ **and** Elliot have finished <u>their</u> homework.

>   The house **and** garage both have cracks in <u>their</u> foundations.

2. If a compound antecedent is connected by *or* or *nor*, and both are singular, the pronoun should be singular. (Notice the singular verbs.)

>   Neither LJ **nor** Elliot has finished <u>his</u> homework.

>   Neither the house **nor** the garage has a crack in <u>its</u> foundation.

If one antecedent is female and the other male, the sentence must be rewritten:

Incorrect:	Neither LJ **nor** Magdalena has finished <u>his</u> homework.
Incorrect:	Neither LJ **nor** Magdalena have finished <u>their</u> homework.
Correct:	Both LJ and Magdalena still have to do <u>their</u> homework.
Correct:	Neither LJ nor Magdalena has finished the assignment.

3. If a compound antecedent is connected by *or* or *nor*, the pronoun must agree with the nearest antecedent.

> Neither LJ **nor** his sisters have finished <u>their</u> homework.
>
> Neither the twins **nor** LJ has finished <u>his</u> homework.

Practice 3
Choose the correct word in the following sentences.

1. The penguins and the walrus have had (its / their) breakfasts.
2. Neither the walrus nor the penguins have had (its / their) breakfast.
3. Neither the penguins nor the walrus has had (its / their) breakfast.
4. Has Maria or Arnold fed (his / her / their / the) animals yet?
5. Have Maria and Arnold fed (his / her / their / the) animals yet?

Collective and Other Singular Nouns
As you learned in chapter 5, collective nouns (e.g., *class, committee, crowd*) are singular unless the context emphasizes the individual members of the group. Titles, phrases, and "singular plurals" (e.g, *economics* and *news*) are also singular antecedents:

> The **class** expressed <u>its</u> approval with loud applause.
>
> The **class** put <u>their</u> signatures on the petition.

> **Delivering pizza** is not a glamorous job, but <u>it</u> pays the bills.
>
> **Physics** is my favorite subject, but <u>it</u> is also my most challenging.

Practice 4
Circle the correct choice from the parenthesis in each sentence below.

1. The committee will announce (its / their) selection tomorrow.
2. I admit the news is bad, but (it / they) could be worse.
3. The team (has its / have their) final playoff game Thursday.

4. I don't feel comfortable with these statistics because I don't trust (its / their) source.

5. *The Three Musketeers* was a popular book long before (it was / they were) made into a film.

Indefinite Pronouns

The following indefinite pronouns require a singular verb and a singular pronoun:

anybody	everybody	nobody	somebody	each
anyone	everyone	no one	someone	either
anything	everything	nothing	something	neither

Unless you know that everyone referred to is of the same gender, you cannot pick one pronoun or the other. Revise the sentence one of three ways:

1. Use two pronouns: Does **everyone** have <u>his or her</u> password?

2. Rewrite the sentence so that the antecedent is plural: Do all of the students have <u>their</u> passwords?

3. Rewrite the sentence to eliminate the pronoun: Does every student have a password?

Generic Nouns

A **generic** noun refers to one or more members of a group *in general*:

A <u>student</u> must work hard to earn good grades.

A <u>customer</u> expects to be treated with respect.

Like collective nouns, singular generic nouns require a singular pronoun. Since in most cases the group includes males and females, the pronoun must agree with both genders, revise as you would for a singular indefinite pronoun.

Incorrect: A student must work hard if <u>she</u> wants to earn good grades.

Incorrect: A student must work hard if <u>they</u> want to earn good grades.

Correct: A student must work hard if <u>he or she</u> wants to earn good grades.

Correct: Students must work hard if <u>they</u> want to earn good grades.

Correct: A student must work hard to earn good grades.

REMEMBER THIS!

Singular indefinite antecedents and generic nouns require *two* third-person singular pronouns, or revise the sentence to have a plural antecedent or to eliminate the pronoun altogether.

Practice 5

How would you correct any pronoun-antecedent agreement errors in the following sentences?

1. I don't know anybody who hasn't had a crush on one of his teachers.
2. A scientist must be guided by her observations, not her emotions.
3. Someone has left their keys on the table.
4. To be great, an artist must listen to his heart and not his critics.
5. Each of the sculptures have their own unique charm.

UNCLEAR REFERENCE

How quickly you can find the problem in this sentence?

Tyler and Leon are going to his house after school.

Ambiguous Reference

Whose house are they going to? The sentence is unclear because the pronoun *his* could refer to either *Tyler* or *Leon*. This is an **ambiguous** reference—a pronoun that has to two or more possible antecedents. In most cases, the best fix is either to rewrite the sentence to avoid the need for a pronoun or to repeat the antecedent.

Tyler and Leon are going to <u>Tyler's</u> house after school.

Vague Antecedents

Sometimes a writer thinks there is a clear antecedent when actually none exists. That's the problem in the following sentence:

After Dylan finished vacuuming, he put <u>it</u> away.

You might have assumed that *it* refers to a vacuum, but the word *vacuum* itself isn't anywhere. The verb is being used as an antecedent; this is a mistake.

After Dylan finished vacuuming, he put <u>the vacuum</u> away.

This next sentence may seem clearer, but it makes the same kind of mistake:

Incorrect: Jules walks to work because <u>it</u> only takes her fifteen minutes.

Correct: Jules walks to work because <u>the trip</u> only takes her fifteen minutes.

Try another common vague antecedent problem:

<u>They</u> predict that it's going to be a very cold winter.

Yesterday <u>they</u> shut down the turnpike because of a serious accident.

Who are *they*? In both sentences, the *they* referred to is unspecified. Of course, these sentences might be correct if *they* refers clearly to an antecedent in a prior sentence. But this structure, often used because the agent is unknown or unimportant, should be avoided. Don't leave it to your reader to decided whether *they* refers to the National Weather

Service or Channel 4 in the first sentence or the police, vigilantes, or emergency workers in the second. Make your sentences clear:

A very cold winter is predicted.

Yesterday <u>the police</u> shut down the turnpike because of a serious accident.

> ### REMEMBER THIS!
> **Don't** make your readers guess what you're talking about. Make your pronoun references **specific** and **clear**.

Practice 6

How would you correct vague pronoun references in the following sentences?

1. The Cobras vs. Stingrays should be no contest because they're at the top of their game.
2. Shonda ran into Isabelle, and she gave her your number.
3. Sami put some thick logs into the fireplace and it burned brightly for hours.
4. I got the application, and it took me over an hour.
5. As Bernice was putting the last toothpick on top of her toothpick Eiffel Tower, it broke.

Overly Broad Reference

Another common pronoun error is to use *this*, *that*, *which*, or *it* to refer to a whole idea or sentence rather than a specific antecedent:

The characters wrestle with matters of race, religion, and free will, and <u>that's</u> what makes the novel so powerful.

Here, *that* refers to the whole first clause, which expresses a broad idea. Pronouns are most effective and clear when they replace a *specific* antecedent. This sentence should be revised:

The characters wrestle with matters of race, religion, and free will, and <u>their struggle</u> is what makes the novel so powerful.

RELATIVE PRONOUNS

- Use *who, whom, whose* (and some authorities permit *that*) to refer to people.
- Use *which* and *that* to refer to animals or things. (Exception: If you are refering to a pet or otherwise beloved creature, you can use *who*.)
  - Use *which* for clauses that are *not* essential to the meaning of the sentence: *I'm going to the laundromat, which is my favorite place for people watching.*
  - Use *that* for clauses that *are* essential to the meaning of the sentence: *I will only go to a laundromat that offers free soap.*

Practice 7

How would you revise the following sentences to correct overly broad or indefinite pronoun references or errors?

1. They have raised the tuition by 2% for next year.
2. Residents of the embattled town have survived two hurricanes and a tornado, which has brought everyone together as a community.
3. On the phone they said to bring three forms of ID.
4. I'm making this sweater for my dog Glenda, which loves to play in the snow.
5. I'm going to the same dermatologist that treated Rashaad's eczema.

PRONOUN CASE

Personal pronouns come in three **cases: subjective, objective,** and **possessive.** Most of us know when to use the possessive, but many confuse the subjective and objective cases.

Subjective Case	Objective Case
I	me
you	you
he, she, it	him, her, it
we	us
you (plural)	you (plural)
they	them
who	whom

Use the **subjective case** when the pronoun is the **subject** or **subject complement** of its clause.

Otherwise, use the **objective case**.

I hope <u>they</u> don't ask <u>me</u> too many questions.
subject / subject / indirect object

It was <u>I</u> who called the police.
subject complement

For <u>me</u>, the most difficult part of the day is just getting out of bed.
object of preposition

REMEMBER THIS!
Use the subjective case when a pronoun is the subject or complement. Otherwise, use the objective case.

Simple enough, right? But we develop bad habits, so what sounds right is actually wrong:

Between you and (I / me), Lotta should keep her opinions to herself.

Between is a preposition, and both pronouns are its objects, so they should be in the objective case: *between you and <u>me</u>*.

Comparative Statements

Pronouns used in comparisions are notorious:

You like chocolate more than <u>me</u>.

You like chocolate more than <u>I</u>.

Both are correct—but they convey very different meanings. In the first sentence, *me* is an object and the sentence means you like chocolate *more than you like me*. In the second, because *I* is a subject, the sentence means that you like chocolate *more than I do*.

As in the second example, the verb of the subjective pronoun is often omitted in comparisons …which is why it's so easy to make a mistake. Look carefully at the context to determine the intended meaning. If adding *I do* or *I am* to the end of the sentence makes sense, then you probably need the subjective case.

Modifiers

When a pronoun is in a modifying phrase or clause, determine whether it is modifying or renaming a subject or an object:

> Though many students were involved in the fight, the principal only called two people to the office: Darlene and me.

> Only two people, Darlene and I, were called to the principal's office, though many students were involved in the dispute.

In the first sentence, the phrase *Darlene and me* refers back to *people*, a direct object; the pronoun should be in the objective case. In the second, the phrase relates to the subject of the sentence, *only two students,* and is in the subjective case.

Practice 8

For each sentence below, determine whether the pronouns are functioning as subjects or objects. Then choose the correct pronoun.

1. Zach is not coming, for (I / me) asked him to wait until tomorrow.
2. This present is not for you but for (I / me).
3. Come and meet my cousin Charles, (who / whom) works as a clown in the circus.
4. You have your interview earlier than (I / me).
5. I assure you, only two people know your secret—Marcus and (I / me).

We vs. Us

Occasionally we put the pronouns *we* or *us* in front of nouns to emphasize our membership in that group or category: *we Americans* or *us snowboarders*. But which pronoun should we use? Again, it depends upon whether the antecedent is a subject in its clause:

Does Uncle Sam think <u>we</u> **taxpayers** have money growing on trees?

Uncle Sam needs to give <u>us</u> **taxpayers** a break.

In the first sentence, *taxpayers* is a subject—*taxpayers have*, so the pronoun must be subjective. In the second, *taxpayers* is an indirect object, therefore objective. To help you determine which case to use, simply eliminate the noun:

Uncle Sam needs to give (we / us) a break.

Who vs. Whom

Use *who* (or *whoever*) for subjects and *whom* (or *whomever*) for objects. In the following sentences, *who* functions as a subject:

The award will be given to the student <u>who</u> earns the highest overall GPA.

Do you know <u>who</u> has the keys to the shed?

In these sentences, on the other hand, the pronoun *whom* is an object:

To <u>whom</u> should I address this letter? (object of preposition)

<u>Whom</u> are you going to ask to the prom? (direct object)

At tomorrow's meeting, we will decide <u>whom</u> to hire.

To see more easily which case to use, replace the pronoun with *he* or *him* (you may need to invert word order in questions and other inverted sentences):

<u>He</u> has the keys to the shed = use *who*.

I am going to ask <u>him</u> to the prom = use *whom*.

Practice 9

Circle the correct pronoun.

1. The reason (we / us) clowns are not smiling is because we've been fired.
2. Can you give (wc / us) clowns another chance?
3. The flu shot will be given to (whoever / whomever) is most at risk.
4. (Who / whom) did you buy this necklace for?
5. We will select the candidate (who / whom) is most qualified.
6. The panel will decide (who / whom) to charge for this offense.

CONSISTENCY

Pronouns should be consistent in person, number and gender.

Inconsistent: If you are thinking of buying a new car, one should carefully consider the safety ratings of the cars they're considering.

Consistent: If you are thinking of buying a new car, you should carefully consider the safety ratings of the cars you're considering.

SUMMARY

Pronouns must **agree** with their antecedents in number (singular or plural), person (first, second or third), and gender (male or female). Rules for pronoun-antecedent agreement are similar to those for subject-verb agreement:

1. Compound antecedents (whether singular or plural) connected by *and* take a plural pronoun.
2. Compound antecedents that are singular and connected by *or* or *nor* use a singular pronoun—unless one antecedent is male and one female. In that case, the sentence must be rewritten.
3. If a singular antecedent and plural antecedent are connected by *or* or *nor*, the pronoun must agree with the closest antecedent.
4. If the antecedent is a collective noun, title, specified word or phrase, or "singular plural," use a singlular pronoun unless the context emphasizes the individuals in the group.

5. If the antecedent is a singular indefinite pronoun such as *anybody*, use a singular pronoun—but *he* or *she* alone will not do, unless it is clear that everyone is of the same gender.

6. Generic nouns refer to one or more members of a group in general, and are singular. Use two pronouns to include both genders, rewrite the sentence to make it plural, or revise it to eliminate the pronoun.

Unclear pronoun reference is a common problem.

- **ambiguous** reference means there are two or more possible antecedents; rewrite the sentence or repeat the correct antecedent to make the sentence clear.

- **vague antecedent** means the antecedent is not present—often the unspecified *they*, which should be replaced by a specific noun. To be grammatically correct, the antecedent needs to be clear.

- **overly broad reference** means a pronoun refers to a whole phrase, clause, or sentence when it should have a specific antecedent.

Who (and according to some authorities *that*) refers to people (and beloved creatures), *which* and *that* to animals and things. Use *who* or *which* for clauses that are not essential to the meaning of the sentence; use *that* for clauses that *are* essential.

Pronouns have three **cases: subjective, objective**, and **possessive**. Use the subjective case (*I, you, he/she/it, we, they, who*) when the pronoun is the subject or subject complement of its clause, and the possessive to show ownership. Otherwise use the objective case (*me, you, him/her/it, us, them, whom*). In **comparisons** and in **modifying clauses and phrases**, be sure the pronoun case accurately reflects your intended meaning. Determine whether the clause or phrase modifies a subject or object in its clause, then use the appropriate case.

Finally, remember to be consistent in pronoun person, number, and gender.

Practice Answers and Explanations

Practice 1

1. Mia
2. keys
3. folder
4. children
5. photographs

Practice 2

1. *their.* The antecedent is *ice skaters*, so the pronoun is third-person plural.
2. *we, our.* The antecedent is *Americans*, so the pronoun is third-person plural.
3. *her.* The antecedent is *LuAnne*, so the pronoun must be third-person singular and feminine.
4. *its.* The antecedent is *male peacock*, so the pronoun is third-person singular.
5. *their.* The antecedent is *photos*, so the pronoun is third-person plural.

Practice 3

1. *their.* The compound antecedents *penguins* and *walrus* are connected by *and*, so the pronoun is plural.
2. *their.* The same antecedents are connected by *or*, so the pronoun agrees with the closest antecedent.
3. *its.* This time the closest antecedent is the singular *walrus*, so the pronoun should be singular.
4. *the.* None of the pronouns work. *Maria* and *Arnold* are different genders, so neither *his* nor *her* is correct. *Their* is also incorrect because *or* calls for a singular pronoun. Only *the* is correct.
5. *their.* This time the antecedents are connected by *and*, so the plural pronoun is correct.

Practice 4

1. *its. Committee* is a singular collective noun.

2. *it. News* is a singular collective noun.

3. *has its. Team* is a singular collective noun.

4. *their.* The word *these* indicates that *statistics* is plural in this context, so the pronoun must be plural.

5. *it was.* The title *The Three Musketeers* is singular.

Practice 5

Here are two possible revisions for each sentence.

1. a. I don't know anybody who hasn't had a crush on one of his or her teachers.

1. b. I think all students have a crush on one of their teachers.

2. a. Scientists must be guided by their observations, not their emotions.

2. b. A scientist must be guided by observation, not emotion.

3. a. Someone has left his or her keys on the table.

3. b. Somebody's keys have been left on the table.

4. a. To be great, an artist must listen to his or her heart and not his or her critics.

4. b. To be great, artists must listen to their hearts and not their critics. (But 4b is a better, less clumsy option.)

5. a. Each of the sculptures has its own unique charm.

5. b. All of the sculptures have their own unique charm.

Practice 6

1. The Cobras vs. the Stingrays should be no contest because <u>the Cobras</u> (*or Stingrays*) are at the top of their game.

2. Shonda ran into Isabelle, and <u>Shonda</u> (*or Isabelle*) gave her your number.

3. Sami put some thick logs into the fireplace and <u>the fire</u> burned brightly for hours.

4. I got the application, and it took me over an hour <u>to fill it out</u>.

5. As Bernice was putting the last toothpick on top of her toothpick Eiffel Tower, <u>the Tower</u> (*or toothpick*) broke.

Practice 7

Answers will vary slightly.

1. <u>The Board of Trustees</u> has raised the tuition by 2% for next year. (The indefinite *they* must be replaced by a specific noun.)

2. Residents of the embattled town have survived two hurricanes and a tornado; <u>these disasters</u> have brought everyone together as a community. (The pronoun *which* refers to an overly broad antecedent.)

3. On the phone <u>the representative</u> said to bring three forms of ID. (The Indefinite *they* should be replaced by a specific noun.)

4. I'm making this sweater for my dog Glenda, <u>who</u> loves to play in the snow. (The pronoun *which* should be *who*, as the dog is named and referred to as a person. *Which* could also be correct because the clause is unnecessary to the meaning of the sentence.)

5. I'm going to the same dermatologist <u>who</u> treated Rashaad's eczema. (While some authorities accept *that*, it's preferable to use *who* to refer to a person.)

Practice 8

1. *I*. Here *for* is not a preposition but a coordinating conjunction, and *I* functions as a subject.

2. *me*. Here *for* is a preposition, so the pronoun is in the objective case.

3. *who*. In this subordinate clause, *who* is a subject.

4. *I*. The subjective case is required.

5. *I*. The modifier *Marcus and I* refers to the subject *two people* (the verb: *know*).

Practice 9

1. *we*. The noun *clowns* is a subject.

2. *us*. Here the noun *clowns* is an indirect object.

3. *whomever*. The pronoun is the object of the preposition *to*.

4. *whom*. The pronoun is the object of the preposition *for*.

5. *who*. The pronoun introduces the subordinate clause *who is the most qualified*, so it is the subject of the verb *is*.

6. *whom*. Remember, use *whom* before an infinitive.

CHAPTER 6 TEST

Choose the best version of the underlined portion of each sentence below.

1. The belief that time is linear, <u>that is</u> a Western notion, contrasts with the Native American belief that time is circular.

    (A) that is   (B) which is   (C) which are
    (D) that are   (E) being

2. When you go to a fancy restaurant, <u>one</u> should always place the napkin on your lap.

    (A) one   (B) people   (C) he   (D) she   (E) you

3. Neither the hydrangea nor the rose bushes have any flowers on <u>it</u> yet.

    (A) it   (B) itself   (C) them   (D) themselves   (E) they

4. This isn't about <u>you and me</u>; it's about our daughter.

    (A) you and me   (B) you and I   (C) yourself and myself
    (D) yourself and I   (E) we

5. This is the house <u>which</u> I was telling you about.

    (A) which   (B) whichever   (C) who   (D) whoever   (E) that

6. <u>A soldier must be loyal to his</u> country.

    (A) A soldier must be loyal to his

    (B) A soldier must be loyal to her

    (C) A soldier must be loyal to one's

    (D) A soldier must be loyal to its

    (E) Soldiers must be loyal to their

7. I was going to go grocery shopping, but <u>it</u> closed early.

    (A) it   (B) they   (C) the store   (D) shopping   (E) that

8. The founders of the club—Tazjeer and I—are the only permanent members.

(A) Tazjeer and I   (B) Tazjeer and me   (C) Tazjeer and myself
(D) Tazjeer himself and me   (E) us

9. They recommend that you floss your teeth every day.

(A) They recommend that you floss
(B) They recommend flossing
(C) Dentists recommend that you flosses
(D) Dentists recommend that you floss
(E) Dentists recommend that we floss

10. Us tenants have about had it with our superintendent.

(A) Us tenants   (B) We tenants   (C) Us tenants ourselves
(D) We ourselves   (E) Our tenants

11. Someone has parked their car illegally in front of the fire hydrant.

(A) their car   (B) his car   (C) her car
(D) his or her car   (E) its car

12. You can give that extra notebook to who wants it.

(A) who wants
(B) who want
(C) whoever want
(D) whoever wants
(E) whomever wants

13. Neither Lisa nor Jennifer has seen the movie.

(A) has seen   (B) have seen   (C) has saw
(D) have saw   (E) did see

14. Either that dog lost his collar, or it doesn't have an owner.

(A) his collar, or it   (B) its collar, or it   (C) his collar, or she
(D) her collar, or he   (E) its collar, or he

15. Imani has always liked sports <u>more than me; I've</u> never been much of an athlete.

    (A) more than me; I've   (B) more than myself; I've

    (C) more than I; I've   (D) more than I; I was

    (E) more than I; while I've

16. Zoe and Elizabeth are coming over <u>after she finishes</u> work.

    (A) after she finishes   (B) after they finishes

    (C) after Zoe finishes   (D) after Zoe and Elizabeth finishes

    (E) after finishing

17. The committee <u>will have their final meeting</u> of the year tomorrow.

    (A) will have their final meeting

    (B) has their final meeting

    (C) will have his or her final meeting

    (D) will have its final meeting

    (E) will has its final meeting

18. I am tired, hungry, and bored, <u>which makes</u> me very grumpy indeed.

    (A) which makes   (B) which make   (C) that makes

    (D) a combination that makes   (E) making

19. Neither the books nor the magazine <u>has its</u> original cover.

    (A) has its   (B) have its   (C) have their

    (D) has their   (E) have the

20. My mom, <u>whom has</u> a degree in early childhood education, will start teaching next fall.

    (A) whom has   (B) who has   (C) who have

    (D) whom have   (E) which has

Answers and Explanations

1. B

The clause is not essential, so it should be introduced by *which*, not *that*. The subject is singular, so the verb must be *is*, eliminating (C) and (D).

2. E

To be consistent, all pronouns should be in the second person.

3. C

When two antecedents are connected by *nor*, the pronoun must agree with the closest. *Rose bushes* is plural, so the correct pronoun is *them*.

4. A

The pronouns are objects of the preposition *about*, so they should be objective.

5. E

The clause is essential to the meaning of the sentence; without it, we wouldn't know which house. So it should be introduced by *that*.

6. E

A generic noun needs to include both genders. Only (E) does so by revising the antecedent to make it plural.

7. C

The pronoun *it* refers to *store*, a word that is not stated in the original sentence.

8. A

This modifier refers to *founders*, which is the subject, so the pronoun must be subjective.

9. D

The pronoun *they* doesn't refer to a specific antecedent; replace it with *dentists*. The verb is subjunctive because it expresses a recommendation.

10. B

Tenants is a subject, so the pronoun must be subjective. Eliminate *tenants* and *we* makes a correct sentence.

11. D

Someone is a singular indefinite pronoun and must include both singular third-person pronouns.

12. D

The underlined words are a clause, which needs a subject and verb—thus the subjective pronoun. *Whoever* fits the context.

13. A

The two singular antecedents are connected by *nor*, so the antecedent and verb must be singular.

14. B

The pronouns must be consistent; only (B) uses the same third-person singular pronoun.

15. C

It's clear from the context that the comparison is between how much Imani and the speaker like sports. The subjective *I* is needed.

16. C

The pronoun *she* is ambiguous because it could refer to either *Zoe* or *Elizabeth*. Only (C) identifies a specific antecedent.

17. D

Committee is a singular collective noun, so it requires a singular pronoun. The verb *have* must be in its base form following *will*, so (E) is incorrect.

18. D

Which makes an overly broad reference to the whole clause *I am tired, hungry, and bored.* What *makes me very grumpy* is the *combination* of the three.

19. A

With a compound antecedent, the pronoun and verb must agree with the closest referent—*magazine.*

20. B

The clause *who has … education* modifies the subject of the sentence, *my mom.* So the pronoun must be subjective and the verb must be singular.

Modifiers and Their Placement

Start with this 10-question Building Block Quiz. The first few questions test material you've already seen.

BUILDING BLOCK QUIZ

Part A: Questions 1–6 refer to the following sentence:

> He who is outside his door already has a hard part of his
> journey behind him.   —*Dutch proverb*

1. [B]ehind him is a/an:

   (A) subordinating conjunction   (B) subordinate clause

   (C) prepositional phrase   (D) subject complement

   (E) infinitive

2. [W]ho is outside his door is a/an:

   (A) independent clause   (B) subordinate clause

   (C) prepositional phrase   (D) predicate   (E) subject

3. The antecedent of who is:

   (A) he   (B) door   (C) journey

   (D) you (unstated)   (E) no antecedent

4. [W]ho is outside his door has which of the following functions?

   (A) describes the action of the sentence

   (B) connects equal parts of the sentence

   (C) indicates the tense of the verb

   (D) modifies the subject of the sentence

   (E) modifies the verb of the sentence

5. Which of the following words is an adverb?

   (A) he   (B) behind   (C) door   (D) hard   (E) already

6. Which of the following words is an adjective?

   (A) who   (B) outside   (C) hard   (D) journey   (E) him

Part B: For questions 7–10, choose the best version of the underlined portion of the sentence.

7. Under hypnosis, many people can access memories buried in the <u>most deepest</u> part of their subconscious.

   (A) No change   (B) deepest   (C) more deep

   (D) deeper   (E) most deep

8. I'm not feeling <u>well</u>, so I won't make it to the party.

   (A) No change   (B) good   (C) best   (D) gooder   (E) goodly

9. <u>Being terrified of heights</u>, that roller coaster is one ride I'll never go on.

   (A) No change

   (B) Terrified of heights

   (C) Since there's terror of heights

   (D) Since I'm terrified of heights

   (E) Since heights terrify

10. Lost deep in the woods, <u>it was impossible to tell</u> which direction was home.

   (A) No change

   (B) it couldn't be told

   (C) we couldn't possibly tell

   (D) telling was impossible

   (E) it wasn't possible to tell

Answers and Explanations

1.   C

Behind is a preposition, *behind him* the prepositional phrase.

2.   B

The relative pronoun *who* introduces a subordinate clause that cannot stand on its own.

3.   A

Who refers to *he*.

4.   D

He is the subject of the sentence, so the clause describes the subject.

5.   E

Already modifies the verb *has*.

6.   C

Hard modifies the noun *part*.

7.   B

Comparatives should only take one form—*er/est* or *more/most, less/least*.

8.   A

Well is an adverb *except* when it refers to health or condition.

9.   D.

The original doesn't make clear who was *being terrified of heights*.

10.   C.

The sentence doesn't tell us who was *lost deep in the woods*.

Without adjectives and adverbs, the world would lack great words like *rambunctious* and *vile*. It would have no color or comparison, no *now* or *later*. It would lack temperature and degree: no *sweltering* or *frigid*, no *totally* or *almost*.

English is rich with modifiers—words, phrases, and clauses that describe or restate. After a brief review, this chapter moves on to comparisions and modifier placement.

ADJECTIVES

Adjectives modify nouns and pronouns. They tell us which one, what kind, or how many, or how someone or something looks, smells, tastes, or feels:

The shopkeeper was <u>helpful</u> and <u>friendly</u>.

I'd like to try <u>that</u> <u>burgundy</u> loafer on the <u>wire</u> rack, please, in size <u>8</u>.

Because they describe people, places, and things, adjectives can function as subject complements:

They said the apartment was <u>charming</u> and <u>cozy</u>; it turned out to be <u>tiny</u> and <u>dank</u>.

ADVERBS

Many adverbs are formed by adding –*ly* to an adjective. Adverbs modify verbs, adjectives, and other adverbs, telling us where, when, how, and to what extent:

We drifted <u>slowly</u> <u>away</u>.

I will <u>never</u> eat <u>here</u> <u>again</u>!

FLASHBACK

Recall from chapter 1: adjectives modify nouns and pronouns, while **ad**verbs modify <u>verbs</u>, **adj**ectives, and other **ad**verbs.

Though often similar in form, adjectives and adverbs are not interchangeable:

Incorrect: The car in front of me was going so <u>slow</u> that I was late for work.

Correct: The car in front of me was going so <u>slowly</u> that I was late for work.

Say What You Mean

Using adjectives and adverbs properly isn't just a matter of being grammatically correct. Using one instead of the other can drastically change your meaning:

Ilka found the test <u>easy</u>.   Ilka found the test <u>easily</u>.

In the first sentence, *easy* is an adjective modifying the noun *test*. In the second sentence, *easily* is an adverb modifying the verb *found*: Ilka had no trouble finding the test.

Good and Bad, Well and Badly

The most commonly confused adjective and adverb pairs are *good/well* and *bad/badly*. *Good* and *bad* are adjectives; *well* and *badly* are adverbs.

Justine took the <u>bad</u> news very <u>well</u>. (*Bad* modifies *news*; *well* modifies *took*.)

Justine took the <u>good</u> news quite <u>badly</u>. (*Good* modifies *news*; *badly* modifies *took*.)

MEMORY TIP

To remember that *well* and *badly* are adverbs, note that both words have an *l*, and *–ly* is a common adverb ending.

The exception: *well*, when referring to health or condition, is an adjective. When someone asks about your health, the correct response is "I'm *well*," not "I'm *good*." In all other cases, use *well* only to modify verbs, adverbs, and adjectives:

Adjective:	The patients are <u>well</u>.
Adverb:	The students did <u>well</u>.
Adverb:	A <u>well</u>-known author will speak.
Adverb:	<u>Well</u> said, Jacob!

Practice 1

Determine which word in the parentheses correctly completes the sentence.

1. How (bad / badly) was he hurt?
2. Please be (careful / carefully)!
3. It's not a (good / well) situation, but we'll get through it.
4. The phone rang so (loud / loudly) it startled us all.
5. You look (good / well) in that dress.

COMPARISONS

Most adjectives and adverbs come in three forms: **positive**, **comparative**, and **superlative**. The positive is used to modify; the comparative and superlative forms are used in comparisons.

For one- and two-syllable adjectives and some one-syllable adverbs, the comparative is formed by adding *–er*, the superlative by adding *–est*. For longer adjectives and most adverbs (including all of those that end in *–ly*), use **more** and **less** for the comparative and **most** and **least** for the superlative.

Positive	Comparative	Superlative
nice	nicer	nicest
sweet	sweeter	sweetest
less	lesser	least
challenging	more challenging	most challenging
desirable	less desirable	least desirable
likely	more likely	most likely

Two sets of words have irregular comparative and superlative forms:

good / well	better	best
bad / badly	worse	worst

Incorrect: excitingest, worser

Correct: most exciting, worst

Practice 2

Write the comparative and superlative forms of the adjectives and adverbs below.

1. scary   _____
2. beloved   _____
3. surprisingly   _____
4. friendly   _____
5. clearly   _____

Comparative vs. Superlative

The comparative is used to compare **two** things; the superlative compares **three or more**.

> **Incorrect:** Zach and Juliana both play chess, but Juliana plays <u>best</u>.
>
> **Correct:** Zach and Juliana both play chess, but Juliana plays <u>better</u>.

Double Comparisons and Double Negatives

The comparative and superlative take only *one* form: **either** the suffix (*-er* or *–est*) **or** *more/less, most/least*. Do not use both forms together:

> **Incorrect:** This is the <u>most fanciest</u> hotel room I have ever seen.
>
> **Correct:** This is the <u>fanciest</u> hotel room I have ever seen.

Similarly, only one negative is necessary to express a negative meaning. (In fact, two negatives make a positive—they cancel each other out.) Therefore, do not use double negatives unless you intend a positive meaning:

> **Negative:** I was <u>unhappy</u> with the contract.
>
> **Positive:** I was <u>not</u> <u>unhappy</u> with the contract.

The adverbs *hardly, barely,* and *scarcely* are inherently negative, so don't pair them with a negative like *not, never,* or *none*:

> **Incorrect:** I ca<u>n't</u> <u>hardly</u> see a thing through this fog.
>
> **Correct:** I can <u>hardly</u> see a thing through this fog.

Practice 3

Correct any modifier errors in the following sentences.

1. I am the most luckiest person in the world.
2. Who is the greatest genius: Einstein or Leonardo da Vinci?
3. This is much more worse than I thought.
4. I don't hardly know what I'm doing anymore.
5. Monaco, Nauru, and Tuvalu are all tiny countries, but Monaco (at just 1.95 square miles!) is by far the smaller of the three.

MODIFIER PLACEMENT

Whether a single word or a lengthy phrase, modifiers should be as close as possible to the word(s) they modify. A **misplaced modifier** may appear to modify a different word or phrase from the one the writer intended—often with humorous effect:

Misplaced:	<u>Lost deep in a daydream</u>, Ed's boss startled him when she walked into his office.
Correct:	<u>Lost deep in a daydream</u>, **Ed** was startled when his boss walked in.

Ed was lost in a daydream, but the modifying phrase in the first sentence seems to modify *Ed's boss*. The possessive pronoun is an adjective, not a noun, so it can't be the word modified.

> ### REMEMBER THIS!
> Modifiers should be as close as possible to the word(s) they modify.

Misplaced modifiers can create an **ambiguous** sentence (one with two possible meanings):

Ambiguous:	The volunteers who help us out <u>occasionally</u> want permanent, paid positions.
Clear:	The volunteers who <u>occasionally</u> help us out want permanent, paid positions.
	<u>Occasionally</u>, the volunteers who help us out want

permanent, paid positions.

Practice 4

How would you correct any misplaced modifiers in the following sentences?

1. After they robbed the jewelry store, the police caught the thieves.
2. Covered in mud from head to toe, Eunice saw her filthy children.
3. Your meal comes with a free drink or dessert on Sunday.
4. In painstaking detail, the deposition required Zelda to describe her accident.
5. The painting depicted a knight on an armor-covered horse throwing a lance.
6. As a baby, my mother said I loved peas, but now I can't stand them.

Dangling Modifiers

A **dangling modifier** is an adjective (word, phrase or clause) that lacks a clear referent: the word or words it modifies are never specifically stated.

Dangling: <u>Lurching violently in the waves</u>, the captain was afraid of capsizing.

Who or what was *lurching … in the waves*? Presumably the captain's boat—but *boat* is not mentioned in the sentence. To correct the problem, the person or thing being modified (in this case, *boat*) must be added. (Sometimes a more substantial revision may be required.)

Correct: <u>With the boat lurching violently in the waves</u>, the captain was afraid of capsizing.

Dangling modifiers often begin with a present participle or gerund, but they come in all shapes and sizes:

Dangling: After seeing the flooded basement, the house was taken off the market.

Correct: After <u>the inspector saw</u> the flooded basement, the house was taken off the market.

Dangling: At four years old, my family moved to Nevada.

Correct: <u>When I was</u> four years old, my family moved to Nevada.

REMEMBER THIS!

Just as pronouns need a clear and specific antecedent, modifiers need a clear and specific referent.

Practice 5

How would you correct any dangling modifiers in the following sentences?

1. Growing up an only child, my parents gave me all of their attention.
2. While preparing dinner, a mouse ran across the counter and disappeared behind the oven.
3. Sleeping peacefully on the beach, the sudden storm took us by surprise.
4. In selecting an outfit for her interview, a conservative look was the first priority.
5. Sandwiched between a woman shouting into her cell phone and a man snoring as loud as thunder, it was impossible to get any work done on the train.

Limiting Modifiers

Limiting modifiers include such adverbs as *almost, even, just, nearly,* and *only.* These modifiers belong in front of the word they limit:

Wrong place: The workers have finished <u>nearly</u> remodeling the kitchen.

Right place: The workers have <u>nearly</u> finished remodeling the kitchen.

Interrupter Modifiers

As you saw in chapter 2, the usual sentence pattern is *subject–verb–object*. As a rule, avoid putting lengthy modifiers between subjects and verbs or between helping and main verbs—and don't put *any* adverbs between verbs and their objects:

Interrupted:	Captain Jones, after fourteen years at sea, finally returned home.
Correct:	After fourteen years at sea, Captain Jones finally returned home.
Interrupted:	Juanita threw down angrily the letter.
Correct:	Juanita angrily threw down the letter.

However, *who, that,* and *which* clauses, if not excessively long, are acceptable between subject and verb:

Acceptable:	My son, who is obsessed with trains, hopes to be an engineer.
Too long:	My son, who has been obsessed with trains since he was two, hopes to be an engineer.
Corrected:	Obsessed with trains since he was two, my son hopes to be an engineer.

Split Infinitives

Today, the occasional split infinitive is acceptable if it is not awkward. In the right context, it is actually better to split the infinitive:

Awkward:	I want you <u>to very carefully think</u> about my offer.
Better:	I want you <u>to think</u> <u>very carefully</u> about my offer.
Awkward:	I would like <u>actually to hear</u> the rest of the story, so please be quiet!
Better:	I would like <u>to actually hear</u> the rest of the story, so please be quiet!

Practice 6

Correct any modifier errors in the following sentences.

1. Be sure to thoroughly chew your food before you swallow it.

2. Are you ready yet? Already it's time to go.

3. Renee Yeager, author of several self-help books and creator of a series of children's workbooks, will be the keynote speaker at the conference.

4. I will only help if you promise to never tell anyone what I told you.

5. The control group will receive each week a placebo, while the experimental group will be given small doses of the new drug.

SUMMARY

The adjectives **good** and **bad** are often confused with the adverbs **well** and **badly**. *Well* functions as an adjective only when it refers to health.

The **comparative** compares two items, and the **superlative** three or more. The comparative is formed by adding *–er* or using *more/less* in front of the word; the superlative by adding *–est* or using *most/least* in front of the word.

Two common modifier errors are **double comparisons** and **double negatives**. Use only one comparative or superlative form and only one negative (unless you intend a positive meaning).

Modifiers should be placed **as close as possible** to the word(s) they modify. Correct **dangling modifiers** by clearly stating the person or thing being described. **Limiting modifiers** such as *almost* and *only* should immediately precede the word(s) they modify. Avoid placing **lengthy modifiers** between subject and verb, between helping verb and main verb, or between verb and object. The occasional **split infinitive** is acceptable if the resulting sentence is not awkward.

Practice: On Your Own

Practice identifying adjectives and adverbs. Look for modifying phrases and clauses as well as single adjectives and adverbs. Identify the referent—who or what is modified. Find instances when infinitives are split and pay attention to the placement of modifiers. Find examples of modifier errors.

Practice Answers and Explanations

Practice 1

1. *badly*. The modifier describes the verb *was hurt*, so it should be an adverb.
2. *careful*. The unstated subject is *you*, and *be* is a linking verb, so an adjective is required in the subject complement position to modify *you*.
3. *good*. The modifier describes the noun *situation*, so it should be an adjective.
4. *loudly*. The modifier describes the verb *rang*, so it should be an adverb.
5. *good*. The subject complement should be an adjective.

Practice 2

1. scarier, scariest
2. more beloved, most beloved
3. more surprisingly, most surprisingly
4. friendlier, friendliest
5. more clearly, most clearly

Practice 3

1. I am the <u>luckiest</u> person in the world. (*Most* must be deleted.)
2. Who is the <u>greater</u> genius: Einstein or Leonardo da Vinci? (The comparative is required.)
3. This is much <u>worse</u> than I thought. (*More* must be deleted.)
4. I <u>hardly</u> know what I'm doing anymore. (*Don't* must be deleted.)
5. Monaco, Nauru, and Tuvalu are all tiny countries, but Monaco (at just 1.95 square miles!) is by far the <u>smallest</u> of the three. (The superlative is required.)

Practice 4

Answers may vary slightly.

1. After the thieves robbed the jewelry store, the police caught them. (The clause *after they robbed the jewelry store* appears to modify *police* because of its placement, and it is ambiguous because *they* could refer to either *police* or *thieves*. *They* should be changed to *thieves* to eliminate the ambiguity.)

2. Eunice screamed when she saw her filthy children covered in mud from head to toe. (The modifying phrase *covered in mud from head to toe* appears to modify *Eunice* in the original; it needs to be moved to the end of the sentence to clearly modify *children*.)

3. On Sunday, your meal comes with a free drink or dessert. (The modifier *on Sunday* needs to be moved to eliminate ambiguity. Does the free drink/dessert come on Sundays, or do you have to come back to the restaurant on Sunday to get that free drink or dessert?)

4. The deposition required Zelda to recount the story of her accident in painstaking detail. (The modifier *in painstaking detail* appears to describe *deposition* in the original and needs to be moved to the end of the sentence.)

5. The painting depicted a knight riding an armor-covered horse and throwing a lance. (The modifier *throwing a lance* appears to modify *horse* in the original.)

6. My mother said that as a baby I loved peas [*or* I loved peas as a baby], but now I can't stand them. (The modifier *as a baby* needs to be moved so it doesn't modify *my mother*.)

Practice 5

Answers may vary as there is more than one way to revise each sentence.

1. Because I was an only child, my parents gave me all of their attention. (The referent *I* needs to be added so we know who was *growing up an only child*.)

2. While I was preparing dinner, a Mouse ran across the counter and

disappeared behind the oven. (The referent *I* needs to be added to the modifier *while preparing dinner*; otherwise the sentence states that the *mouse* was cooking!)

3. As we slept peacefully on the beach, the sudden storm took us by surprise. (The referent *we* needs to be added so we know who was *sleeping peacefully on the beach*.)

4. In selecting an outfit for her interview, Susan's first priority was a conservative look. (A clear referent needs to be added to the sentence—who was selecting an outfit? *Susan* [or any other name you choose].)

5. Sandwiched between a woman shouting into her cell phone and a man snoring as loud as thunder, I couldn't possibly get any work done on the train. (The referent *I* needs to be added so we know who was *sandwiched* between two loud passengers.)

Practice 6

1. Be sure to chew your food thoroughly before you swallow it. (The infinitive should not be split in this sentence.

2. Are you ready yet? It's already time to go. (The limiting modifier *already* should precede *time*.)

3. Author of several self-help books and creator of a series of children's workbooks, Renee Yeager will be the keynote speaker at the conference. *Another option is to break this into two sentences*: Renee Yeager will be the keynote speaker at the conference. She is the author of several self-help books and creator of a series of children's workbooks. (The modifier *author…workbooks* is too long to interrupt the subject-verb pattern.)

4. I will help only if you promise never to tell anyone what I told you. (The limiting modifier *only* should precede the *if* clause.)

5. The control group will receive a placebo each week, while the experimental group will be given small doses of the new drug. (The modifier *each week* cannot be between the verb and its object.)

CHAPTER 7 TEST

Choose the best version of the underlined portion of each sentence.

1. There's nothing <u>gooder</u> than a bowl of hot soup on a cold, rainy day.

    (A) No change   (B) better   (C) best
    (D) betterer   (E) more good

2. The fire is burning <u>bright</u>.

    (A) No change   (B) more brighter   (C) brighter
    (D) most brightly   (E) brightly

3. You are <u>badly</u> mistaken if you think I'm to blame.

    (A) No change   (B) bad   (C) worse
    (D) badder   (E) most bad

4. Let's go with the <u>least expensive</u> of the two options.

    (A) No change   (B) lesser expensive   (C) less expensiver
    (D) less expensive   (E) least expensiver

5. We have it on <u>well</u> authority that you will win the award.

    (A) No change   (B) good   (C) best
    (D) gooder   (E) more good

6. Yogurt is a much <u>more healthy</u> snack than potato chips.

    (A) No change   (B) healthy   (C) healthier
    (D) more healthier   (E) healthiest

7. There <u>isn't nothing</u> wrong with the phone itself; let me check the wires.

    (A) No change   (B) is anything   (C) is nothing
    (D) isn't anything   (E) is a thing

8. Please <u>give me now that paper</u>.
   - (A) No change
   - (B) give me that paper now
   - (C) give now me that paper
   - (D) now give me that paper
   - (E) give me that now paper

9. <u>Wilson, unlike all the other governors before him, chose to continue living in his own home</u>.
   - (A) No change
   - (B) Wilson chose to continue living in his own home, unlike all other governors before him.
   - (C) Wilson, choosing to continue living in his own home, was unlike all other governors before him.
   - (D) Unlike all the other governors before him, Wilson chose to continue living in his own home.
   - (E) Choosing to continue living in his own home, and unlike all the other governors before him, was Wilson.

10. <u>The next step is to carefully hammer the nail into the base</u>.
   - (A) No change
   - (B) Into the base, the next step is to carefully hammer the nail.
   - (C) The next step is into the base to carefully hammer the nail.
   - (D) The next step is to hammer carefully into the base the nail.
   - (E) The next step is carefully to hammer the nail into the base.

11. <u>I'm going to soundly sleep tonight</u>.
   - (A) No change
   - (B) Soundly I'm going to sleep tonight.
   - (C) I'm soundly going to sleep tonight.
   - (D) I'm going soundly to sleep tonight.
   - (E) I'm going to sleep soundly tonight.

12. <u>We barely were through the door</u> when the phone rang.
   (A) No change
   (B) We were barely through the door
   (C) Barely we were through the door
   (D) We were through the door barely
   (E) We weren't barely through the door

13. <u>There is one stipulation only in the contract</u>.
   (A) No change
   (B) There is one stipulation in the contract only.
   (C) There only is one stipulation in the contract.
   (D) There is one stipulation in the only contract.
   (E) There is only one stipulation in the contract.

14. <u>Sitting at my computer, the screen suddenly went blank</u>.
   (A) No change
   (B) While sitting at my computer, the screen suddenly went blank.
   (C) As I sat at my computer, the screen suddenly went blank.
   (D) While sitting at my computer, my screen suddenly went blank.
   (E) My screen suddenly went blank while sitting at my computer.

15. <u>I went to the mall with Hannah wearing my new black shoes</u>.
   (A) No change
   (B) Wearing my new black shoes, I went to the mall with Hannah.
   (C) I went to the mall wearing my new black shoes with Hannah.
   (D) I went with Hannah wearing my new black shoes to the mall.
   (E) To the mall I went with Hannah wearing my new black shoes.

16. <u>Being sick, we didn't want to visit Erika</u>.
    (A) No change
    (B) Being sick, we didn't want Erika to visit.
    (C) We didn't want Erika to visit, being sick.
    (D) Because we were sick, we didn't want to visit Erika.
    (E) Because of being sick, we didn't want to visit Erika.

17. <u>The elderly patients we visit every week ask us to stay longer</u>.
    (A) No change
    (B) Every week, the elderly patients we visit ask us to stay longer.
    (C) The elderly patients we visit weekly ask us to stay longer.
    (D) The elderly patients every week we visit ask us to stay longer.
    (E) The elderly patients we visit ask us to stay every week longer.

18. <u>The dreams I have from time to time are disturbing</u>.
    (A) No change
    (B) I have dreams from time to time that are disturbing.
    (C) Being disturbing, I have dreams from time to time.
    (D) From time to time my dreams are disturbing.
    (E) I have dreams that are disturbing from time to time.

19. <u>Standing in the shower, the water suddenly became ice cold</u>.
    (A) No change
    (B) As I stood in the shower, the water suddenly became ice cold.
    (C) While standing in the shower, the water suddenly became ice cold.
    (D) Suddenly becoming ice cold, I stood in the shower.
    (E) The water suddenly became ice cold while standing in the shower.

20. The novel tells the story <u>of a woman with a dog who is an aspiring painter</u>.
    (A) No change
    (B) of a woman with a dog and an aspiring painter.
    (C) of a woman who has a dog and is an aspiring painter.
    (D) of a dog, a woman, and an aspiring painter.
    (E) of an aspiring painter who is a woman and a dog.

Answers and Explanations

1. B
The sentence compares two things: *a hot bowl of soup* and *nothing*; the comparative is correct.

2. E
The underlined word modifies the verb *is burning*, so it should be an adverb.

3. A
The underlined word modifies the verb *mistaken*, so it should be an adverb.

4. D
There are two options, so use the comparative. (B), (C), and (E) incorrectly use two comparative or superlative forms.

5. B
The underlined word modifies the noun *authority*, so it should be an adjective.

6. C
The positive comparative form is needed here. *Healthy* has only two syllables so it takes the *–er* form, not *more*.

7. C *or* **D**
A trick question: Both (C) and (D) are acceptable; both avoid the double negative.

8. B

The modifier *now* cannot be between verb and object and is awkward before the verb or before *paper*. It is most logical *after* the object.

9. D

The modifier *unlike ... before him* is too long to safely interrupt the subject (*Wilson*) and verb (*chose*). It's best placed at the beginning, where it clearly modifies *Wilson*.

10. A

This split infinitive is logical, because it helps to emphasize the modifier *carefully*.

11. E

The modifier *soundly* should immediately follow *sleep*.

12. B

The limiting modifier *barely* should be immediately before *through*.

13. E

The limiting modifier *only* should be immediately before *one*.

14. C

This dangling modifier needs a specific referent—*who* was *sitting at my computer*? Only (C) adds the referent.

15. B

The placement of the modifier *wearing ... shoes* in (A), (D), and (E) means *Hannah* was wearing them. (C) seems to say both the speaker and Hannah were wearing them.

16. D

We can't tell who is sick: *we* or *Erika*. Only (D) adds the needed referent, *we*.

17. B

Do we visit the patients every week or do they ask us to stay longer every week? Only (B) clarifies the meaning. (E) incorrectly splits the infinitive.

18. D

Does the speaker have dreams from time to time, or are the dreams disturbing from time to time? Only (D) clarifies the sentence. (C) is simply illogical.

19. B

We don't know *who* was standing in the shower. Only (B) corrects the problem.

20. C

In the original sentence the *dog* is an aspiring painter! (B) corrects this. (E) says that the aspiring painter is both a woman and a dog!

CHAPTER 8

Sentence Fragments and Run-Ons

Start with this 10-question Building Block Quiz. The first few questions test material you've already seen.

BUILDING BLOCK QUIZ

Part A: Choose the best answer for questions 1–7.

1. Which of the following is a complex sentence?
   - (A) Do four-leaf clovers really bring good luck?
   - (B) Four-leaf clovers were once believed to ward off evil spirits.
   - (C) These clover charms were considered quite powerful against evil.
   - (D) Over the years, this belief transformed from keeping away the bad to bringing the good.
   - (E) Today, many people believe they are lucky if they find a four-leaf clover.

2. Which of the following is a coordinating conjunction?
   - (A) yet   (B) however   (C) since   (D) because   (E) as

3. Which of the following is a conjunctive adverb?
   - (A) yet   (B) however   (C) since   (D) because   (E) as

4. Which of the following is <u>not</u> a sentence fragment?
   - (A) Many products made from soy beans.
   - (B) More than most people realize.
   - (C) Including milk, yogurt, tofu, cheese, ice cream, and, of course, soy sauce.
   - (D) Because of its incredible versatility and nutritional value.
   - (E) Soy has many important health benefits.

5. Which of the following <u>is</u> a sentence fragment?

   (A) Full-grown male cats are usually larger than full-grown females.

   (B) Feeding cats dog food can cause blindness.

   (C) Studies show that cats can see some colors.

   (D) Not just black and white.

   (E) Cats have only four toes on their back paws.

6. Which of the following is <u>not</u> a run-on sentence?

   (A) Each Zodiac sign corresponds to a planet, for example, Libra corresponds to Venus.

   (B) Some people think these astrological signs mean nothing, however others put great stock into astrological predictions.

   (C) Some people believe that only certain signs are compatible, such as Libras should only marry Scorpios or Leos should stay away from Capricorns.

   (D) Libra is the only sign whose symbol is not a human or animal, it is a scale.

   (E) Andy Warhol and Robert DeNiro are Leos, Clint Eastwood and John F. Kennedy are Geminis.

7. Which of the following <u>is</u> a run-on sentence?

   (A) "Netiquette" is a code of network (or cyberspace) etiquette, it is the rules you should follow when communicating online.

   (B) These rules include respecting other people's time as well as their privacy.

   (C) Other guidelines are more specific, such as do not write in all capitals, which is the online equivalent of shouting.

   (D) Many guidelines deal with the problem of "flaming" or expressing strong emotions or opinions online.

   (E) Flaming is not forbidden by Netiquette, but "flame wars" should be strictly avoided.

Part B: For questions 8–10, choose the best version of each sentence. If the original is best, choose (A).

8. UNO is a very popular card game, the object is to get rid of all your cards before the other players.

    (A) No change

    (B) In UNO, a very popular card game, the object is to get rid of all your cards before the other players.

    (C) UNO is a very popular card game, you must try to get rid of all your cards before the other players.

    (D) Get rid of your cards before the other players, that is the object of UNO, a very popular card game.

    (E) Trying to get rid of your cards before the other players in UNO; a very popular card game.

9. Watching the season finale of my favorite television show.

    (A) No change

    (B) Watching my favorite television show's season finale.

    (C) The season finale of my favorite television show.

    (D) I was watching the season finale of my favorite television show.

    (E) While I was watching the season finale of my favorite television show.

10. Banks used to be open only during business hours, now many banks have extended weekday and weekend hours.

    (A) No change

    (B) While banks used to be open only during business hours, now many banks have extended weekday and weekend hours.

    (C) Once open only during business hours; many banks now have extended weekday and weekend hours.

    (D) Once open only during business hours. Many banks now have extended weekday and weekend hours.

    (E) Banks used to be open only during business hours, however, now many banks have extended weekday and weekend hours.

Answers and Explanations

1. E

(A)–(D) are simple sentences with only one independent clause (one subject-predicate pair). (E) has one independent clause and two subordinate clauses.

2. A

Yet is one of the seven coordinating conjunctions (*and, or, nor, for, so, but* and *yet*) that connect grammatically equivalent elements.

3. B

However is a conjunctive adverb used to introduce independent clauses.

4. E

(E) contains both a subject and verb and expresses a complete thought. (A) lacks a subject; (B) and (D) are subordinate clauses; and (C) lacks a subject and verb.

5. D

(D) is a phrase; it does not have a subject or verb and it does not express a complete thought.

6. C

(A), (B), (D), and (E) are comma splices, a type of run-on sentence. (C) is a complete sentence.

7. A

This is also a comma splice. The other sentences are correct.

8. B

(A), (C), and (D) are run-ons (comma splices). In (E), the semicolon creates a fragment.

9. D

(A), (B), (C), and (E) are fragments. (A)–(C) lack a subject and helping verb; (E) is a subordinate clause.

10. B

(A) and (E) are run-on sentences. (C) incorrectly uses the semicolon between a phrase and an independent clause, creating a fragment. The first "sentence" in (D) is a fragment.

Imagine that as you read there are no periods on a page every sentence seems to run together into the next one they are blended into one big sentence you can't really tell where one idea ends and the next begins.

Or imagine. The opposite. That periods keep. Popping up in places. They don't belong. So you are always stopping. Before an idea is. Complete. Like this paragraph.

Not very pleasant reading, is it? That's because neither paragraph respects sentence boundaries.

UNDERSTANDING SENTENCE BOUNDARIES

To recognize and correct fragments and run-ons—two of the most common writing errors—you must identify kinds of phrases and clauses and determine the best way to join them.

Phrases and Clauses

A **phrase** *does not* contain a subject and predicate. It may contain one or the other or neither, but not both.

    to the store   sleeping soundly   once upon a time

A **clause** does contain both a subject and predicate. An **independent clause** expresses a complete thought and can stand alone. A **subordinate (or dependent) clause** cannot stand by itself; it does not express a complete thought and depends upon another clause to complete its idea. These clauses begin with a **subordinating conjunction** or **relative pronoun** (see chapter 1):

Independent: I / <u>went</u> to the store.

  Dependent: while I / <u>was</u> at the store <u>who</u> / <u>likes</u> to go shopping

Practice 1

Determine whether each of the following is a phrase or a clause, and decide whether each clause is independent or subordinate.

1. Freud divided the mind into three levels.
2. The id, the ego, and the superego.
3. The id is the most important part of our personality.
4. Because it allows us to meet our basic needs.
5. Such as food, drink, and shelter.
6. The id functions on what Freud called "the pleasure principle."
7. Which means it only cares about its own needs and satisfaction.
8. Not the satisfaction or needs of others.

Practice 2

Determine whether each underlined segment is a phrase or a clause; decide whether each clause is independent or subordinate.

<u>On the other hand,</u> <u>the ego functions on the reality principle</u>.
    1   2

<u>The ego is the awareness of the self</u> in relationship to others.
               3

Thus the ego must balance the needs of the id <u>with the needs and</u>
                                              4

<u>desires of others</u>. <u>As we grow older,</u> the third part of our
                    5

personality, the superego, develops. The superego is the moral

conscience <u>that helps us determine right from wrong</u> and keeps
                              6

us from seeking too much satisfaction <u>for our id</u>.
                                       7

A **sentence** contains at least one independent clause—so it (1) contains a **subject** and a **predicate** and (2) expresses a **complete thought**. To be grammatically correct, a sentence must meet *both* criteria. (The big exceptions are the **imperative** sentence, which has the unstated but understood subject *you*, and **interjections**; see chapters 1 and 2). If it lacks a subject or a predicate (or both) or does not express a complete thought, it is a **fragment**.

> Fragment: Thinking of you.
>
> Complete: <u>I was</u> thinking of you.

But a sentence should express only *one* complete thought; it may consist of several clauses, but each clause must be closely related and contribute to a unified idea. When clauses are not properly connected, the result is a **run-on** sentence.

> Run-on: I was thinking of you again, I couldn't help it.
>
> Correct: I was thinking of you again; I couldn't help it.

SENTENCE FRAGMENTS

A fragment either is missing an essential part (subject and/or predicate) or does not express a complete idea. Sometimes you write fragments because you think of something to add after you've already ended a sentence. Sometimes it's because you think that a sentence is already too long.

Types of Fragments

Most fragments will be one of four types:

1. **Subordinate clause.** These fragments have a subject and verb, but they do not express a complete thought. The fragments are underlined in the examples below:

   In the futuristic society of *Brave New World*, everyone is happy. <u>Because they all take a drug called *soma*.</u> Unlike the others, however, Bernard, the protagonist of the novel, refuses to take the drug. <u>So that he can feel both pleasure and pain.</u>

2. **Phrase missing a subject or verb**. These fragments have one essential element but lack the other. They are often a participial phrase or the second part of compound predicate that got separated from the original sentence:

   <u>Believing that happiness means nothing without unhappiness</u>. Bernard rejects *soma*. <u>Thereby ostracizing himself from society</u>. <u>Being the only one who is not happy</u>.

3. **Phrase missing both subject and verb**. These fragments can be any kind of phrase, including prepositional phrases, modifiers, lists, and examples:

   In Bernard's world, everyone is predestined to be happy. <u>Through genetic engineering and psychological conditioning</u>. <u>For example, exposing the bottled fetus to cold to condition that person to enjoy cold weather</u>. <u>Also, hypnopedia or "sleep teaching" (brainwashing during sleep)</u>.

4. **Fragment used for effect**. Writers may deliberately use fragments *for effect*—for emphasis, for transitions, or to answer a question. Fragments are also frequently used in advertising, and most interjections are fragments:

For emphasis:	Everyone is happy. <u>Except Bernard</u>.
To transition:	<u>First, a fundamental question</u>.
Answer to a question:	Can we be happy if there is no unhappiness? <u>Probably not</u>.
Ad:	<u>Soma: Happiness today, tomorrow, and always</u>.

Practice 3

Determine whether any of the following are fragments and, if so, which type.

1. This brave new world sounds like a scary place. Because people don't have free will.

2. They are born already predestined to be a plumber or pilot or factory worker.

3. And love what they do.

4. Also, the children. They are raised in group homes. Not with their parents.

5. Because emotional attachment is considered dangerous.

How to Correct Fragments

1. **Subordinate clause**. To fix this kind of fragment: (1) attach the subordinate clause to an independent clause or (2) make the clause independent.

   In the futuristic society of *Brave New World*, everyone is <u>happy because</u> they all take a drug called *soma*. Unlike the others, however, Bernard, the protagonist of the novel, refuses to take the drug. <u>He wants to feel</u> both pleasure and pain.

2. **Phrase missing a subject or verb**. Attach the phrase to an independent clause or add the missing element.

   Believing that happiness means nothing without <u>unhappiness, Bernard</u> rejects *soma*. <u>He</u> thereby <u>ostracizes</u> himself from society.

3. **Phrase missing both subject and verb**. Attach the phrase to an independent clause or add the missing elements.

   In Bernard's world, everyone is predestined to be <u>happy through</u> genetic engineering and psychological conditioning. For example, <u>a fetus may be exposed</u> to cold to condition that person to enjoy cold weather. Also, <u>everyone was subjected to</u> hypnopedia or "sleep teaching" (brainwashing during sleep).

Practice 4

Correct any fragments in the following paragraph.

Francis Ford Coppola's visually stunning and deeply disturbing film *Apocalypse Now*. Set in Vietnam during the war, it is an adaptation of Joseph Conrad's 1902 novel *Heart of Darkness*. Which takes place in the Belgian Congo. Conrad's novel is based on his own experience as a riverboat captain. During a time of widespread corruption and slaughter. Of both elephants (for their ivory) and natives. Ironically, the most human characters in Conrad's novel are the "savages." While the "civilized" Europeans behave like animals. *Apocalypse Now* adds new characters and makes many significant changes. Such as Marlow's murder of Kurtz. Yet the film remains true to the themes of Conrad's novel. Both are equally haunting. And instead of indicting the Europeans for their imperialism and greed. *Apocalypse Now* indicts America for its wrongheaded and imperialistic involvement in Vietnam.

RUN-ON SENTENCES

Two or more improperly joined independent clauses need to be connected in certain ways so that the boundaries of a sentence and the relationship between its parts are clear.

Think of each sentence as a color. If you paint a red sentence and immediately paint a blue sentence after it—without doing anything to show the boundary between them—you end up with one purple sentence rather than a red one and a blue one. The ideas blur together rather than remaining distinct.

Types of Run-Ons

There are only two types of run-on sentences:

1. **Fused sentences:** Two (or more) independent clauses run together.

   Japanese *anime* is Japanese animation there are several important differences between *anime* and American animated comics and cartoons. For one thing, *anime* comes in dozens of genres for adults as well as children here in America comics and cartoons are almost exclusively for kids.

2. **Comma splices:** Two (or more) independent clauses separated only by a comma.

   Another important difference is that *anime* tends to be more realistic and sophisticated than American versions, our animation often avoids real life issues such as death or important aspects of daily life such as school and work. And *anime* characters are more human than the typical American comic book hero, they aren't superhuman exaggerations but people much more like you and me.

REMEMBER THIS!

Two independent clauses cannot be separated by a comma alone. If you use a comma, you must also have a coordinating conjunction (*and, or, nor, for, so, but, yet*).

Practice 5

Identify any comma splices or fused sentences in the following.

1. Perhaps the greatest comic book superhero of all time, Superman debuted in June of 1938, this "man of steel" was the creation of two young men, Jerry Siegel and Joe Shuster.

2. Siegel and Shuster were still in high school when they created their hero, whom they dubbed "champion of the oppressed."

3. Their timing couldn't have been better, the nation was still suffering from the Great Depression and the world was on the brink of World War II.

4. Part of Superman's appeal was that he was dedicated "to helping those in need," and many in the nation were needy.

5. In fact, nearly a quarter of Americans still lived below the poverty line, in addition unemployment was still near record highs at 15%.

How to Correct Run-Ons

There are five ways to correct run-on sentences, depending upon the context of the run-on and the relationship between the independent clauses.

1. **Separate clauses with a period.** Break the clauses in two, with or without a transitional word or phrase:

   Japanese *anime* is Japanese <u>animation. There</u> are several important differences between *anime* and American animated comics and cartoons. For one thing, *anime* comes in dozens of genres for adults as well as <u>children. Here</u> in America, comics and cartoons are almost exclusively for kids.

2. **Separate clauses with a comma + coordinating conjunction.** A comma alone cannot separate two independent clauses.

   For one thing, *anime* comes in dozens of genres for adults as well as <u>children, but here</u> in America, comics and cartoons are almost exclusively for kids. And *anime* characers are more human than the typical American comic book <u>hero, for </u>they aren't superhuman exaggerations but people much more like you and me.

Note: Many people confuse coordinating conjunctions with conjunctive adverbs. *But* is a coordinating conjunction and can safely separate two independent clauses with just a comma. *However* has a similar meaning, but it is a conjunctive adverb.

Run-on: For one thing, *anime* comes in dozens of genres for adults as well as children, however here in America, comics and cartoons are almost exclusively for kids.

Correct: For one thing, *anime* comes in dozens of genres for adults as well as children, but here in America, comics and cartoons are almost exclusively for kids.

3. **Separate clauses with a semicolon.** Use this option only if the two sentences are closely related. The semicolon is a strong punctuation mark: it means that the two ideas are distinct but important enough to each other that they need a strong physical connection. Semicolons may be followed by a conjunctive adverb such as *however*:

   For one thing, *anime* comes in dozens of genres for adults as well as children; here in America, comics and cartoons are almost exclusively for kids.

If you use a semicolon to join a phrase or independent clause to a clause, you create a fragment:

Fragment: While *anime* uses many of the same technological conventions as American animation; it is more advanced and stylistically unique.

Correct: *Anime* uses many of the same technological conventions as American animation; however, it is more advanced and stylistically unique. (Two independent clauses connected by a semicolon.)

4. **Separate clauses with a colon or dash.** If the second independent clause summarizes or explains the first, then use a colon; if the idea in the second clause is strongly connected to the first and deserves emphasis, use a dash (see chapter 16).

   And *anime* characters are more human than the typical American comic book hero: they aren't superhuman exaggerations but people much more like you and me.

5. **Turn one clause into a subordinate clause or modifier.** Add an appropriate subordinating conjunction to one clause, or make it a modifying phrase.

> **Modifier:** There are several important differences between *anime, or Japanese animation,* and American animated comics and cartoons.

> **Subordinate clause:** For one thing, <u>while</u> *anime* comes in dozens of genres for adults as well as children, here in America comics and cartoons are almost exclusively for kids.

FLASHBACK

There are four kinds of conjunctions: **coordinating, correlative, subordinating, and conjunctive adverbs** (see chapter 1).

Practice 6

How would you correct any run-ons in the following paragraph?

One of the most popular means of transportation for teens and young adults today is the skateboard, it was first invented back in the early 1900s, though no one knows exactly who made the first board or when. The earliest skateboards were more like scooters, they were roller skate wheels attached to wooden boxes or boards. These early skateboards were not very safe, many people got hurt in those first years. Skateboards got a big boost in the 1950s, that's when California surfers started to popularize skateboards and refine the design, they wanted to "surf" on the street. In 1963, a surfboard company began mass manufacturing skateboards, in the same year the first skateboard contest was held in California.

SUMMARY

A **sentence** (1) contains both a subject and predicate and (2) expresses a complete thought. Sentences must contain both elements; otherwise, they are fragments. **Run-ons** are independent clauses that are not properly connected. **Fragments** come in four types: subordinate clauses, phrases missing a subject or verb, phrases missing a subject and verb, and fragments used for effect (like interjections and imperatives).

Correct a fragment by attaching it to an independent clause or adding the missing element. If the fragment is a subordinate clause, the subordinating conjunction or relative pronoun can be removed to make the clause independent.

Depending upon the relationship between the clauses, run-ons can be corrected by:

1. separating the clauses with a period
2. separating the clauses with comma and coordinating conjunction
3. separating the clauses with a semicolon, if the clauses are strongly connected
4. separating the clauses with a colon (if the second clause explains the first) or a dash (for emphasis)
5. turning one of the clauses into a subordinate clause or modifier

Practice: On Your Own

Advertisements are a great place to find fragments (and occasionally a run-on). Look through a newspaper or magazine to find examples of different kinds of fragments. Practice correcting them using the different strategies outlined in this lesson. You're less likely to find run-ons in published writing, but you can find examples on websites, especially personal sites or chat rooms.

Practice Answers and Explanations

Practice 1

1. independent clause
2. phrase
3. independent clause
4. dependent clause
5. phrase
6. independent clause
7. dependent clause
8. phrase

Practice 2

1. phrase
2. independent clause
3. independent clause
4. phrase
5. dependent clause
6. dependent clause
7. phrase

Practice 3

1. Fragment: *because … free will* is a dependent clause.
2. No fragment.
3. Fragment: *and love what they do* is missing a subject (it's the second part of a compound predicate).
4. Fragment: *also, the children* and *not with their parents* are phrases missing subject and verb.
5. Fragment: *Because … dangerous* is a subordinate clause.

Practice 4

Answers may vary. In A below, all fragments are underlined, and B offers one corrected version.

A. <u>Francis Ford Coppola's visually stunning and deeply disturbing film</u> *Apocalypse Now*. Set in Vietnam during the war, it is an adaptation of Joseph Conrad's 1902 novel *Heart of Darkness*. <u>Which takes place in the Belgian Congo.</u> Conrad's novel is based on his own experience as a riverboat captain. <u>During a time of widespread corruption and slaughter. Of both elephants (for their ivory) and natives.</u> Ironically, the most human characters in Conrad's novel are the "savages." <u>While the "civilized" Europeans behave like animals</u>. *Apocalypse Now* adds new characters and makes many significant changes. <u>Such as Marlow's murder of Kurtz</u>. Yet the film remains true to the themes of Conrad's novel. Both are equally haunting. <u>And instead of indicting the Europeans for their imperialism and greed</u>. *Apocalypse Now* indicts America for its wrongheaded and imperialistic involvement in Vietnam.

B. Set in Vietnam during the war, Francis Ford Coppola's visually stunning and deeply disturbing film *Apocalypse Now* is an adaptation of Joseph Conrad's 1902 novel *Heart of Darkness,* which takes place in the Belgian Congo. Conrad's novel is based on his own experience as a riverboat captain during a time of widespread corruption and slaughter of both elephants (for their ivory) and natives. Ironically, the most human characters in Conrad's novel are the "savages" while the "civilized" Europeans behave like animals. *Apocalypse Now* adds new characters and makes many significant changes, such as Marlow's murder of Kurtz. Yet the film remains true to the themes of Conrad's novel. Both are equally haunting. And instead of indicting the Europeans for their imperialism and greed, *Apocalypse Now* indicts America for its wrongheaded and imperialistic involvement in Vietnam.

Practice 5

1. Run-on: comma splice.
2. No run-on.
3. Run-on: fused sentence.
4. No run-on.
5. Run-on: comma splice.

Practice 6

Every sentence in this paragraph is a comma splice run-on. The fourth sentence (*Skateboards … street*) has three independent clauses. Answers may vary. <u>One of the most popular means of transportation for teens and young adults today,</u> [*turned into a modifier*] the skateboard was first invented back in the early 1900s, though no one knows exactly who made the first board or when. The earliest skateboards were more like <u>scooters: they</u> [*a colon is best here as the second sentence explains the first*] were roller skate wheels attached to wooden boxes or boards. These early skateboards were not very <u>safe; many</u> [*these closely related sentences can be connected with a semicolon, colon or dash, depending upon desired effect*] people got hurt in those first years. Skateboards got a big boost in <u>the 1950s when California surfers</u> [*delete subordinating conjunction "that"*], <u>who wanted to "surf" on the street,"</u> [*turned independent clause into a modifier*] started to popularize skateboards and refine the design. In 1963, a surfboard company began mass manufacturing <u>skateboards. In</u> [*a period is fine here; a semicolon would also do*] the same year, the first skateboard contest was held in California.

CHAPTER 8 TEST

Read each proverb carefully, correcting punctuation and conjunctions as needed.

1. After three days without reading; talk becomes flavorless. —*Chinese*

2. Don't be too sweet lest you be eaten up, don't be too bitter lest you be spewed out. —*Jewish*

3. A closed mind is like a closed book. Just a block of wood. —*Chinese*

4. Don't run too far you will have to return the same distance. —*Biblical*

5. The eyes believe themselves; the ears believe other people. —*German*

6. From a thorn comes a rose, from a rose comes a thorn. —*Greek*

7. When spiders unite, they can tie down a lion. —*Ethiopian*

8. Goodness shouts, evil whispers. —*Balinese*

9. If you can't go over. You must go under. —*Jewish*
10. Life is not separate from death, it only looks that way.
    —*Native American*
11. Man has responsibility. Not power. —*Native American*
12. Since we cannot get what we like; let us like what we can get.
    —*Spanish*
13. To know the road ahead. Ask those coming back. —*Chinese*
14. Vision without action is a daydream, action without vision is
    a nightmare. —*Japanese*
15. What the heart thinks. The tongue speaks. —*Romanian*
16. When you go to buy, use your eyes. Not your ears. —*Czech*
17. Tell me who your friends are, I'll tell you who you are.
    —*Russian*
18. You've got to do your own growing. No matter how tall your
    grandfather was. —*Irish*
19. Shared joy is a double joy shared sorrow is half a sorrow.
    —*Swedish*
20. Never do anything standing that you can do sitting. Or
    anything sitting that you can do lying down. —*Chinese*

Answers and Explanations

1. After three days without reading, talk becomes flavorless. A semicolon can only separate *independent* clauses. *After … reading* is a subordinate clause.

2. Don't be too sweet lest you be eaten up; don't be too bitter lest you be spewed out. The original is a run-on.

3. A closed mind is like a closed book: just a block of wood. The orginal is a fragment.

4. Don't run too far, for you will have to return the same distance. The original is a run-on.

5. Correct as written.

6. From a thorn comes a rose, and from a rose comes a thorn. The original is a run-on.

7. Correct as written.

8. Goodness shouts while evil whispers. The original is a run-on.

9. If you can't go over, you must go under. The original is a fragment. *If … over* is a subordinate clause.

10. Life is not separate from death—it only looks that way. The original is a comma splice.

11. Man has responsibility, not power. The original is a fragment. *Not power* is a phrase.

12. Since we cannot get what we like, let us like what we can get. The original is a fragment; *since … like* is a subordinate clause.

13. To know the road ahead, ask those coming back. The original is a fragment; *to know the road ahead* is a phrase.

14. Vision without action is a daydream; action without vision is a nightmare. The original is a run-on.

15. What the heart thinks, the tongue speaks. The original is a fragment; *what the heart thinks* is a subordinate clause functioning as the subject of the sentence.

16. When you go to buy, use your eyes, not your ears. The original is a fragment; *when you go to buy* is a subordinate clause and *not your ears* is a phrase.

17. Tell me who your friends are, and I'll tell you who you are. The original is a run-on.

18. You've got to do your own growing, no matter how tall your grandfather was. The original is a fragment. *No matter … was* is a phrase.

19. Shared joy is a double joy, and shared sorrow is half a sorrow. The original is a run-on.

20. Never do anything standing that you can do sitting, or anything sitting that you can do lying down. The original contains a fragment. *Or anything … down* is part of the predicate.

CHAPTER 9

Parallelism; Active vs. Passive Voice

Start with this 10-question Building Block Quiz. The first few questions test material you've already seen.

BUILDING BLOCK QUIZ

Part A: For questions 1–5, choose the best correction. If the sentence is correct, choose (E).

1. I'm glad we have the whole day together, for you and me have a lot of catching up to do.

   (A) Change *glad* to *happy*.   (B) Change *have* to *has*.

   (C) Change *me* to *I*.   (D) Change *to do* to *doing*.

   (E) No change

2. Neither rain nor snow have fallen in months; it is the driest winter on record.

   (A) Change the semicolon to a comma.

   (B) Move *in months* to the beginning of the sentence.

   (C) Change *driest* to *most dry*.

   (D) Change *have* to *has*.

   (E) No change

3. Bounding gracefully across the field, the hunter saw the deer.
   (A) Move *bounding gracefully across the field* to the end of the sentence.
   (B) Move only *bounding gracefully* to the end of the sentence.
   (C) Change the comma to a period or semicolon.
   (D) Change *saw* to *seen*.
   (E) No change

4. Raj's New Year's resolutions included spending more time with his girlfriend, spending less time in front of the television, and to spend less money on gourmet coffee.
   (A) Change *included* to *including*.
   (B) Put a semicolon after *girlfriend*.
   (C) Change *less* to *fewer*.
   (D) Change *to spend* to *spending*.
   (E) No change

5. Kira swears she will marry for love, not because of money.
   (A) Change *swears* to *swear*.
   (B) Change *she* to *her*.
   (C) Change the comma to a semicolon.
   (D) Change *because of money* to *for money*.
   (E) No change

Part B: For questions 6–10, choose the best answer *or answers*.

6. Use the active voice
   (A) always   (B) most of the time   (C) sometimes
   (D) rarely   (E) never

7. Use the passive voice
   (A) always   (B) most of the time   (C) sometimes
   (D) rarely   (E) never

8. Which of the following is an example of the active voice?
   (A) The pollution in the river has been brought under control.
   (B) Who has been eating my porridge?
   (C) Stop right there!
   (D) The thief was caught red-handed.
   (E) The students have put together a fabulous yearbook.

9. Which of the following is an example of the passive voice?
   (A) Check it out!
   (B) We donate 2% of all profits to charities.
   (C) The charities are chosen by our employees.
   (D) Doctors Without Borders won the most votes this year.
   (E) We donate to five different charities each year.

10. In which situation is the passive voice preferred?
    (A) Whenever there is a direct object
    (B) When the agent of action is unknown
    (C) When the subject is unstated but understood
    (D) When emphasis on the agent of action is desired
    (E) When the verb is in the subjunctive mood

Answers and Explanations

1. C
The pronoun should be in the subjective case; *for* is a coordinating conjunction and *you and I ... to do* is an independent clause.

2. D
The compound subject *rain* and *snow* is connected by *nor*, so the verb must be singular.

3. A
The phrase *bounding ... field* is a misplaced modifier; it belongs next to *deer*.

4. D
The verb should be *spending* for parallel structure.

5. D

For love will create parallel structure; the two items connected by *not* now have the same format.

6. B

In general, use the active voice as it is clearer and more direct.

7. D

There are some instances in which the passive is preferred.

8. B, C, and E

(B) is a question, but the subject and agent is *who*. (C) is imperative, the implied subject *you*. (E) has a clear agent of action (*students*) directly performing the action of the verb (*put together*). In (A) and (D) the subjects receive the action; the agent is unknown.

9. C

The *employees* are the agent of action, but they are not the subject. (A) is an interjection. (B), (D), and (E) are all active sentences with clear agents of action.

10. B

It is necessary to use the passive when the agent of action is unknown.

Congratulations! This is your last lesson in Section I: The Building Blocks of Better Grammar and Sentence Structure.

Happily, the two subjects of this chapter—parallel structure and the active and passive voice—are not only a fitting conclusion to this section but also an introduction to the next. Both parallelism and active/passive voice are matters of structure *and* style.

PARALLEL STRUCTURE

One of the basic principles of art is **symmetry**: the balancing or mirroring of two sides or parts through repetition of patterns or forms. In writing, symmetry is achieved through **parallel structure**: expressing related ideas in similar form. Many proverbs, like the following Chinese one, are excellent examples of parallel structure:

> Give a man a fish and you feed him for a day. Teach a man to fish and you feed him for a lifetime.

Both sides of the sentence follow the same grammatical pattern:

Give / a man / a fish / and / you / feed / him / for a day.
verb /   indirect   /   object / coordinating / subject / verb /   direct / prepositional phrase.
            object   conjunction   object

Teach / a man / to fish / and / you / feed / him / for a lifetime.

Consider this proverb without parallel structure; it loses rhythm and rhetorical impact:

Give a man a fish and you feed him for a day; he'll be fed for the rest of his life if he's taught how to fish.

Parallel structure may be used in a series of sentences or within a single sentence:

Not parallel: Wally is quite a scholar, but he's not very good at teaching.

Parallel: Wally is <u>quite a scholar</u>, but <u>not much of a teacher</u>.

GRAMMAR SPEAK

Parallelism means that two or more sentences (or parts of sentences) have the same grammatical structure.

Practice 1

Determine which version of each sentence uses parallel structure, and underline the parallel items.

Example:

a. The computer screen flickered, turned blue, and then it was just blank.

b. The computer screen *flickered*, <u>turned blue</u>, and then <u>went blank</u>.

1. a. There is no eating or drinking, and do not chew gum.

   b. There is no eating, drinking, or chewing gum.

2. a. I will either dance or sing, but I will not dance *and* sing.

   b. I will either dance or sing, but dancing *and* singing together I will not do.

3. a. The song starts off soft and slow, but by the end it is loud and fast.

   b. The song starts off soft and slow, but it's different at the end, being loud and fast.

4. a. In addition to stretching the body, yoga also stretches the mind.

   b. In addition to stretching the body, yoga is good for stretching the mind.

When to Use Parallel Structure

Use parallel structure any time you have two or more comparable or analogous ideas or items.

Items in a Series

Items in a list should be in parallel form.

Not parallel: It will be an evening of singing, dancing, and there will be food to eat.

Parallel: It will be an evening of <u>singing</u>, <u>dancing</u>, and <u>eating</u>.

Items in Pairs

Items connected by coordinating or correlative conjunctions or other pairing constructions should be in parallel form.

Not parallel: The test measures reasoning skills as well as students' ability to solve problems.

Parallel: The test measures <u>reasoning skills</u> as well as <u>problem-solving ability</u>.

FLASHBACK

Coordinating conjunctions include *and, or, nor, for, so, but,* and *yet.* They connect grammatically equivalent elements.
Correlative conjunctions have the same function and include *either…or* and *neither…nor* constructions.

Items Compared

When two or more items are compared, they should have parallel structure.

Not parallel: Jin Lee thinks only with her heart; you, however, also use your brain to think.

Parallel: Jin Lee thinks only with her heart; you, however, also think with your brain.

REMEMBER THIS!

Use parallel structure for items in lists, pairs, or comparisons—whenever two or more items are comparable or analogous.

Signpost Readers

Parallel structure—especially in lists—is often introduced by a signal word such as *that, to,* or *of.* Sometimes it's necessary to repeat these signal words to make your parallel structure clear.

I love you because you're smart and you're compassionate.

I love you <u>because</u> you're smart and <u>because</u> you're compassionate.

Repeating *because* makes it clear that *I love you* for both characteristics.

Correcting Faulty Parallelism

If just one of several items is faulty, change it to match the structure of the others. If you have two items with different structures, choose the structure that is more concise or eloquent.

Not parallel: I am <u>industrious</u>, <u>creative</u>, and <u>I always tell the truth</u>.

Parallel: I am <u>industrious</u>, <u>creative</u>, and <u>honest</u>.

Here's another example:

Not parallel: Erich von Daniken's book *Chariots of the Gods* sold over seven million copies; several million copies of its follow-up *Gods from Outer Space* were also sold.

The first clause is title-verb-number sold. The second clause is number sold-title-verb. The first clause uses the active voice and is more powerful and concise:

Parallel: Erich von Daniken's book *Chariots of the Gods* sold over seven million copies; its follow-up *Gods from Outer Space* also sold several million.

Practice 2

Correct any faulty parallelism in the following sentences.

1. Before we go, I need to make a few phone calls and the dishwasher needs to be turned on.

2. According to moral relativism, we each determine for ourselves what is right or wrong; according to utilitarianism, right and wrong is determined by the principle of "the greatest good."

3. The study revealed that most people vote based on a politician's personality, not where the politician stands on issues.

4. If we go to the diner now, we can beat the dinner crowd and money will be saved with the early bird special.

5. Bob Dylan captivates me with his lyrics, while Neil Young's music is what mesmerizes me.

ACTIVE VS. PASSIVE VOICE

In active sentences the subject directly performs the action. The active agent is removed or displaced in passive sentences (see chapter 4).

Active: Sherman Alexie wrote my favorite novel, *Reservation Blues.*

Passive: *Reservation Blues*, my favorite novel, was written by Sherman Alexie.

The subject of the active sentence, *Sherman Alexie*, becomes the *object* of the prepositional phrase *by Sherman Alexie* in the passive version, and the object *Reservation Blues*, becomes the subject. The novel didn't *do* the writing; it *was written*, hence the term *passive*.

FLASHBACK

As you saw in chapter 4, in most cases the active voice is better than the passive.

Practice 3

Determine whether the following sentences are active or passive.

1. The judges have selected a winner.
2. The winner will be announced tomorrow.
3. A prize of $10,000 will be given to the winner.
4. The winner will also receive an all-expense paid trip to Hawaii.
5. Included in the package are scuba-diving lessons.

Because they have a clear agent of action, active sentences are more direct and engaging. They are also more concise—an important element of style you'll review in the next section. Note the significant difference between the active and passive versions of this paragraph:

Passive: In the ancient Greek myth of Icarus, wings of feathers and wax are built by Icarus and his father. Icarus is told by his father not to fly too close to the sun, for the wax will be melted by the heat. Unfortunately, this warning is not heeded. A height too great is reached by Icarus, and destruction is faced by the wings. Death is then faced by Icarus, who is drowned in the sea below.

Active: In the ancient Greek myth of Icarus, Icarus and his father build wings of feathers and wax. Icarus's father tells him not to fly too close to the sun, for the heat will melt the wax. Unfortunately, Icarus does not heed this warning. He flies too high, the wings fall apart, and Icarus falls to his death in the sea below.

A Note about Word Count

We just said that one of the reasons the active voice is better than the passive is that it is more concise. But what about word count? What if you have to write a 300-word essay but are stuck at 250? Why not boost your word count by using the passive voice?

You could, but it's a bad idea. Yes, your essay would be longer, but it would also be much less effective. Instead of using the passive to fill out your essay, add more details or expand an explanation.

Practice 4

How would you make the following passive sentences active?

1. Eugene should be given another chance by the coach.
2. Due to circumstances beyond our control, the brochures can't be delivered today.
3. The test will be taken by over 3,000 students statewide.
4. The art school was given a donation of $10,000 from Wilson Banks.
5. Several volunteers are needed for Friday's pot-luck dinner.

When the Passive Is Preferred

That said, the passive has its place.

To Minimize the Significance of the Agent or Emphasize the Receiver

Sometimes, we want to downplay the role of the agent of action or emphasize the receiver. We can accomplish this by using the passive voice.

> **Active:** Henrietta fired Charlotte today.
>
> **Passive:** Charlotte was fired today.

Henrietta disappears in the passive version; all the emphasis is on Charlotte. Here's another example:

> **Active:** The storm badly damaged the house.
>
> **Passive:** The house was badly damaged by the storm.

When the Agent Is Unknown

When we don't know the agent of action, the passive voice is a logical choice.

Active: Someone found the scrolls in a cave in the desert.

Passive: The scrolls were found in a cave in the desert.

REMEMBER THIS!

Use the passive to minimize the significance of the agent, to emphasize the receiver, or when the agent is unknown.

Practice 5

Which version—the active or passive—is most appropriate?

1. **Active:**   The noise of the fireworks frightened Hannah.
   Passive: Hannah was frightened by the noise of the fireworks.
2. **Active:**   Builders completed the bridge in 1902.
   Passive: The bridge was completed in 1902.
3. **Active:**   Investigators found wire taps on the house telephones.
   Passive: Wire taps on the house telephones were found by investigators.
4. **Active:**   The panel of judges gave Janel top honors.
   Passive: Janel received top honors from the panel of judges.

SUMMARY

Parallel structure means comparable or analogous items follow the same grammatical pattern. Items in lists, pairs, and comparisons should be expressed in parallel form. Sometimes the word(s) that introduce the parallel items must be repeated for clarity.

In the **active voice** the subject is a clear agent of action. In **passive** sentences, that agent is displaced or removed. In most cases, the active voice is preferable. However, the passive voice is best when you want to minimize the significance of the agent of action, when you want to emphasize the receiver, or when the agent of action is unknown.

Practice: On Your Own

News articles are an excellent place to look for examples of parallel structure and the passive and active voice. Choose a few articles and find several examples of parallelism. Look for a variety of uses of parallelism—in short phrases, long clauses, a series of sentences. Then find examples of passive sentences, and see if you can determine why the author decided to use the passive.

Practice Answers and Explanations

Practice 1

1. b. There is no <u>eating</u>, <u>drinking</u>, or <u>chewing gum</u>.
2. a. <u>I will either dance or sing</u>, but <u>I will not dance *and* sing</u>.
3. a. The song starts off <u>soft and slow</u>, but by the end it is <u>loud and fast</u>.
4. a. In addition to stretching <u>the body</u>, yoga also stretches <u>the mind</u>.

Practice 2

Answers may vary. The revised portion is underlined.

1. Before we go, I need to make a few phone calls and <u>turn on the dishwasher</u>.
2. According to moral relativism, we each determine for ourselves what is right or wrong; according to utilitarianism, <u>the principle of "the greatest good" determines what is right and wrong</u>.
3. The study revealed that most people vote based on a politician's personality, not <u>the politician's stance on issues</u>.
4. If we go to the diner now, we can beat the dinner crowd and <u>save money</u> with the early bird special.
5. Bob Dylan captivates me with his lyrics while Neil Young <u>mesmerizes me with his music</u>.

Practice 3

1. active
2. passive
3. passive
4. active
5. passive

Practice 4

Answers may vary. The agent of action is underlined.

1. The <u>coach</u> should give Eugene another chance.
2. Due to circumstances beyond our control, <u>we</u> cannot deliver the brochures until tomorrow.
3. Over <u>3,000 students</u> statewide will take the test.
4. <u>Wilson Banks</u> donated $10,000 to the art school.
5. <u>We</u> need several volunteers for Friday's pot-luck dinner.

Practice 5

1. **Passive.** The emphasis should be on *Hannah*, the receiver.
2. **Passive.** Because the agent of action is the generic *builders*, it's probably best to use the passive and emphasize the receiver—*the bridge*.
3. **Active.** The passive would only be acceptable if the writer wanted to emphasize *wire taps*.
4. **Passive.** Here, the receiver (*Janel*) should be emphasized, not the agent (*the panel of judges*).

CHAPTER 9 TEST

Choose the version of the underlined portion of the sentence that best corrects any error(s) in the original (including any grammar error covered in Section I). If the original is correct, choose (A). (There may be more than one correct answer!)

1. Sam likes to spend his Sundays <u>reading the paper, watching sports, and he'll make a gourmet dinner</u>.
   - (A) No change
   - (B) reading the paper, watching sports; and he'll make a gourmet dinner.
   - (C) reading the paper, watching sports, and making a gourmet dinner.
   - (D) to read the paper, watch sports, and to make a gourmet dinner.
   - (E) reading the paper. Watching sports, and making a gourmet dinner.

2. <u>Without electricity and not having any candles, we</u> were stuck in total darkness for hours.
   - (A) No change
   - (B) Without electricity and not having no candles, we
   - (C) Without electricity or candles, we
   - (D) Without electricity and no candles; we
   - (E) We, without electricity or candles,

3. <u>To be honest, being fair, and being kind are the three principles</u> I try to live by.
   - (A) No change
   - (B) Being honest, being fair, and being kind are the three principles
   - (C) Being honest, being fair, and being kind. Are the three principles
   - (D) The three principles, to be honest, fair, and kind, are what
   - (E) Honesty, fairness, and being kind are the three principles

4. <u>Nearly 300,000 children in the United States are affected by juvenile arthritis</u>.
   - (A) No change
   - (B) Juvenile arthritis affects nearly 300,000 children in the United States.
   - (C) By juvenile arthritis, nearly 300,000 children in the United States are affected.
   - (D) Affected by juvenile arthritis, nearly 300,000 children are in the United States.
   - (E) Juvenile arthritis affect nearly 300,000 children in the United States.

5. The keynote speaker seemed <u>nervous; he kept adjusting his tie and shuffling his papers as he spoke</u>.
   - (A) No change
   - (B) nervous, he kept adjusting his tie and shuffling his papers as he spoke.
   - (C) nervous; he kept adjusting his tie and shuffling his papers. As he spoke.
   - (D) nervous, he kept adjusting his tie as he spoke and shuffling his papers.
   - (E) nervous; he adjusted his tie a lot and was shuffling his papers as he spoke.

6. <u>*Or, The Modern Prometheus* was the subtitle given by Mary Shelley to her novel *Frankenstein*</u>.
   - (A) No change
   - (B) *Or, The Modern Prometheus* was the subtitle of the novel *Frankenstein* given by Mary Shelley.
   - (C) *Or, The Modern Prometheus* was the subtitle Mary Shelley gave to her novel *Frankenstein*.
   - (D) Mary Shelley gave the subtitle *or, The Modern Prometheus* to her novel *Frankenstein*.
   - (E) To her novel *Frankenstein*, Mary Shelley gave the subtitle *or, The Modern Prometheus*.

7. Take what Justin says with a grain of salt, <u>for he has been known to embellish his stories and he exaggerates</u>.

   (A) No change
   (B) for he has been known to embellish his stories and exaggerate.
   (C) for he has been known to embellishing his stories and exaggerating.
   (D) for him has been known to embellish his stories and to exaggerate.
   (E) for he has been known to embellish his stories. And exaggerate.

8. My five-year-old nephew says he wants to be a <u>fireman because firemen help people, they save animals, and he'd get to ride in a firetruck</u>.

   (A) No change
   (B) fireman. Because firemen help people, save animals, and he'd get to ride in a firetruck.
   (C) fireman, because firemen help people, save animals, and get to ride in a firetruck.
   (D) fireman; because firemen help people, save animals, and get to ride in a firetruck.
   (E) fireman, because people are helped and animals are saved by firemen, who also get to ride in a firetruck.

9. <u>The senator's office was inundated with calls from angry constituents</u>.

   (A) No change
   (B) From angry constituents, the senator's office was inundated with calls.
   (C) Calls from angry constituents inundated the senator's office.
   (D) The senator's office, with calls from angry constituents, was inundated.
   (E) The senator's office were inundated with calls from angry constituents.

10. The witch told Dorothy <u>to click her heels together three times and then "There's no place like home" is what she should say.</u>

    (A) No change

    (B) clicking her heels together three times and saying "There's no place like home."

    (C) to click her heels together three times. Then say "There's no place like home."

    (D) to click her heels together three times and say "There's no place like home."

    (E) her heels should be clicked together three times and then "There's no place like home" should be said.

11. <u>The meal was thoroughly enjoyed by all of us.</u>

    (A) No change

    (B) By all of us, the meal was thoroughly enjoyed.

    (C) The meal was thoroughly enjoyed by all of we.

    (D) Us all thoroughly enjoyed the meal.

    (E) We all thoroughly enjoyed the meal.

12. Renee is definitely a good <u>friend, but she is not my best friend.</u>

    (A) No change

    (B) friend, however, she is not my best friend.

    (C) friend, but she is not my most best friend.

    (D) friend, but we're not best friends.

    (E) friend. Although she is not my best friend.

13. <u>The mansion was home to several original works by Picasso, van Gogh, and Matisse.</u>

    (A) No change

    (B) The mansion was home to several original works; by Picasso, van Gogh, and Matisse.

    (C) Several original works by Picasso, van Gogh, and Matisse were housed in the mansion.

    (D) Housed in the mansion were several original works by Picasso, van Gogh, and Matisse.

    (E) Housed in the mansion was several original works by Picasso, van Gogh, and Matisse.

14. When fluoride was first introduced into the water supply in the United <u>States, it was believed to be a government conspiracy by some.</u>
    - (A) No change
    - (B) States. It was believed to be a government conspiracy by some.
    - (C) States. Some people believed it was a government conspiracy.
    - (D) States, some people believed it was a government conspiracy.
    - (E) States, it was a government conspiracy, some people believed.

15. Approximately one-fifth of the world's population lives in <u>China, while in India there is another one-fifth</u>.
    - (A) No change
    - (B) China. While in India there is another one-fifth.
    - (C) China, while another fifth lives in India.
    - (D) China, another fifth lives in India.
    - (E) China, while India has another fifth.

16. As you prepare your resume, <u>remember that items in lists and pairs should be expressed in parallel form</u>.
    - (A) No change
    - (B) remember to express items in list and pairs in parallel form.
    - (C) remember that parallel form should be used for items in lists and pairs.
    - (D) remember. Items in lists and pairs should be expressed in parallel form.
    - (E) remember that for items in lists and pairs, parallel form should be used.

17. For me, a doctor's bedside manner is as important as <u>his knowledge and experience</u>.
    (A) No change
    (B) their knowledge and experience.
    (C) how much he knows and how much experience he has.
    (D) the knowledge and expertise they have.
    (E) his or her knowledge and experience.

18. <u>Feeling fully prepared and having confidence,</u> Elliot entered the courtroom prepared to win the case.
    (A) No change
    (B) Feeling fully prepared and with confidence,
    (C) Feeling fully prepared and confident,
    (D) Feeling fully prepared and confident.
    (E) Feeling fully prepared and confident;

19. College students are a favorite target of credit card companies because students need to establish a credit <u>history but often have little experience managing money.</u>
    (A) No change
    (B) history but often having little experience managing money.
    (C) history. But often have little experience managing money.
    (D) history, but their experience managing money is often little.
    (E) history, but often he or she lacks experience managing money.

20. <u>The jury submitted its verdict, and the judge sentenced Carlson to five months of community service</u>.
    (A) No change
    (B) The jury submitted its verdict, and Carlson was sentenced to five months of community service.
    (C) The verdict was submitted by the jury, and Carlson was sentenced to five months of community service.
    (D) Submitted by the jury, the verdict was in, and five months of community service was the sentence received by Carlson.
    (E) The jury submitted its verdict, and Carlson was sentenced. To five months of community service.

Answers and Explanations

1. C

This version corrects the faulty parallelism. (E) is a fragment.

2. C

This is the only version that corrects the faulty parallelism of the original. (B) has a double negative; (D) creates a fragment. (E) awkwardly inserts a modifier between the subject and verb.

3. B

(A) and (E) lack parallel structure. (C) creates a fragment. (D) is parallel but unnecessarily interrupts the subject-verb structure.

4. B

The original is grammatically correct, but the active is preferable unless the writer wants to emphasize the children. (C) and (D) misplace modifiers. (E) lacks subject-verb agreement.

5. A

The original is correct, with clear parallel structure. (B) and (D) are run-ons. (C) has a fragment. (E) lacks parallel structure.

6. D

(D) uses the active voice. (A), (B), and (C) are wordy and awkward. (E) awkwardly places the phrase *to her novel* Frankenstein.

7. B

(A) and (C) lack parallel structure. (D) uses the objective pronoun *him* instead of the subjective *he*. (E) creates a fragment.

8. C

(A), (B), and (E) lack parallel structure. (B) and (D) are also fragments. (E) uses the passive voice when the active is better.

9. A or C

(A) is an acceptable use of the passive voice, if the emphasis is on the senator's office. (C) uses the active voice, which is also correct but emphasizes the angry constituents. (B) has a misplaced modifier. (D) inserts a modifier between subject and verb. (E) has an error in subject-verb agreement.

10. D

(A) and (B) lack parallel structure. (C) has a fragment. (E) unnecessarily uses the passive voice.

11. E

(A), (B), and (C) use the passive voice inappropriately. (B) misplaces a modifier. (C) and (D) contain pronoun case errors.

12. A

The original has correct parallel structure. (B) creates a run-on. (C) has a double superlative. (D) lacks parallel structure and (E) is a fragment.

13. A

(A) is best because it is in the active voice. (B) creates a fragment. (C), (D), and (E) are all passive. (E) also has an error in subject-verb agreement.

14. D

The original unnecessarily uses the passive, as does (B), which also creates a fragment. (C) uses the active voice but creates a fragment. (E) awkwardly places the object (what people believed) before the subject and verb.

15. C

(A) and (E) lack parallel structure. (B) is a fragment and lacks parallel structure. (D) is a run-on.

16. B

(A), (C), (D), and (E) all use the passive voice. (B) is the most direct and concise because it is active. (D) is a fragment.

17. E

(A) does have parallel structure, but the pronoun *his* does not acknowledge both genders. (B) incorrectly uses a plural pronoun. (C) has faulty parallelism and (D) places the object before the subject and verb.

18. C

(A) and (B) lack parallel structure. (D) and (E) correct the faulty parallelism in the same way as (C) but create fragments.

19. A

(B) and (D) lack parallel structure. (C) is a fragment. (E) uses the singular *he or she* to refer to a plural antecedent.

20. A

(A) uses the active voice for both clauses. (B) is fine if the writer wants to emphasize Carlson. (C) uses the passive voice and this is awkward and unnecessary. (D) misplaces modifiers and (E) is a fragment.

SECTION II

Style and Usage

CHAPTER 10

Effective Word Choice

Start with this 10-question Building Block Quiz. The first few questions test material you've already seen.

BUILDING BLOCK QUIZ

For questions 1–7, choose the answer that will most improve the sentence.

1. Toby promised his sister he'd take her bowling, but he had went without her.
   (A) Change the comma to a semicolon.
   (B) Change *her* to *she*.
   (C) Delete *had*.
   (D) Change *had went* to *gone*.
   (E) Change *but* to *however*.

2. If you love someone, set them free.
   (A) Change *them* to *him or her*.
   (B) Change *them* to *he or she*.
   (C) Change the comma to a semicolon.
   (D) Change *you* to *one*.
   (E) Change *set them free* to *release them*.

3. I am willing to try your solution, however, I must tell you I don't think it will work.

   (A) Change *however* to *for*.

   (B) Change *work* to *succeed*.

   (C) Change the comma between *solution* and *however* to a semicolon.

   (D) Change the comma between *however* and *I* to a semicolon.

   (E) Change *must* to *need to*.

4. I've had enough of Cameron being so laid back; he never does anything around here and we have to pick up his slack.

   (A) Change *anything* to *nothing*.

   (B) Change *pick up* to *endure*.

   (C) Change the semicolon to a comma.

   (D) Change *laid back* to *lazy*.

   (E) Change *I've had enough of* to *I'm done with*.

5. Ilya walked loudly across the floor, trying to make as much noise as possible.

   (A) Change *walked loudly* to *stomped*.

   (B) Change *floor* to *carpet*.

   (C) Change *noise* to *sound*.

   (D) Change *walked* to *traversed*.

   (E) Change *trying to* to *try to*.

6. Tallulah sat hunched in the corner until the air raid sirens stopped.

   (A) Change *sat* to *set*.

   (B) Change *stopped* to *no longer sounded*.

   (C) Move *until the air raid sirens stopped* to the beginning of the sentence.

   (D) Move *in the corner* to the beginning of the sentence.

   (E) Change *sat hunched* to *cowered*.

7. Unfortunately, government is often corrupt and it uses a lot of unnecessary resources, too.

   (A) Change *wastes* to *waists*.
   (B) Change *it uses a lot of unnecessary resources, too* to *wasteful.*
   (C) Change *uses* to *consumes*.
   (D) Change *uses a lot of unnecessary resources* to *wastes a lot of resources*.
   (E) Change *unfortunately* to *sadly*.

For questions 8–10, answer the questions that follow.

8. Which of the following is NOT an element of style?

   (A) word choice
   (B) sentence structure
   (C) level of detail
   (D) agreement
   (E) parallelism

9. *Connotation* refers to

   (A) a writer's style
   (B) the literal meaning of a word
   (C) figurative language
   (D) a word's implied or suggested meaning
   (E) the level of detail in a text

10. *Green* is a _____ for *inexperienced*.

   (A) euphemism
   (B) dysphemism
   (C) connotation
   (D) tone
   (E) homonym

Answers and Explanations

1. C

The simple past tense should be used in both clauses; *had* should be followed by the past participle *gone*, not the simple past *went*.

2. A

The indefinite pronoun *someone* is singular, so the pronoun should be *him or her*. (B) uses the subjective case when the objective case is required.

3. C

The sentence is a run-on; a comma alone cannot separate two independent clauses. *However* is a conjunctive adverb and needs a semicolon or period.

4. D

Laid back has a positive connotation—casual and not easily stressed. The context of the sentence requires a negative word. (A) creates a double negative. (B) changes the meaning and doesn't quite make sense. (C) creates a run-on sentence. (E) doesn't improve the sentence.

5. A

Stomped is more precise than *walked loudly*. (B) doesn't improve the sentence; (C) uses two words that are too close in meaning. (D) sounds pretentious. (E) is grammatically incorrect.

6. E

To sit hunched is to *cower*, a more precise and concise verb. (B) adds words without adding precision. (C) and (D) create misplaced modifiers.

7. B

Wasteful is precise and concise, and uses parallel structure. (A) uses the wrong homophone. (C) uses a more sophisticated word but it is unnecessary (and may sound pretentious). (D) is still bulky and lacks parallel structure. (E) makes no significant change.

8. D

Agreement is a grammar issue, not a matter of style. Parallelism is both grammar and style.

9. D

Connotation refers to a word's suggested or implied meaning.

10. A

A euphemism replaces a negative term with a positive or neutral word or phrase. *Green* is a color suggesting youth or spring; it carries a more positive connotation than *inexperienced*.

Good writing has three characteristics: (1) it has something to say, (2) it says it correctly, and (3) it says it with style. Style refers to the kinds of words and sentences we use to express our ideas. Is a movie *suspenseful* or *riveting*? Are your sentences compact or long and complex? Do you offer figurative language or stick to unadorned facts?

While sentence structure plays a large role in shaping our style, the greatest impact comes from the individual words we use. So we begin this section with **diction**.

GRAMMAR SPEAK

Diction is simply the grammatical term for **word choice**. Because it is more concise, you may come across it often in grammar and style textbooks.

WHY WORD CHOICE MATTERS

You may never have thought of it this way before, but writing is a series of decisions. What should you write about? How should you organize your ideas? What is the best punctuation?

And the one decision that you make in every part of every sentence is which word to use. Poor word choice distorts your ideas and misleads your readers; the right word leaves no room for misinterpretation, because it is:

- precise
- appropriate
- concise
- correct

This chapter focuses on the first quality: precision.

PRECISE LANGUAGE

Want to elevate your style to the next level? **Be precise**. Notice how the following sentence is enhanced by substituting one of the precise verbs listed below for the imprecise *looked at*:

Sebastian <u>looked at</u> the woman seated next to him.

stared at	studied	peered at	regarded
glared at	admired	watched	scrutinized
leered at	gazed at	surveyed	inspected

Because they create vivid and exact pictures, exact words are far more powerful than general terms.

Exact Verbs

Use an exact verb whenever possible. If you have a *verb + modifier* phrase, you can often find a single verb to express that idea more powerfully, precisely, and concisely.

Imprecise: "Hurry up!" Jolene <u>said</u>.

Precise: "Hurry up!" Jolene <u>shrieked</u>.

Precise: "Hurry up!" Jolene <u>begged</u>.

Precise: "Hurry up!" Jolene <u>bellowed</u>.

Imprecise: Xavier <u>drove quickly</u> to the hospital.

Precise: Xavier <u>raced</u> to the hospital.

Precise: Xavier <u>zoomed</u> to the hospital.

Precise: Xavier <u>flew</u> to the hospital.

Exact Nouns

Name people, places, and things as precisely as possible: *modifier + noun* combinations can often be replaced by a single, more precise noun.

Imprecise: The <u>flowers</u> are beginning to bloom.

Precise: The <u>geraniums</u> are beginning to bloom.

Imprecise: Ansel's <u>car</u> is in the garage—again.

Precise: Ansel's <u>Volkswagen</u> is in the garage—again.

Exact Modifiers

Describe people, places, things, and actions precisely. You can often replace a modifying phrase or clause with just the right word.

Imprecise: Harold makes me <u>very mad</u>.

Precise: Harold makes me <u>furious</u>.

More precise: Harold <u>infuriates</u> me.

Imprecise: Myra is <u>always coming up with original ideas</u>.

Precise: Myra is very <u>innovative</u>.

Imprecise: Hans is <u>the kind of person who has his own business</u>.

Precise: Hans is <u>an entrepreneur</u>.

> ### REMEMBER THIS!
> Be precise. Use exact words to convey your meaning.

Practice 1

In each sentence below, replace the underlined section with a more precise word or phrase.

Example: The contract ~~does not have~~ lacks a specific deadline.

1. It's <u>really cold</u> outside today.
2. I think Hillary would be a <u>good</u> manager.
3. The car <u>made a noise</u>, then stopped.
4. The cake is <u>really good</u>.
5. The <u>lack of light</u> made it difficult to see what I was doing.

The Right Connotation

Each word has a **denotation**—its dictionary meaning—and a **connotation**—the suggested or implied meaning, the set of assumptions or associations carried by that word. You're headed for trouble if you open up a thesaurus and randomly pick a synonym. Words with similar denotations have vastly different connotations. Consider this list of synonyms for *smart*:

| intelligent | gifted | brainy | sharp | astute |
| clever | bright | keen | sagacious | |

Brainy is the most informal and suggests the person is more comfortable with books than people. *Sagacious* connotes wisdom and insight, while *clever* implies craftiness. A *gifted* person has a special talent and is not interchangeable with someone who is *sharp* or *keen*. Like the verbs we examined earlier, adjectives convey very specific meaning.

> **GRAMMAR SPEAK**
>
> **Denotation** is a word's literal or dictionary meaning.
> **Connotation** refers to its implied meaning and associations.

In the most general terms, connotations can be positive, negative, or neutral. The term *politician* is neutral; *public servant* and *statesman* are positive; and *influence peddler* is decidedly negative. Within these categories, there are degrees and cultural associations. *Public servant* connotes responsibility to constituents, while *statesman* suggests respect, even nobility.

Practice 2

Rank the following word groups according to connotation, 1 being weakest or most negative, 2 the most neutral, and 3 the strongest or most positive.

1. ___ happy   ___ ecstatic   ___ content
2. ___ furious   ___ angry   ___ upset
3. ___ exaggerated   ___ lied   ___ fibbed
4. ___ boring   ___ routine   ___ tedious
5. ___ worried   ___ preoccupied   ___ anxious

Practice 3

Which word in parenthesis has a connotation that best fits the context?

1. The twins, finally reunited after ten years, stayed up all night (talking / getting reacquainted).

2. Unable to convince Hector to help, Adele (resorted to / tried) begging and pleading.

3. "That's the last straw!" Belinda (hissed / remarked) as she (fled / stormed out of) the room.

4. I admire Kendra's (distinct / peculiar) style.

5. At first, Nadia felt (self-conscious / ashamed) in her new glasses, but now she won't go anywhere without them.

Word Choice and Tone

Word choice is the key factor in establishing **tone**: the mood or attitude conveyed by words or speech—heavy or light, informative or mysterious:

> 1. I'd like to be alone.   2. Go away.   3. Get lost!

All three say essentially the same thing—but each has a different tone and sends a very different message. The first is polite and respectful, the second curt, and the third rude.

Practice 4

Match the following sentences with the word that best describes their tone.

Sentence	Choice	Tone
1. "Hurry up!" Jolene shrieked.	_____	a. angry
2. "Hurry up!" Jolene demanded.	_____	b. cheerful
3. "Hurry up!" Jolene snapped.	_____	c. impatient
4. "Hurry up!" Jolene sang.	_____	d. serious
5. "Hurry up!" Jolene seethed.	_____	e. fearful

Euphemisms and Dysphemisms

Have you ever considered buying a *pre-owned vehicle*? Would you prefer that to a *used car*? Do you know anyone in his or her *golden years*—that is, a *senior citizen*? In other words, someone who is *elderly* or just plain *old*? The use of words and phrases like *pre-owned vehicle* and *golden years* is called **euphemism**: the substitution of a neutral or positive term for one that is harsh or offensive.

Euphemisms can make difficult or unpleasant subjects easier to discuss. Saying that a loved one has *passed away* is often easier than saying someone *died*. But euphemisms can be used to mask reality or to put an ideological spin on a concept. The military speaks of *collateral damage*—a glaring euphemism for *civilian casualties* (and *casualty* is a euphemism for someone injured or killed). In a war, enemy fighters are called *rebels* or *insurgents*—two **dysphemisms** (the opposite of euphemisms)—while the rebels call themselves *freedom fighters* or *liberators*.

Precise and *honest* writing avoids euphemisms and dysphemisms unless the context or audience requires a certain delicacy. In any case, remember that careful readers tend to be wary of them.

GRAMMAR SPEAK

A **euphemism** is the use of a neutral or positive term instead of one that is unpleasant or offensive. A **dysphemism** does the opposite, substituting a negative term for one that is neutral or positive.

Practice 5

Replace the euphemisms and dysphemisms in the sentences below with a more neutral word or phrase.

Example: Lito was released from ~~the correctional institution~~. *jail*

1. Gerry wants to be a <u>law enforcement officer</u> when he grows up.
2. Inez was <u>sacked</u> after she admitted to "borrowing" office supplies.
3. Helene works at a home for <u>visually impaired</u> children.
4. Ulysses visits his <u>shrink</u> every Thursday at noon.

Be Specific and Concrete

Being precise means providing real, tangible **details** and using **concrete** rather than abstract nouns.

Abstract nouns refer to ideas or qualities: *love, duty, misery, convenience.* Concrete nouns refer to physical objects or things you can experience with your senses: *book, olive, dancer, message.*

Abstract time, disapproval, justice

Concrete watch, frown, judge

Use concrete, rather than abstract, nouns whenever possible. Concrete nouns are vivid and exact.

Okay: The car veered into opposing traffic on the highway.

Better: The <u>green hatchback</u> veered into opposing traffic on <u>Route 6</u>.

Okay: Xavier has achieved great <u>success</u> as a writer.

Better: Xavier has won <u>rave reviews and two awards for his short stories</u>.

Practice 6

Replace the underlined words or phrases with specific, concrete details.

hamster (or newt, etc.)

Example: Emily takes good care of her ~~pet~~ .

1. I only use organic <u>products</u> for doing my laundry.

2. Richie has <u>so much stuff</u> in his backpack that he can't even close it.

3. That <u>bag over there</u> belongs to Lauren.

4. Akim was devastated to learn that Candy's letters were filled with <u>deceit</u>.

5. The <u>atmosphere</u> is oppressive.

SUMMARY

Style is controlled largely by **word choice** and sentence structure. Effective diction means that words are exact, appropriate, concise and correct. **Exact language** means using just the right word to replace a bulky, imprecise verb, noun, or modifying phrase.

Effective word choice also requires sensitivity to **connotation**. Words have positive or negative connotations and a range of social and cultural associations.

Word choice also controls the **tone:** the mood or attitude conveyed.

Euphemisms are positive words or phrases that replace negative or unpleasant terms; **dysphemisms** replace positive or neutral terms with negative ones. But both should be avoided in honest, precise writing.

Finally, precise language means including specific **details** and using **concrete nouns** whenever possible.

Practice: On Your Own

Books (either fiction or non-fiction), major magazines, and newspapers are great places to look for examples of effective word choice. Find instances of precise language as you look through chapters or articles. Alternatively, find examples of writing that lacks precise language—perhaps a workplace memo, the draft of an essay, or a letter you received in the mail. How much can you improve that text.

Practice Answers and Explanations

Practice 1

Answers will vary. We provide two options for each question below.

1. freezing, frigid
2. effective, excellent
3. sputtered, hissed
4. delicious, buttery
5. darkness, shadows

Practice 2

1. 2, 3, 1
2. 3, 2, 1
3. 1, 3, 2
4. 2, 1, 3
5. 2, 1, 3

Practice 3

1. *getting reacquainted*. If the twins have been separated for ten years, they'll want to do more than just *talk*.
2. *resorted to*. The context tells us that Adele already *tried* other means; *resorted to* tells us that she's moving to an option she didn't want to use, but has to.
3. *hissed, stormed out*. The quote tells us that Belinda is angry, so *hissed* is appropriate. *Fled* connotes fear instead of anger, which is clearly implied by *stormed out*.
4. *distinct*. If Kendra's style is something we admire, we need a positive word. *Peculiar* has a slightly negative connotation.
5. *self-conscious*. The connotation of *ashamed* is too strong for the context of the sentence. *Self-conscious* is more accurate and appropriate.

Practice 4

1. **e.** *Shrieked* suggests fear.
2. **d.** *Demanded* suggests the situation is serious.
3. **c.** *Snapped* suggests impatience.
4. **b.** *Sang* suggests cheerfulness.
5. **a.** *Seethed* suggests anger.

Practice 5

1. police officer (euphemism)
2. bathroom, rest stop (euphemism)
3. fired (dysphemism)
4. blind (euphemism)
5. psychiatrist (dysphemism)

Practice 6

Answers will vary. We provide two possibilities for each question.

1. detergent, cleaner
2. so many papers; so much clothes
3. purse, backpack; on the table, under the bench
4. lies, empty words
5. heat, room

CHAPTER 10 TEST

Choose the best answer to fill the blank in the sentence.

1. The id is always there, ____ just under the surface of our consciousness.

   (A) being   (B) hiding   (C) lurking

   (D) hanging out   (E) waiting

2. With holes in his shirt, pants, and shoes, Connor looked ____.

   (A) messy   (B) unpolished   (C) sloppy

   (D) bedraggled   (E) untidy

3. Irfan's ____ makes him unpleasant to be around.

   (A) negative attitude   (B) pessimism   (C) unoptimistic nature

   (D) bleak outlook   (E) feelings of negativity

4. I enjoy the ____ of the lake.

   (A) tranquility   (B) quiet   (C) peace and quiet

   (D) lack of noise   (E) muteness

5. The car ____ out of control.

   (A) swerved back and forth   (B) went   (C) swiveled

   (D) zigzagged   (E) careened

6. Rajesh was feeling so ____ that he went to the hospital.

   (A) unwell   (B) ill   (C) under the weather

   (D) unhealthy   (E) bad

7. I like that Ike is ____ when it comes to getting what he wants.

   (A) a person who always keeps trying   (B) obstinate

   (C) persistent   (D) relentless   (E) single-minded

8. When I leaned closer, I could hear the old man ___, "Thank you."
   (A) say quietly   (B) say in a hushed tone of voice   (C) hiss
   (D) request   (E) whisper

9. I don't like Ed's ___ attitude, he thinks he's better than everyone else.
   (A) superior   (B) confident   (C) self-assured
   (D) overbearing   (E) stuck-up

10. Cody refuses to sleep without a light on because he ___ the dark.
    (A) doesn't like   (B) is terrified of   (C) dislikes
    (D) gets nervous in   (E) is alarmed by

11. Ahmed is so ___ that I'm afraid he'll have a heart attack.
    (A) excitable   (B) uptight   (C) tense
    (D) preoccupied   (E) stressed out

12. Jasmine's outfit ___ the new dress code.
    (A) violates   (B) does not accord with   (C) counters
    (D) breaks   (E) disagrees with

13. Lowell's office is so ___ with papers that you literally can't see the floor.
    (A) messy   (B) bursting   (C) littered
    (D) replete   (E) full

14. According to the letter, James will not be ___ until the disputed balance is paid in full.
    (A) gratified   (B) pleased   (C) content
    (D) satiated   (E) satisfied

15. Rwanda's 1994 ___ of Tutsis left an estimated 800,000 dead.
    (A) ethnic cleansing
    (B) termination
    (C) selective elimination
    (D) mass murder
    (E) purging

16. American Sign Language translators will be available for the ___.
    (A) hard of hearing (B) deaf (C) hearing impaired
    (D) unhearing (E) auditorily disadvantaged

17. The acoustics in Stan's new ___ are quite amazing.
    (A) place (B) apartment (C) loft
    (D) residence (E) abode

18. The overwhelming success of the experiment ___ even Jing Lee, who had been the most optimistic about the results.
    (A) startled (B) alarmed (C) flabbergasted
    (D) surprised (E) dumbfounded

19. What happened to the ___ you left on the table?
    (A) thing (B) instrument (C) tool
    (D) equipment (E) hammer

20. Because of my consistently low grades in math, my parents have decided to send me to a ___.
    (A) learning consultant
    (B) tutor
    (C) educational assistant
    (D) academic counselor
    (E) achievement aide

Answers and Explanations

1. C

Lurking is the most precise word with the most appropriate connotation.

2. D

Bedraggled is the most precise word with the strongest connotation (required here given the context).

3. B

Pessimism is most precise and concise. *Bleak* has a very strong connotation, and *bleak outlook* is less concise than *pessimism*.

4. A

Tranquility is most precise, concise, and appropriate. *Muteness* has an inappropriate negative connotation and *lack of noise* is not positive enough.

5. E

Careened is the most precise verb with the strongest connotation.

6. B

Ill carries the strongest connotation and is the most precise of the choices.

7. C

The correct word must have a positive connotation. (A) is wordy and imprecise; (B)–(E) are all precise, but only (C) is positive.

8. E

Whisper is the most precise and concise choice. Because the speaker has to *lean close*, neither *hiss* nor *request* are appropriate.

9. A

The best word will be negative and show Ed's sense of being better than others. *Superior* is best. *Confident* and *self-assured* are positive; *overbearing* and *stuck-up* are negative, but don't convey the idea of being above others.

10. B

Cody feels strongly about the dark, so we need a word or phrase with a strong connotation. *Terrified* is powerful and precise.

11. E

We need a strong word—something powerful enough to send Ahmed to the hospital. *Stressed out* has the strongest connotation.

12. A

Violates is clearly the most precise word with the strongest connotation (and note how wordy (B) is in comparison).

13. C

Littered is the most precise choice. (A), (B), and (E) have appropriate connotations, but (A) and (E) are not as precise, and (B) doesn't fit the context. (D) has an inappropriate connotation.

14. E

Though all the words are precise and have similar meanings, *satisfied* best fits the context. (A)–(C) are too positive. (D) has too strong a connotation.

15. D

Only *mass murder* is clear, straightforward language (and the only concrete noun). All other choices offer euphemisms.

16. B

Deaf is the most straightforward choice. The others are awkward and/or euphemisms.

17. C

Loft is the most precise choice. *Residence* and *abode* are more sophisticated, but not precise. *Apartment* is specific, but *loft* is a precise kind of apartment. (A) is imprecise.

18. D

Surprised is precise and fits the context. (A) and (B) both suggest fear and are negative. (C) and (E) suggest an inability to understand.

19. E

Hammer is the only specific, concrete choice. (A) is about as imprecise as you can get. (B)–(D) offer only categories of things, not specific items.

20. B

Tutor is the only honest and precise choice. The other choices are all euphemisms.

| CHAPTER 11 |

Being Appropriate

Start with this 10-question Building Block Quiz. The first few questions test material you've already seen.

BUILDING BLOCK QUIZ

Choose the answer that best explains the grammar or style error in each sentence below. (We've tinkered with quotations to create the error.)

1. Life is the art of drawing sufficient conclusions from premises that are insufficient. —*Samuel Butler*

   (A) run-on sentence   (B) lacks subject-verb agreement

   (C) incorrect pronoun case   (D) incorrect verb tense

   (E) lacks parallel structure

2. The trouble with the rat race is that even if you win. You are still a rat. —*Lily Tomlin*

   (A) misplaced modifier   (B) sentence fragment

   (C) incorrect use of passive voice   (D) incorrect helping verb

   (E) use of infinitive instead of gerund

3. The eternal silence of those infinite spaces strike me with terror. —*Blaise Pascal*

   (A) use of adjective instead of adverb

   (B) lacks pronoun agreement

   (C) lacks parallel structure

   (D) lacks subject-verb agreement

   (E) misplaced modifier

4. The best thing a person can do in an emergency is to keep calm so he can think clearly and act decisively.
   (A) imprecise word choice   (B) use of slang   (C) use of jargon
   (D) pretentious language   (E) sexist language

5. The child vociferously vocalized her discontent.
   (A) imprecise word choice   (B) use of slang   (C) use of jargon
   (D) pretentious language   (E) sexist language

6. When Ravi returned to his computer, he saw a message from his old friend Nadia: "LTNS, friend. I've been thinking of you. I hope all's well. TCOY, Nadia."
   (A) imprecise word choice   (B) use of slang   (C) use of jargon
   (D) pretentious language   (E) sexist language

7. "I'd really like to know what makes Nathan tick," Shani said.
   (A) imprecise word choice   (B) use of slang   (C) use of jargon
   (D) pretentious language   (E) sexist language

8. The foregoing events have necessitated our premature departure.
   (A) imprecise word choice   (B) use of slang   (C) use of jargon
   (D) pretentious language   (E) sexist language

9. Is there a waitress nearby? I need some ketchup.
   (A) imprecise word choice   (B) use of slang   (C) use of jargon
   (D) pretentious language   (E) sexist language

10. Although I do not wish to have a confrontation, I'm ready to play hardball if I have to.
    (A) inconsistent tense   (B) inconsistent voice
    (C) inconsistent level of formality   (D) inconsistent pronouns
    (E) inconsistent level of precision

Answers and Explanations

1.   E

The two comparable items—*sufficient conclusions* and *premises that are insufficient*—are not parallel. The latter should be *insufficient premises*.

2.   B

In the first sentence, the dependent clause *even if you win* needs the clause *you are still a rat* to complete its thought.

3.   D

The subject of the verb *strike* is *eternal silence*, not *infinite spaces* (which is part of a prepositional phrase); the verb should be singular, *strikes*.

4.   E

The sentence uses the generic *he*; it should be revised to include both genders.

5.   D

Vociferously vocalized is pretentious language—fancy words designed to impress readers, which are often confusing and unclear, and sometimes downright obnoxious.

6.   C

Internet chat room jargon makes no sense to readers who are not chat room regulars. (*LTNS* means *long time no see*; *TCOY* is *take care of yourself*).

7.   B

The phrase *what makes Nathan tick* is slang and inappropriate for most forms of writing.

8.   D

This is another example of pretentious language. In plain English, the sentence is *Because of what happened we must leave early.*

9.   E

Help wanted ads for restaurants now ask for *servers* rather than *waiters* or *waitresses,* which is sexist language.

10.   C

This sentence has a rather marked shift in its level of formality. The first clause is quite formal, the second informal, with contractions and slang.

So, it's like, we were talking about word choice and stuff in the last lesson, and we covered exact language, because that was numero uno on our list. Now we're gonna do number two, being appropriate—which this here intro sure ain't!

Effective style means that your word choice is **appropriate:** your language *suits* your subject, audience, and purpose.

LEVEL OF FORMALITY

What sort of style would you use in a letter to describe an experience to a friend? Probably relaxed, informal, sprinkled with slang—the way you and your friend might talk to each other. How would you describe the same experience in a college or job application essay? You'd use more formal language and more carefully structure each sentence and paragraph.

Chances are you make this adjustment in formality level automatically. Some audiences and subjects require more formal treatment than others; if you write at the wrong level of formality, you risk confusing or offending your audience.

To determine what level is appropriate, ask yourself the following questions:

- **What sort of style does your subject deserve?** Is it something sensitive or weighty that requires formal treatment (nuclear proliferation or global warming)? Is it something humorous or light, suitable for a relaxed style (the latest fashion trends or a review of a new sitcom)? Or does it fall somewhere in between?

- **What style best fits your purpose?** If you aim to make readers laugh, your writing will be more relaxed than if you want to convince readers of your professionalism and expertise.

- **Who is your audience?** Be as specific as possible: is it a general reader, a prospective employer, a newspaper editor? Do you have two or more levels of readers—your primary audience (people who will definitely read what you write) and a secondary audience (others who may also read it)?

- **What is your relationship to the audience?** Do you know your readers well enough to assume a tone of familiarity? Are your readers strangers? Or do you want to invite readers in with a style that finds a middle ground?

Practice 1

For each writing task below, determine the appropriate level of formality on the following scale:

> 1 very informal
> 2 somewhat informal
> 3 middle ground
> 4 somewhat formal
> 5 very formal

___1. An essay for your sociology class.

___2. A letter informing the Department of Motor Vehicles of an address change.

___3. A note thanking your neighbor for taking care of your cats while you were away.

___4. A note thanking your landlord (whom you know well but with whom you aren't friendly) for getting the kitchen sink fixed promptly.

___5. A memo to your new boss requesting a schedule change.

> ### REMEMBER THIS!
> Level of formality is determined primarily by word choice.

Once you've determined the level of formality, simply choose appropriate words. If an informal style is right, use *party* instead of *celebration* or *festivities*; use *keep at it* instead of *persist*. For a more formal style, choose words like *attempt* instead of *try*, or *evaluate* rather than *size up*. In most writing, there are three word choice pitfalls to avoid: slang, jargon, and pretentious language.

Slang

In normal conversation, you probably use **slang**: the very casual and often playful language used by a particular group. It is prone to frequent change (what was *groovy* in the '60s became *phat* or *hot* in 2000, and who knows what ten years from now).

While slang has its place, it should be avoided in most writing for two reasons. First, it is highly informal, so it is inappropriate for most academic or workplace writing. Second, it has a limited accessibility (not everyone knows what *phat* means).

> **Slang:** Jules, <u>I've gotta give you props</u> for how you handled that situation.
>
> **Standard:** Jules, <u>congratulations</u> on how you handled that situation.

The standard version lacks the vitality of everyday speech, but *all* readers can understand it—and that's essential for effective writing.

Regionalisms and Dialects

Like slang, **regional expressions** and **dialects** have their place but in general should be avoided because they are not familiar to all readers. If you want to convey the nature of your characters' speech, that's one thing—but in most contexts, stick to standard English.

> **Regional:** My dad <u>saws gourds</u> so loudly <u>ain't no one can</u> sleep at night.
>
> **Standard:** My dad <u>snores</u> so loudly that <u>no one can</u> sleep at night.
>
> **Dialect:** My grandpa never <u>think</u> about <u>hisself</u>; he only <u>think</u> about others.
>
> **Standard:** My grandpa never <u>thinks</u> about <u>himself</u>; he only <u>thinks</u> about others.

Practice 2

How would you revise the following sentences to eliminate slang?

1. I love your idea, Hank, but it'll never fly.
2. Please tell me straight up what's going on.
3. You wouldn't know it from the clothes he wears, but Antonio has really deep pockets.
4. We've been on a roll since Hendricks stepped up to the plate.
5. I totally bombed the math test—my mom's gonna kill me.

Jargon

Jargon is technical language shared by those engaged in a shared activity—members of a certain profession or people who share a hobby. Computer experts can toss around such terms as *compile*, *jpeg*, and *firewall* and economists can speak to each other of *aggregate demand* and *monopsony*, but average readers are likely to be lost.

As a general rule, then, avoid jargon unless you are writing for a specialized audience. Use plain English that all readers can understand; if you must use a technical or specialized term, define it:

Jargon:	The patient has an <u>internal rotation ROM of the shoulder</u> of 15 degrees.
Plain English:	The patient <u>can fold his arm in from the shoulder</u> at 15 degrees.
Defined:	The patient has an internal rotation <u>ROM (range of motion)</u> of the shoulder at 15 degrees.

GRAMMAR SPEAK

Slang is very casual, playful language used by a particular group. **Jargon** is technical or specialized language relating to a particular activity.

Practice 3

How would you revise the following sentences to eliminate the underlined jargon?

1. Paul's two <u>periorbital hemotomas</u> made him look like a raccoon.
2. Before we got our jobs at the mall, Irma and I just <u>IMed</u> each other all afternoon.
3. The newspaper's <u>byline</u> attributed the article to the wrong author.
4. The <u>PA system</u> wasn't working, so Gus's band had to reschedule the show.
5. Olga's convinced we need a <u>hired gun</u>, but I don't think an outsider can cure our problems.

Pretentious and Inflated Language

Pretentious language is big words and fancy phrases where simple language will do, often used in an attempt to sound smart or sophisticated.

Pretentious: The edifice erected at the transversion of Main and Walnut Streets reflects the aesthetic architectural form of the classical era.

Plain English: The building on the corner of Main and Walnut Streets is neoclassical.

Inflated language is a lesser offense but still something to avoid. This chart offers some of the most common instances of inflated language and their plain English counterparts.

Inflated	Plain English
at this point in time	now
commence	begin
endeavor	try
facilitate	help, aid
in close proximity to	near
instrument	tool
transpire	happen

Practice 4

What simple familiar words are hidden in these pretentious or inflated sentences?

1. Avoid placement of the wheeled medium of transportation anterior to the mammal of the equine family.

2. The experience of temporality elapses at an expeditious rate while one is enjoying diversions.

3. Purveyors of benevolent deeds perpetually terminate in the rearmost position.

> ## REMEMBER THIS!
> Unless you are writing for an audience that is certain to understand you, **avoid slang and jargon. Pretentious language** is obnoxious and confusing, not impressive.

Be Consistent

Add level of formality to your list of things that must be consistent. Mixing formal and informal language suggests that you aren't clear about your subject, audience, or purpose.

SEXIST AND OFFENSIVE LANGUAGE

We've come a long way in eliminating bias in our language, but there is still work to be done. As Jeane J. Kirkpatrick put it: "Words can destroy. What we call each other ultimately becomes what we think of each other, and it matters." To continue to work toward a fair and just society, be careful to avoid sexist or biased language.

What Exactly *Is* Sexist Language?

Sexist language includes any word or phrase that reflects a disrespect or contempt for women *or* men. This includes blatantly sexist terms such as *broad* or sentences that reflect stereotypical roles or behaviors.

The Generic *He*

Before the 1970s, it was considered correct to use the masculine pronoun if a person's gender was unknown. This "solution" neglects an entire gender, so its use is no longer acceptable.

Except where a single gender is clearly meant, both genders or neither should be referred to. As with pronoun agreement errors (see chapter 6), use *he or she* (if it isn't too awkward), or revise your sentence to make the pronoun plural or to eliminate the need for a pronoun.

Unacceptable: When a doctor sees a new patient, <u>he</u> must review that patient's full medical history.

Revised: Before they see new patients, doctors must review each patient's full medical history.

Unacceptable: A nursing student will have several hospital internships before <u>she</u> is certified.

Revised: A nursing student will have several hospital internships before being certified.

Use Gender-Free Terms

Any word with *man* or *woman* in it can be revised to eliminate the inherent gender reference. Similarly, most words that have a masculine and feminine version are no longer acceptable; use a gender-neutral version instead. The chart offers a short list of sexist terms and their gender-free counterparts.

Sexist	Gender-Free
businessman	executive
chairman, chairwoman	chairperson, chair, coordinator
congressman, congresswoman	member of Congress, representative
fireman	firefighter
foreman	supervisor
mailman	mail carrier, letter carrier
mankind	people, humans
policeman, policewoman	police officer
salesman, saleswoman	sales clerk, sales representative
stewardess, steward	flight attendant
waitress, waiter	server, wait staff
weatherman	forecaster, meteorologist

REMEMBER THIS!

To avoid sexist language: use gender-free terms, avoid stereotypes, and avoid the generic *he*.

Be PC

Some may argue that "PC"—political correctness—has gone too far, and that our language has become filled with inflated euphemisms (e.g., *vertically challenged*). While there may be some truth to this, it's best to be very sensitive to how language can offend others. **Biased language** can be blatant or subtle; it can come across in name-calling or stereotypes, either positive or negative (e.g., *Like most Chinese, Yi was good at science and math.*).

To avoid biased language, be extra careful when describing cultural groups and use terms that fairly and accurately describe the population.

Inappropriate: Raul is very proud of his Indian heritage.

Revised: Raul is very proud of his <u>Navajo</u> heritage. (*Indian* means from India.)

Practice 5

How would you eliminate sexist and biased language in the following sentences?

1. The anchorman said the death toll from the earthquake will exceed 20,000.

2. When an astronaut is in space, his muscles will atrophy quickly if he does not exercise regularly.

3. A person who is always criticizing others is terrified that others will criticize him.

4. Chantal works as a hostess at Chez Chez.

SUMMARY

Appropriate language comes from having the right level of formality and avoiding sexist or otherwise offensive language. To find the appropriate level of formality, consider: (1) What style does your subject deserve? (2) What style best fits your purpose? (3) Who is your audience? (4) What is your relationship to that audience?

Slang and **jargon** are only appropriate when the audience consists only of readers who will understand it *and* it is suitable to the subject. **Pretentious** or **inflated language** is the use of fancy, wordy language in an attempt to impress readers.

Avoid **sexist** or **biased language**. To include both genders, use gender-free terms and avoid the generic *he*. Avoid stereotypes (positive or negative) of either sex and any ethnic, racial, or cultural group.

Practice: On Your Own

Browse through a variety of texts and identify their different levels of formality. Consider *why* each author used that level of formality. Search for examples of slang and jargon in the texts you read. Is it appropriate? Did you have any difficulty understanding it?

Practice Answers and Explanations
Practice 1

1. **4 or 5**. Somewhat to very formal is called for in an academic assignment for a general reader. Write at the highest level of formality, but try not to sound too stuffy.

2. **5**. Because you have no relationship with the reader and the reader is in a position of authority, your letter should be highly respectful.

3. **1 or 2**. Depending upon just how close you and your neighbor are, this note can be somewhat to very informal.

4. **3**. Because you do have a relationship with your landlord, even if it is not particularly friendly, and because the message is positive, the note can be somewhere in the middle.

5. **4 or 5**. Because it's a new boss, we can assume you don't have a particularly close relationship, so it's best to show distance and respect.

Practice 2

Answers will vary. We've provided one sample revision for each.

1. *it'll never fly*. I love your idea, Hank, but <u>it'll never work</u>.
2. *straight up*. Please tell me <u>honestly</u> what's going on.
3. *has really deep pockets*. You wouldn't know it … but Antonio *is really rich*.

4. *on a roll, stepped up to the plate*. We've been <u>very successful</u> since Hendricks <u>began doing his share</u>.
5. *totally bombed, gonna kill me*. I failed the math test—my mom will be furious.

Practice 3

Answers may vary.

1. Paul's two <u>black eyes</u> made him look like a raccoon.
2. Before we got our jobs at the mall, Irma and I just <u>sent e-mail instant messages to</u> each other all afternoon.
3. The newspaper's <u>byline, which names the author of the article, was incorrect</u>.
4. The <u>sound system</u> wasn't working, so Gus's band had to reschedule the show. [*PA* means *public address*.]
5. Olga's convinced we need a <u>consultant</u>, but I don't think an outsider can cure our problems.

Practice 4

1. Don't put the cart before the horse.
2. Time flies when you're having fun.
3. Good guys always finish last.

Practice 5

1. Change *anchorman* to *newscaster*.
2. Make the sentence plural to include both genders: When astronauts are in space, their muscles will atrophy quickly if they do not exercise regularly.
3. Make this sentence plural too: People who are always criticizing others are terrified that others will criticize them.
4. Change *hostess* to *host*.

CHAPTER 11 TEST

Read the following sentences carefully to identify inappropriate language. If the sentence is correct, choose (E).

1. Vanessa has been down in the dumps since her best friend moved to California.
   - (A) slang (including regionalisms or dialect)
   - (B) jargon
   - (C) pretentious or inflated language
   - (D) sexist or biased language
   - (E) No error

2. Someone purloined Jordan's backpack.
   - (A) slang (including regionalisms or dialect)
   - (B) jargon
   - (C) pretentious or inflated language
   - (D) sexist or biased language
   - (E) No error

3. Listen, I'm going to just lay my cards on the table here and tell you I love you.
   - (A) slang (including regionalisms or dialect)
   - (B) jargon
   - (C) pretentious or inflated language
   - (D) sexist or biased language
   - (E) No error

4. From the beginning of time, mankind has wondered about his place in the universe.
   - (A) slang (including regionalisms or dialect)
   - (B) jargon
   - (C) pretentious or inflated language
   - (D) sexist or biased language
   - (E) No error

5. Miko was flustered by the interviewer's inappropriate question.
   (A) slang (including regionalisms or dialect)
   (B) jargon
   (C) pretentious or inflated language
   (D) sexist or biased language
   (E) No error

6. We doesn't have nothin' to say to ya'll, so skedaddle!
   (A) slang (including regionalisms or dialect)
   (B) jargon
   (C) pretentious or inflated language
   (D) sexist or biased language
   (E) No error

7. Your boyfriend is a *persona non grata* in this house!
   (A) slang (including regionalisms or dialect)
   (B) jargon
   (C) pretentious or inflated language
   (D) sexist or biased language
   (E) No error

8. I still think Wendell is the best man for the job.
   (A) slang (including regionalisms or dialect)
   (B) jargon
   (C) pretentious or inflated language
   (D) sexist or biased language
   (E) No error

9. "The girls from my office are always asking me to join them for lunch," Hayden bragged.

   (A) slang (including regionalisms or dialect)

   (B) jargon

   (C) pretentious or inflated language

   (D) sexist or biased language

   (E) No error

10. Unfortunately, the company's assets didn't amount to a hill of beans, and the owners had to call it quits.

   (A) slang (including regionalisms or dialect)

   (B) jargon

   (C) pretentious or inflated language

   (D) sexist or biased language

   (E) No error

11. Though the pain was excruciating, Eunice didn't cry.

   (A) slang (including regionalisms or dialect)

   (B) jargon

   (C) pretentious or inflated language

   (D) sexist or biased language

   (E) No error

12. I Googled my high school sweetheart and found out he married my best friend from grade school.

   (A) slang (including regionalisms or dialect)

   (B) jargon

   (C) pretentious or inflated language

   (D) sexist or biased language

   (E) No error

13. All of the freshmen are invited to an ice cream social in the student center.
    (A) slang (including regionalisms or dialect)
    (B) jargon
    (C) pretentious or inflated language
    (D) sexist or biased language
    (E) No error

14. This product will finally put us on the map.
    (A) slang (including regionalisms or dialect)
    (B) jargon
    (C) pretentious or inflated language
    (D) sexist or biased language
    (E) No error

15. After a harrowing drive up the mountain in a rickety cart, Kurt decided to hike back down.
    (A) slang (including regionalisms or dialect)
    (B) jargon
    (C) pretentious or inflated language
    (D) sexist or biased language
    (E) No error

16. When the market is bullish again, I will sell my stocks and invest in real estate instead.
    (A) slang (including regionalisms or dialect)
    (B) jargon
    (C) pretentious or inflated language
    (D) sexist or biased language
    (E) No error

17. With her multi-hued raiment, Eloise is sure to turn heads at the party.
    (A) slang (including regionalisms or dialect)
    (B) jargon
    (C) pretentious or inflated language
    (D) sexist or biased language
    (E) No error

18. With all of his accounts in the red, Andres decided it was time to get off his duff and get a job.
    (A) slang (including regionalisms or dialect)
    (B) jargon
    (C) pretentious or inflated language
    (D) sexist or biased language
    (E) No error

19. The boisterous sounds of the party echoed down the hallway and into my apartment.
    (A) slang (including regionalisms or dialect)
    (B) jargon
    (C) pretentious or inflated language
    (D) sexist or biased language
    (E) No error

20. These are all man-made materials; how about something natural?
    (A) slang (including regionalisms or dialect)
    (B) jargon
    (C) pretentious or inflated language
    (D) sexist or biased language
    (E) No error

Answers and Explanations

1. A

The phrase *down in the dumps* is slang for *depressed* or *upset*.

2. C

The word *purloined* is pretentious; *stole* would do just fine.

3. A

The phrase *lay my cards on the table* is slang for *be honest*.

4. D

The use of *mankind* and *his* is sexist; *humans* and *their* would correct the problem.

5. E

Flustered is a precise, effective verb; there is no inappropriate language.

6. A

This sentence includes regionalisms (*y'all, skedaddle*) and dialect (a double negative).

7. C

Persona non grata is pretentious; *unwelcome* would be precise and clear.

8. D

The word *man* excludes the possibility that a woman could be best for the job. Change *man* to *person*.

9. D

Calling the women in his office *girls* is sexist.

10. A

The phrases *a hill of beans* (*small amount*) and *call it quits* (*stop* or *quit*) are slang.

11. E

The sentence is correct; *excrutiating* is precise and effective.

12. B

The word *Googled* is computer jargon for using the Internet search engine Google.

13. D

Freshmen is a sexist term that acknowledges only one gender.

14. A

The phrase *put us on the map* is slang for *gain us recognition*.

15. E

The sentence is correct. *Harrowing* and *rickety* are precise words.

16. B

Bullish is finance jargon for rising stock prices.

17. C

The phrase *multi-hued raiment* is pretentious; *colorful, gaudy,* or *loud* could replace *multi-hued* and *outfit* should replace *raiment.*

18. B

The phrase *in the red* is financial jargon for *in debt* or *operating at a deficit.*

19. E

The sentence is correct. *Boisterous* is an effective, precise word choice.

20. D

The word *man-made* is sexist. Replace it with *manufactured* or *synthetic.*

CHAPTER 12

Being Concise

Start with this 10-question Building Block Quiz. The first few questions test material you've already seen.

BUILDING BLOCK QUIZ

Determine which change, if any, will most improve each sentence below. If no change offers improvement, choose (E).

1. Unlike some reptiles, hermit crabs are social creatures whom thrive only in the company of other crabs.

   (A) Change the comma to a semicolon.

   (B) Change *whom* to *who*.

   (C) Change *thrive* to *thrives*.

   (D) Move *unlike some reptiles* to the end of the sentence.

   (E) No change

2. Sound asleep at last, Edwin gently laid the baby in the crib and tiptoed out of the room.

   (A) Move *sound asleep at last* to after *baby*.

   (B) Add *with the baby* to the beginning of the sentence and change *the baby* to *her*.

   (C) Change *laid* to *lay*.

   (D) Change *tiptoed* to *walked lightly*.

   (E) No change

3. I thought I sat my glasses on the coffee table, but now I can't find them anywhere.
   (A) Change *sat* to *set*.
   (B) Change the comma to a semicolon.
   (C) Change *but* to *however*.
   (D) Change *anywhere* to *nowhere*.
   (E) No change

4. Due to the fact that my flight has been cancelled, I won't be home until Tuesday.
   (A) Change the comma to a period.
   (B) Change *until* to *before*.
   (C) Add *airplane* before *flight*.
   (D) Change *due to the fact that* to *because*.
   (E) No change

5. There are many good reasons that I can think of for Cassandra's erratic behavior.
   (A) Change *many good reasons* to *numerous plausible explanations*.
   (B) Change *there are many good reasons that I can think of* to *I can think of many good reasons*.
   (C) Change *there are many good reasons that I can think of* to *many good reasons can be imagined*.
   (D) Change *erratic behavior* to *behavior that has been erratic*.
   (E) No change

6. Have you noticed that Mr. Barker has been acting really weird lately?
   (A) Change *noticed* to *observed*.
   (B) Change *really* to *very*.
   (C) Change *lately* to *of late*.
   (D) Change *really weird* to *abnormal*.
   (E) No change

7. Clearly, it is obvious that Shana has a serious crush on you.
   (A) Delete *clearly*.
   (B) Delete *it is obvious that*.
   (C) Change *serious* to *major*.
   (D) Change *crush on* to *infatuation with*.
   (E) No change

8. It has been announced by the principal that a new absentee policy will go into effect next month.
   (A) Change *it has been announced by the principal* to *the principal has announced*.
   (B) Change *a new absentee policy will go into effect* to *going into effect next month will be*.
   (C) Change *next month* to *in the month that follows*.
   (D) Change *will go into effect* to *will be implemented*.
   (E) No change

9. What is bothering me is that I am the only one of my friends who doesn't have a license.
   (A) Change *I am the only one of my friends who doesn't have* to *I am alone among my friends for not having*.
   (B) Change *doesn't* to *don't*.
   (C) Change *bothering me* to *ticking me off*.
   (D) Change *is bothering* to *bothers*.
   (E) No change

10. I saw a boy who is in my class at the concert.
    (A) Change *boy* to *person*.
    (B) Change *boy who is in my class* to *classmate*.
    (C) Change *who* to *that*.
    (D) Change *saw* to *espied*.
    (E) No change

Answers and Explanations

1. B

Who is the subject of the clause *who thrive … other crabs*, so it needs to be in the subjective case.

2. B

It wasn't Edwin who was sound asleep but the baby, but just moving the clause doesn't work. Add the subject, and change *the baby* to avoid repetition.

3. A

The verb *set* means to put or place something.

4. D

The phrase *due to the fact that* is wordy. (A) makes a sentence fragment, (B) does not fix the problem, and (C) adds an unnecessary word.

5. B

There are many good reasons that I can think of is wordy; (B) addresses the problem. (A) is pretentious, (C) is passive, and (D) is wordy.

6. D

The modifier *weird* is not precise, and the intensifier *really* is weak. A more precise and concise modifier significantly improves the sentence. Note that *abnormal* is an adjective, the complement—not an adverb modifying the verb (see chapter 2).

7. B

Clearly and *it is obvious that* say the same thing. (A) chooses the less concise version. (C) and (D) don't address the repetition; the informal *crush* is fine in a conversation between friends.

8. A

The original sentence is passive; the active is more effective and concise. (C) adds wordiness.

9. D

Replacing the progressive form *is bothering* with the more direct *bothers* makes the sentence more vigorous and concise. (A) is a bit awkward and pretentious, (B) lacks subject-verb agreement, and (C) introduces slang.

10. B

Replacing the clause *who is in my class* with the noun *classmate* makes the sentence more concise. (A) is less precise; in (C) *who* should be used to refer to people; and (D) is pretentious.

Some writing—from academic essays to workplace proposals or reports—have length requirements. Writers often have trouble getting to the required word count or find they go well beyond the limit. In either case, the stylistic problem in the resulting texts is often the same: wordiness.

How, you might wonder, can a piece that initially falls short of its word count be wordy? Writers "fill out" the text by adding words instead of ideas:

> In my opinion, I believe that the fact that Frankenstein abandons his creature is the main reason that causes him (that is, the creature) to become violent and hurt people. (30 words)

And essays that goes over the word count are likely to have exactly the same problem: they're loaded with repetition, full of clutter. Note how much more effective this version of the Frankenstein sentence is:

> I believe the creature becomes violent mainly because Frankenstein abandons him. (11 words)

GRAMMAR SPEAK

Concise means expressing much in few words—succinct.

LESS IS MORE

Wordy sentences waste your reader's time, and clutter often clouds the meaning. Less is more. Concise writing shows that you have control over your words and ideas and that you have respect for your readers.

There are five specific strategies for writing clear, concise sentences:

1. Be precise.
2. Use active action verbs.
3. Simplify structure.
4. Eliminate clutter.
5. Avoid unnecessary repetition.

BE PRECISE

You've heard this one before. Exact words are often also concise:

> After Wynona <u>took all the stuff out of</u> her closet, she gave it a fresh coat of paint.

> After Wynona <u>emptied</u> her closet, she gave it a fresh coat of paint.

(This also avoids the ambiguous pronoun, "it".)

Avoid Intensifiers; Don't Be Wishy-Washy

Such intensifiers as *really, very, quite, totally* and *extremely* add unnecessary bulk. Find the right word, instead, for a more powerful sentence:

Imprecise:	The desert was <u>totally empty</u> as far as we could see.
Precise and concise:	The desert was <u>barren</u> as far as we could see.

Likewise, such wishy-washy and informal modifiers as *sort of, pretty,* and *kind of* suggest uncertainty. Find a more precise word to replace the modifier and modified word:

Wishy-washy:	Sheila was <u>pretty upset</u> when she found out that Janell was lying to her.
Precise and concise:	Sheila was <u>livid</u> when she learned that Janell lied to her.

Practice 1

Use more precise word(s) to make each sentence more concise.

1. The way Nina kept walking back and forth across the room made Tula nervous, too.
2. Everyone on the island was ordered to get away from the area because of the approaching hurricane.
3. Cheyenne was pretty embarrassed when her mom told everyone at the party her middle name.
4. The Tigers beat the Ravens by a lot.

USE ACTIVE ACTION VERBS

Whenever possible, use the action verbs in the active voice.

Active Verbs

Most sentences should be written in the active voice, because it's more direct, powerful, and concise than the passive (see chapter 9):

Passive:	Aboriginal art <u>has finally been given</u> the respect it deserves <u>from art critics</u>.
Active:	<u>Art critics have finally given</u> aboriginal art the respect it deserves.

FLASHBACK

Use the active voice for most sentences. But the passive voice is actually preferred: (1) when you want to minimize the significance of the agent, (2) when you want to emphasize the receiver, (3) when the agent of action is unknown.

Action Verbs

Don't over-rely on the state of being verb *be*. Use vigorous, active verbs wherever possible.

Indirect (*be*) verb:	Charles Darwin's trip to the Galapagos Islands <u>is what inspired</u> him to develop his theory of evolution. (17 words)
Direct verb:	Charles Darwin's trip to the Galapagos Islands <u>inspired</u> him to develop his theory of evolution. (15 words)

Avoid *It Is/There Is* Constructions

Notorious word wasters include the *it is/are (was/were)* and *there is/are (was/were)* constructions.

Indirect (*be*) verb:	<u>There are many factors that</u> contribute to weight gain, not just a poor diet.
Direct verb:	<u>Many factors</u> contribute to weight gain, not just a poor diet.

Practice 2

Use active action verbs to make the following sentences more concise.

1. Several artists were commissioned by the State Council on the Arts to create a series of murals for the subway.

2. Carly's report is what I will use as a model for other students.

3. It was Nanny's chicken noodle soup that made me feel better when I was sick.

4. There is still a chance that I'll win the poetry contest.

SIMPLIFY STRUCTURE

Wordiness is often the result of unnecessarily bulky sentence constructions.

Turn Clauses and Phrases into Modifiers

Many clauses and phrases can be reduced to modifiers, especially *that*, *who*, and *which* clauses and prepositional phrases.

> **Wordy:** The school <u>that I go to</u> is undergoing major renovations. (10 words)
>
> **Concise:** <u>My</u> school is undergoing major renovations. (6 words)
>
> **Wordy:** People <u>who visit Internet chat rooms regularly</u> are familiar with chat room slang. (13 words)
>
> **Concise:** <u>Chat room regulars</u> are familiar with Internet jargon. (8 words)

Combine Sentences

When one sentence adds a detail to the preceding one, the second sentence can often be turned into a modifier:

> **Wordy:** One of the problems in early childhood education is high turnover among teachers and assistants. <u>This high turnover is</u> due primarily to long hours and low wages. (29 words)
>
> **Concise:** One problem in early childhood education is high turnover among teachers and <u>assistants due</u> primarily to long hours and low wages. (23 words)

> # REMEMBER THIS!
> Clauses and phrases—especially *that, which* and *who* clauses—can often become concise modifiers.

Practice 3

Simplify the structure of the following sentences to eliminate wordiness.

1. There are 40 children registered for the class. However, the classroom can only accommodate 35 people.
2. My sociology class meets at 8 o'clock, which is unfortunate.
3. I was shocked to learn that 130 pounds of sugar is consumed by the average American each year.
4. A typical can of soda contains about nine teaspoons of refined white sugar. Refined white sugar is so chemically processed that it contains no vitamins, minerals, protein, fiber, or water.

ELIMINATE CLUTTER

Some words merely add clutter. The word *that* is a frequent offender.

Cluttered: The face <u>that</u> is on the $20 bill <u>is that of</u> Andrew Jackson.

Concise: The face on the $20 bill is Andrew Jackson's.

As you've probably noticed, with each succeeding chapter, the information has become more and more interrelated. In chapter 11 you learned some common inflated phrases. Clutter is closely related, as this chart shows.

Cluttered	Concise	Cluttered	Concise
in the event that	if	for the purpose of	for
in spite of the fact that	although	due to the fact that	because
until such time as	until	for the reason that	because
at that point in time	then	at this point in time	now
in the neighborhood of	about	has the appearance of	looks like, seems like

Less is more, and simpler is clearer.

Practice 4

Cross out clutter in the following sentences.

1. I hope that you find that these accommodations are acceptable.
2. In spite of the fact that he can't see without his glasses, Ted almost never wears them.
3. I have always believed that the here and now is more important than the future or the past.
4. I will keep this job until such time as I complete my degree, at which point I will look for an internship.

AVOID UNNECESSARY REPETITION

Repetition is a common cause of wordy sentences.

> **Redundant:** As a bonus, you'll receive a <u>free</u> pen <u>at no extra charge</u>! (12 words)
>
> **Concise:** As a bonus, you'll receive a <u>free</u> pen! (8 words)

Redundant	Concise	Redundant	Concise
red in color	red	12 midnight	midnight
circular in shape	circular	2 A.M. in the morning	2 A.M. or 2 in the morning
large in size	large	shorter in length	shorter
refer back to	refer to	repeat again	repeat
return back to	return to	revert back to	revert to
completely unanimous	unanimous	In my opinion, I believe	In my opinion or I believe
circle around	circle	surrounded on all sides	surrounded
end result	result	each and every	each or every
cooperate together	cooperate	biography of his life	biography
true fact	fact	personal opinion	opinion

Some abbreviations can lead to unnecessary repetition, for example: *There are no ATM machines around here.* ATM stands for Automated Teller Machine—so the sentence states *machine* twice.

Practice 5

Eliminate repetition.

1. I worked until 3 A.M. in the morning, but I still didn't finish my report.
2. These statistics refer back to the chart on page 181.
3. Carmen is a pianist who plays the piano with great skill.
4. Under different circumstances, if we weren't in the situation we're in now, I'd quit my job and go back to school.
5. The airplane circled around the airport several times before it received clearance to land.

SUMMARY

Effective writing is **concise**: it conveys its ideas without unnecessary words. To be concise:

1. **Be precise**. Use exact words and phrases. Avoid weak intensifiers and wishy-washy language. Find an exact word instead.
2. **Use active action verbs**. Most sentences should be in the active voice. When possible, choose a vigorous action verb over the state of being verb *be*. Avoid *there is* and *it is* constructions.
3. **Simplify structure**. Turn clauses and phrases into modifiers, especially *that, who,* and *which* clauses and prepositional phrases. Combine sentences that have repeating elements.
4. **Eliminate clutter**. *That* often unnecessarily clutters sentences, and common clutter phrases should be replaced by clearer alternatives.
5. **Avoid unnecessary repetition**. Common redundant phrases include *end result* and *in my opinion, I believe*. Watch out for redundancies when using abbreviations.

Practice: On Your Own

Wordy writing is everywhere, so you're bound to find examples now that you know what to look for. Amateur publications or websites and everyday communications such as workplace memos are good places to search. Think about how you'd make them more concise.

Practice Answers and Explanations

Practice 1

Answers may vary. We underlined the word that replaces an imprecise word or phrase.

1. The way Nina <u>paced</u> the room was making Tula nervous, too.

2. Everyone on the island was ordered to <u>evacuate</u> because of the approaching hurricane.

3. Cheyenne was <u>mortified</u> when her mom told everyone at the party her middle name.

4. The Tigers <u>crushed</u> the Ravens.

Practice 2

Answers may vary.

1. The State Council on the Arts commissioned several artists to create a series of murals for the subway.

2. I will use Carly's report as a model for other students.

3. Nanny's chicken noodle soup made me feel better when I was sick.

4. I still have a chance to win the poetry contest.

Practice 3

Answers may vary.

1. Forty children are registered for the class, but the room can only accommodate thirty-five.

2. Unfortunately, my sociology class meets at 8 A.M.

3. I was shocked to learn that the average American consumes 130 pounds of sugar per year.

4. A typical can of soda contains about nine teaspoons of refined white sugar, which is so chemically processed that it contains no vitamins, minerals, protein, fiber, or water.

Practice 4

Answers may vary.

1. I hope you find these accommodations acceptable.
2. Although he can't see without his glasses, Ted almost never wears them.
3. I have always believed the present is more important than the future or past.
4. I will keep this job until I complete my degree; then I will look for an internship.

Practice 5

1. I worked until 3 am ~~in the morning~~, but I still didn't finish my report.
2. These statistics refer ~~back~~ to the chart on page 181.
3. Carmen is a pianist ~~who plays the piano with~~ of great skill.
4. Under different circumstances, ~~if we weren't in the situation we're in now,~~ I'd quit my job and go back to school.
5. The airplane circled ~~around~~ the airport several times before it received clearance to land.

CHAPTER 12 TEST

Choose the version that has precise, concise, and appropriate language as well as correct grammar. If the original is the best, choose (A).

1. Because of the fact that he was surrounded on all sides, Cody decided to surrender.
   - (A) No change
   - (B) Because of the fact that he was surrounded on all sides, Cody decided to call it quits.
   - (C) Because he was surrounded on all sides; Cody decided to surrender.
   - (D) Because he was surrounded, Cody decided to surrender.
   - (E) Due to the fact that he was surrounded, Cody decided to surrender.

2. Guy de Maupassant wrote the short story "The Necklace."
   This is one of the most famous short stories ever written.

   (A) No change

   (B) The short story "The Necklace" was written by Guy de
   Maupassant, and this story is one of the most famous
   stories ever written.

   (C) Guy de Maupassant wrote "The Necklace," one of the
   most famous short stories ever written.

   (D) Composed by the writer Guy de Maupassant, the short
   story "The Necklace" is one of the most famous ever
   written.

   (E) Guy de Maupassant wrote "The Necklace," one of the
   phattest stories ever written.

3. Did you know the fact that the first motion pictures were
   created and developed by Louis Aimé Augustin Le Prince
   back in the year 1888?

   (A) No change

   (B) Did you know the first motion pictures were created by
   Louis Aimé Augustin Le Prince back in 1888?

   (C) Were you aware of the fact that Louise Aimé Augustin Le
   Prince developed the first motion pictures? He did this
   back in the year 1888.

   (D) Did you know the fact that back in the year 1888, the
   first motion pictures were created and developed by
   Louis Aimé Augustin Le Prince?

   (E) Created by Louis Aimé Augustin Le Prince, did you
   know that the first motion pictures were developed back
   in the year 1888?

4. Dragonflies are the "helicopters" of the insect world. They are like helicopters in that they can hover, fly forward and backward, and change direction rapidly.

   (A) No change

   (B) Dragonflies are the "helicopters" of the insect world. This is because they can hover, fly forward and backward, and change direction rapidly.

   (C) Dragonflies are the "helicopters" of the insect world, this is so because they can hover, fly forward and backward, and have the ability to change direction rapidly.

   (D) Dragonflies are the "helicopters" of the insect world; they can hover, fly forward and backward, and change direction rapidly.

   (E) Dragonflies can be deemed the "helicopters" of the insect realm; exhibiting a striking resemblance to these hovercraft, the dragonfly can hover, aviate forward and backward, and change trajectory rapidly.

5. A law passed in England in 1865 limited the speed of steam cars to two miles per hour.

   (A) No change

   (B) A law which was passed in England in the year 1865 limited the speed of steam cars to two miles per hour.

   (C) In England, a law passed in 1865 restricted the speed of steam cars, allowing them to travel no more than two miles per hour.

   (D) In 1865, British lawmakers passed a law that allowed steam cars to travel at no more than two miles per hour.

   (E) Restricted to the speed of no more than two miles per hour were steam cars, according to a law passed in England in 1865.

6. The babies of most animal species are hatched from eggs, and the newborns are not taken care of by their parents after they hatch.

   (A) No change

   (B) The progeny of the majority of zoological creatures are hatched from eggs, and these descendants are not nurtured by their progenitors upon emergence.

   (C) Most animal species hatch their offspring from eggs and do not nurture the hatchlings after they are born.

   (D) Not taken care of upon birth are the majority of babies of animal species, which are hatched from eggs.

   (E) The babies of most animal species are born from eggs, and these new beings do not get any care from their parents after they come out.

7. Mozart composed his first symphony when he was only at the age of eight years old.

   (A) No change

   (B) Mozart composed his first symphony when he was only eight years old.

   (C) Mozart, when he was only eight years old, composed his first symphony.

   (D) Only at the age of eight years old was when Mozart composed his first symphony.

   (E) The first symphony of Mozart was composed by him when he was at the age of eight.

8. Requests will be taken by the deejay during dinner.

   (A) No change

   (B) During dinner is when requests will be taken by the deejay.

   (C) The deejay will take requests during dinner.

   (D) During the repast, the deejay shall accept requests.

   (E) Tell the deejay what you want to hear while we chow.

9. The longest fangs of any snake are on the gaboon viper, whose fangs are up to two inches long.

   (A) No change

   (B) With fangs that are up to two inches long, the gaboon viper has the longest fangs of any snake.

   (C) The gaboon viper's fangs—the longest of any snake—can grow up to two inches long.

   (D) Having the longest fangs of any snake is the gaboon viper, whose fangs are up to two inches in length.

   (E) At two inches long, the gaboon viper has the longest fangs of any snake.

10. I'm pretty hungry, so you should get two pizzas.

    (A) No change

    (B) I'm sort of starving, so you should get two pizzas.

    (C) I'm famished, so you should order two pizzas.

    (D) I'm hungry, order two pizzas.

    (E) As I am in a ravenous state, I recommend that you request two pizzas.

11. In the event that the baby wakes up before I return back, please give her a bottle.

    (A) No change

    (B) In the event the baby awakens before I return, please feed her with the bottle.

    (C) Should the baby wake up before I return, she should be given a bottle.

    (D) If the baby wakes before I get back, please give her a bottle.

    (E) If I am not back before the baby wakes, the bottle should be given to her.

12. Zizi said she's just dying for a pedicure for her birthday.
    - (A) No change
    - (B) Zizi said that she would really like a pedicure for her birthday.
    - (C) Zizi has articulated an intense desire for a pedicure for her birthday.
    - (D) Zizi said she wants a pedicure for her birthday.
    - (E) Zizi said she'd love a pedicure for her birthday.

13. There are few American writers as prolific as Mark Twain.
    - (A) No change
    - (B) There are few American writers who are or were as prolific as Mark Twain.
    - (C) Most American writers have not written as much as Mark Twain did.
    - (D) The number of American writers achieving the status of Mark Twain in terms of the number of texts they have written is very few.
    - (E) Not many American writers share being prolific with Mark Twain.

14. Fossils show that the stegosaurus was in the neighborhood of about six feet tall in height.
    - (A) No change
    - (B) Fossils indicate that the stegosaurus was about six feet tall.
    - (C) According to fossil evidence, the height of the stegosaurus was in the neighborhood of six feet.
    - (D) Shown by fossils is the fact that the stegosaurus reached a height of approximately six feet.
    - (E) Fossils show that stegosaurus dinos maxed out around six feet up.

15. This is the email that I have been waiting for.
    (A) No change
    (B) I have been anticipating the arrival of this email.
    (C) I have been waiting for this email.
    (D) The arrival of this email is what I have been awaiting.
    (E) This email is wh... I have been waiting for.

16. Chelsea is an area in Manhattan that is located in the area of
    the Lower West Side in the 20s.
    (A) No change
    (B) Located in the Lower West Side in the 20s, Manhattan
        has the area known as Chelsea.
    (C) Found in the 20s on the Lower West Side of Manhattan
        is the area known as Chelsea.
    (D) On Manhattan's Lower West Side, you'll find the
        neighborhood called Chelsea, in the 20s.
    (E) The area known as Cheslea is located the 20s on
        Manhattan's Lower West Side.

17. The ETA for the arrival of Chad's flight is 8:15.
    (A) No change
    (B) The ETA for Chad's flight is 8:15.
    (C) Chad's flight's arrival has an ETA of 8:15.
    (D) The arrival of Chad's flight has an ETA of 8:15.
    (E) Eight-fifteen is the approximate ETA of Chad's flight.

18. A thick wooly coat protected mammoths from subzero temperatures.
    (A) No change
    (B) Enveloped in a coat of thick wool, mammoths were protected from subzero temperatures.
    (C) It was a thick wooly coat that protected mammoths from subzero temperatures.
    (D) A thick wooly coat kept mammoths warm despite subzero temperatures.
    (E) Mammoths had thick wooly coats. This protected them from subzero temperatures.

19. Missy's poem is what inspired me to start writing my own poetry.
    (A) No change
    (B) Missy's poem is what inspired me starting to write my own poetry.
    (C) Missy's poem inspired me to start writing my own poetry.
    (D) Missy's poem gave me the inspiration to start writing my own poetry.
    (E) Missy's poem gave me the inspiration and motivation to begin to write poetry of my own.

20. The office that is in the corner is finally up for grabs.
    (A) No change
    (B) The office that is in the corner is finally available.
    (C) At last, the office in the corner is finally available.
    (D) Finally available is the corner office.
    (E) The corner office is finally available.

Answers and Explanations

1. D

Because of the fact that is wordy and *surrounded on all sides* is repetitious. (E) replaces one with an equally wordy phrase.

2. C

Combine the sentences as concisely as possible. (A) and (B) both repeat *store* and use the unnecessary *this is*. (D) uses *composed* instead of *written*, a diction error. (E) uses slang.

3. B

The original sentence is wordy, as are (D) and (E). (B) eliminates the problems. (C) adds unnecessary words.

4. D

The original sentences can be combined, as (D) does. (E) is wordy and pretentious.

5. A

(A) is the most concise. (B) adds unnecessary words. (C) and (D) are wordy. (E) is awkward and passive.

6. C

(A) and (D) are wordy and passive. (B) is pretentious. (E) doesn't use precise verbs.

7. B

The original is redundant. (B) is the most clear and concise. (C) inserts a clause between subject and verb. (D) is awkward. (E) is passive and wordy.

8. C

The original sentence is passive, as is (B). (C) is the most direct and concise. (D) is pretentious, and (F) uses slang.

9. C

(A) and (B) are grammatically correct but not concise. (D) is awkward and uses *in length* instead of *long*. (E) has a misplaced modifier.

10. C

(A) and (B) use wishy-washy intensifiers. (C) uses the precise verb *order*. (D) is a run-on. (E) is wordy and pretentious.

11. D

(A) and (B) use the clutter phrase *in the event that*. (A) uses the redundant phrase *return back*. (B) is awkward and imprecise. (C) and (E) use the passive voice.

12. E

(A) uses slang. (B) uses a weak intensifier and verb. (C) is pretentious. (D)'s word choice is not as precise as (E)'s.

13. A

Here, the *there are* construction is the most effective way to convey the idea. (B) unnecessarily adds a *who* clause. (C) uses *have not written as much* instead of the precise *prolific*. (D) is wordy and pretentious. (E) is awkward, indirect, and unclear.

14. B

(A) uses the clutter phrase *in the neighborhood of* and the redundant *in height*. (C) is passive. (D) uses several wordy constructions. (E) uses slang.

15. C

(C) has only one clause; (A) and (E) have two clauses. (B) has one clause but is wordy. (D) keeps the indirect *be* verb of the original.

16. E

(E) is the clearest and most concise version. (C) also uses the passive voice.

17. B

ETA stands for estimated time of arrival; (A), (C), and (D) repeat arrival. (E) adds *approximate*, which repeats *estimated*.

18. A

(B) is passive. (C) uses an unnecessary *it was* clause. (D) is less precise, and (E) causes unnecessary repetition.

19. C

(A) and (B) use a wordy *be* construction. (D) and (E) use the wordy phrase *gave me the inspiration*, and (E) also uses the redundant *inspiration and motivation*.

20. E

(E) turns the clause *that is in the corner* into *corner office*. (C) turns the clause into a prepositional phrase, while (D) is awkward.

Clear and Engaging Sentences

Start with this 10-question Building Block Quiz. The first few questions test material you've already seen.

BUILDING BLOCK QUIZ

Identify the grammar or style error in each sentence below. If the sentence is correct, choose (E).

1. The water on the road had froze into black ice, making the highway treacherous for drivers.

   (A) subject-verb agreement error   (B) incorrect verb form

   (C) inappropriate word choice   (D) misplaced modifier

   (E) No error

2. A professional sports team is a wise investment for a city, if successful, it can bring in billions of dollars in revenue a year.

   (A) unclear pronoun reference   (B) subject-verb agreement error

   (C) run-on sentence   (D) wordiness   (E) No error

3. I felt real bad about calling Sophia the wrong name at dinner.

   (A) double negative   (B) incorrect verb tense

   (C) pretentious language

   (D) confusing adjective and adverb forms   (E) No error

4. Tyra and Diane made a beautiful cake for the party but left it at her house.

   (A) ambiguous pronoun reference   (B) incorrect pronoun case

   (C) run-on sentence   (D) wordiness   (E) No error

5. Alf really threw me a curve when he said he wanted to resign.
   (A) unclear pronoun reference   (B) wishy-washy language
   (C) pretentious language   (D) use of cliché   (E) No error

6. Scanning the horizon, there was no sign of the impending storm.
   (A) dangling modifier   (B) incorrect use of passive voice
   (C) lack of parallel structure   (D) use of slang
   (E) No error

7. The detective caught the thief before he could commit
   another crime.
   (A) incorrect helping verb   (B) ambiguous pronoun reference
   (C) confusing adjective and adverb forms   (D) use of cliché
   (E) No error

8. After driving in the wrong direction for an hour, Jared finally
   made the right turn.
   (A) wordiness   (B) run-on sentence
   (C) ambiguous word choice   (D) repetitive word choice
   (E) No error

9. If you are sick with a sickness that is contagious, you should
   stay away from others so you don't get them sick, too.
   (A) unnecessary repetition   (B) run-on sentence
   (C) inappropriate language   (D) lack of parallel structure
   (E) No error

10. There are many myths about George Washington. Here is one
    example. He did not chop down a cherry tree.
    (A) repetitive word choice   (B) repetitive sentence structure
    (C) sentence fragments   (D) incorrect use of passive voice
    (E) No error

Answers and Explanations

1. B

The past participle of *freeze* is *frozen*. *Froze* is the simple past tense.

2. C

This is a run-on sentence. The comma after *city* needs to be a period or semicolon.

3. D

Real modifies *bad* and *bad* modifies *felt,* so they should be adverbs: *really* and *badly*.

4. A

Her could refer to either Tyra or Diane. The sentence needs to make it clear *whose* house.

5. D

The phrase *threw me a curve* is a cliché. It's not particularly effective because it is overused and slangy, but it is not wishy-washy (B) or pretentious (C).

6. A

The phrase *scanning the horizon* is a dangling modifier; we don't know *who* was scanning. *Scanning the horizon, I saw no sign....* (The sentence also uses the wordy *there was* construction.)

7. B

The pronoun *he* could refer to either the detective or the thief.

8. C

The word *right* is ambiguous. Did Jared *turn* right or make the *correct* turn?

9. A

The writer uses *sick* twice and *sickness* once. Variety and concision would make the sentence much more readable: *If you have a contagious illness, stay away from others so you don't get them sick, too.*

10. B

These three short, simple sentences all begin with the subject followed immediately by the verb. This makes for dull, monotonous writing.

If your local newspaper runs the headline "Local Teens Make Delicious Snacks," would you worry that people are eating *teens* as snacks? No; you'd probably know it meant the teens *prepared* snacks. But the fact that it *could* be misinterpreted is a problem. Effective writing is precise, appropriate, concise, and **clear**, leaving no room for misinterpretation. It is also **lively** and **engaging**.

AVOID AMBIGUITY

One of the wonderful things about language is also one of the things that can make it problematic: the number of words that have more than one possible meaning:

Ambiguous: Gabriella saw Ian down at the <u>bank</u>.

Did Gabriella see Ian down at the *river* bank or at a financial institution? The sentence is **ambiguous**. To make it clear, this ambiguity needs to be eliminated:

Revised: Gabriella saw Ian down at <u>Commerce Bank</u>.
Revised: Gabriella saw Ian down at the <u>riverbank</u>.

Words with just one meaning can also create ambiguity if their *function* isn't clear:

Ambiguous: I hate <u>annoying</u> people.

Is *annoying* a gerund—what the speaker hates *doing*—or an adjective describing *people* the speaker hates?

Revised: I hate <u>to annoy</u> people.
Revised: I hate <u>people who are</u> annoying.

True, this seems to contradict the previous lesson. But concision never requires deleting necessary words.

Modifier Placement

Misplaced modifiers cause trouble (see chapter 7):

Ambiguous: Thomas saved the woman with a cane.

Did Thomas *use* a cane to save a woman, or save a woman who *had* a cane?

> **FLASHBACK**
> A **misplaced modifier** creates a confusing sentence because it seems to modify the wrong word or phrase.

Ambiguous Pronoun Reference

A pronoun may seem to refer to two different antecedents (see chapter 6):

Ambiguous: Wallace grimaced when Toby pulled his splinter out.

Revised: Wallace had a splinter and grimaced when Toby pulled it out.

Practice 1

Revise the following sentences to eliminate ambiguity.

1. Selena enjoys challenging professors.
2. What an amazing shot!
3. Take the bus from the corner to the end of Willow Street.
4. You'll be lucky if he works for you.
5. *Headline*: Twins Reunited after Fifteen Years in Convenience Store

AVOID VAGUENESS

Of course, you might choose to be intentionally vague. But generally, the more specific you are, the better. **Vague** sentences are unclear because words or phrases either aren't specific enough or lack specific referents (see chapter 10 for diction):

Vague: I can't stay; I have lots of <u>stuff</u> to do at home.

Revised: I can't stay; I have a lot of <u>cooking and cleaning</u> to do at home.

Pronouns

Vague antecedent means a pronoun's antecedent is suggested but not specifically stated anywhere. Closely related are pronouns that make **overly broad references**: they refer not to a specific word or phrase but to a whole sentence or idea (see chapter 6).

Dangling Modifiers

Dangling modifiers lack a clear referent, so we don't know who or what they modify (see chapter 7).

>   Vague: After waiting in line for hours, my number was finally
>   called.

>   Revised: After I waited in line for hours, my number was finally
>   called.

GRAMMAR SPEAK

An **ambiguous** word or sentence has more than one possible meaning. A **vague** word or sentence is unclear.

Practice 2

How would you eliminate vagueness in the following sentences?

1. Nadine hasn't been doing well lately.
2. Believing it would boost sales and increase market share, the company launched a new ad campaign.
3. New York City is always loud, always crowded, always in motion. That's what I love about it.
4. Beneath the painting they found an original copy of the Declaration of Independence.
5. Colin is having trouble at school.

OFFER VARIETY

Varied Word Choice

Some repetition of key words is good. Consider the following excerpt from his 1963 "I Have a Dream" speech, Martin Luther King, Jr.:

> There are those who are asking the devotees of civil rights, "When will you be satisfied?" We can never be satisfied as long as our bodies, heavy with the fatigue of travel, cannot gain lodging in the motels of the highways and the hotels of the cities. We cannot be satisfied as

long as the Negro's basic mobility is from a smaller ghetto to a larger one. We can never be satisfied as long as a Negro in Mississippi cannot vote and a Negro in New York believes he has nothing for which to vote. No, no, we are not satisfied, and we will not be satisfied until justice rolls down like waters and righteousness like a mighty stream.

The word *satisfied* is used six times, to emphasize the point. But more often than not, repetition is a failure of vocabulary:

The cost of the new test is significantly higher than the cost of the old test. Both tests contain the same number of questions, but the new test has more sections. This means there are fewer questions per section on the new test. The new test also gives test takers an additional half hour to complete the test.

The writer used the word *test* eight times, an average of twice in each sentence. Such sentences become monotonous and suggest that you don't have a sufficiently developed word base, that you're lazy, or that you just don't care.

Use synonyms wisely and revise or combine sentences if possible to minimize repetition:

The cost of the new <u>test</u> is significantly higher than that of the old <u>one</u>. Both <u>tests</u> contain the same number of questions, but the new <u>version</u> has more sections and therefore fewer questions per section. <u>Test</u> takers also have an additional half hour to complete the new <u>exam</u>.

Practice 3

Revise the following sentences to eliminate repetition and add variety in word choice.

1. My sister Eleanor is very price conscious. She never pays full price for anything. She will only buy something if it is at least half of the original price.

2. To live a healthy lifestyle, you must eat healthy foods. Avoid unhealthy foods such as sodas and chips. Instead, opt for healthy foods such as nuts and yogurt.

3. I've been looking for a new apartment for months now, but every time I look at one I'm disappointed. Nothing I've looked at comes close to my current apartment.

Varied Sentence Structure

Too many sentences with the same pattern lead to tedious writing. This is *not* to say that you should avoid parallel structure. When ideas are comparable, parallel structure is a must.

> **FLASHBACK**
>
> **Parallel structure** means comparable or analogous items follow the same grammatical pattern. Items in lists, pairs, and comparisons should always be expressed in parallel form.

But when you *don't* have parallel ideas, try these three strategies.

1. Vary Sentence Type

Mix simple, compound, complex, and compound-complex sentences. (See chapter 2 for a review.) If the problem is too many simple sentences, combine them to form compound, complex, or compound-complex ones. This also clarifies the relationships between your ideas. Some clauses can be turned into modifiers to make the text more concise.

Same type: About 20 inmates at the San Quentin State Prison practice yoga. The prison is in California. The class meets one night a week for 90 minutes. It includes 20 minutes of meditation. The class is part of a special initiative to reduce prison violence. The results so far have been impressive.

Varied: About 20 inmates at California's San Quentin State Prison practice yoga. The class, which meets one night a week for 90 minutes and includes 20 minutes of meditation, is part of a special initiative to reduce prison violence. The results so far have been impressive.

The rhythm of the varied paragraph is much more interesting. The information about when and how long the class meets is subordinate to the more important fact that the class has a specific goal.

2. Vary Sentence Length

Mix long, medium, and short sentences. Since short sentences tend to stand out, save them for ideas that you want to emphasize. Avoid having too many long sentences in a row: that can strain readers' eyes and attention.

Same length: The ancient practice of yoga has become an official part of the curriculum in school districts in 19 states across the country, and for good reason: evidence from a 2003 study shows what yogis have known for centuries—that yoga improves concentration, discipline, and self-awareness. Participating schools have recorded fewer discipline problems and improved test scores while students report feeling more confident, less stressed, and more comfortable in their bodies.

Varied: The ancient practice of yoga has become an official part of the curriculum in school districts in 19 states across the country, and for good reason. Evidence from a 2003 study shows what yogis have known for centuries: that yoga improves concentration, discipline, and self-awareness. Participating schools have recorded fewer discipline problems and improved test scores. At the same time, participating students report feeling more confident, less stressed, and more comfortable in their bodies.

3. Vary Sentence Openers

The typical sentence begins with the subject followed by the verb. Alternative openers include adverbs and modifying phrases and clauses.

Same opener: About 20 inmates at the San Quentin State Prison practice yoga. The prison is in California. The class meets one night a week for 90 minutes. It includes 20 minutes of meditation. The class is part of a special initiative to reduce prison violence. The results so far have been impressive.

Varied: At the San Quentin State Prison in California, about 20 inmates practice yoga. The class meets one night a week for 90 minutes. For 20 of those minutes, the students meditate. The class is part of a special initiative to reduce prison violence. So far, the results have been impressive.

Of couse, if you move a modifier, *do not* create ambiguity.

Practice 4

Use the strategies outlined in this section to add variety in sentence structure to the following paragraph.

Most Americans have heard of the Dalai Lama. They don't know much about him, however. They may know he is a holy man. But that is about it. The Dalai Lama is revered by people all over the world. He is the spiritual and political leader of Tibet. He is the 14th Dalai Lama of Tibet. His real name is Tenzin Gyatso. He lives in India. He was exiled there in 1959. The Tibetan people rose up against Chinese rule that year. The Dalai Lama had to flee as a result. The Dalai Lama is a Buddhist monk. He advocates nonviolence like other Dalai Lamas before him. He has fought tirelessly for the freedom of his people. He won the Nobel Peace Prize in 1989.

REMEMBER THIS!

Your writing will be much stronger if you have variety in word choice and sentence structure.

USE FRESH LANGUAGE

Let's try a quick experiment. See how quickly you can fill in the blanks in the following sentences:

(a) Last night I slept like a _____.

(b) The yard is as pretty as a _____.

Did you answer (a) *log* or *baby* and (b) *picture*. Each is a cliché: a tired or hackneyed saying, one that has lost its vitality through overuse. A lively style avoids clichés, preferring original figures of speech.

Here is a very partial list of some of the more common expressions to avoid.

beat around the bush	like a sore thumb
behind the eight ball	neat as a pin
better late than never	nose to the grindstone
blind as a bat	one in a million
by hook or by crook	pretty as a picture
cold shoulder	set the record straight
cute as a button	tough/hard as nails
down in the dumps	under the gun
let the cat out of the bag	water under the bridge
light as a feather	whole new ball of wax
a bull in a china shop	

Alternatives

Fresh figurative language enlivens writing. Take the following sentences from one of America's best contemporary writers:

> Nenny and I don't look like sisters…not right away. Not the way you can tell with Rachel and Lucy who have the same fat popsicle lips like everybody else in their family. But me and Nenny, we are more alike than you would know. Our laughter for example. Not the shy ice cream bells giggle of Rachel and Lucy's family, but all of a sudden and surprised like a pile of dishes breaking. (From *The House on Mango Street* by Sandra Cisneros)

Original, beautiful, powerful. Need we say more? A **figure of speech** is an expression used to suggest an image or comparison. It is not literal. If you say *the trees at the foot of the mountain were destroyed by the mudslide*, you don't mean that the mountain actually has feet. You're comparing the mountain to a person and using a figure of speech to mean *bottom*.

A **simile** is figurative language that uses *like* or *as* and compares dissimilar items—a butterfly to a curtain, not a butterfly to a moth.

> Your eyes are *like* the deep blue sea.

A **metaphor,** a more direct comparison, does not use *like* or *as*:

> The deep blue sea of your eyes…

If you can't think of a fresh comparison, you can simply express your ideas literally to avoid clichés.

> **Cliché:** Without my glasses, I am blind as a bat.
>
> **Revised:** Without my glasses, I can't see a thing.

But avoiding clichés doesn't mean you have to avoid figurative language. You can come up with an original comparison or image instead. Yes, it means you'll have to think a little harder—but it also means your writing will be much more engaging.

Practice 5

Revise the following sentences to eliminate clichés. Use a mix of literal revisions and original figurative language in your answers.

1. I know you wanted the party to be a surprise, Josh, but the cat's out of the bag.
2. Oliver definitely walks to the beat of a different drum.
3. I think it's time we had a heart-to-heart talk.
4. Please don't beat around the bush, Adele. Get to the point.
5. The ball is in your court now, so I will wait to hear your proposal.

SUMMARY

Effective writing is precise, appropriate, and concise. It is also clear and engaging.

Ambiguous sentences are caused by a word that can mean two different things; by a word that can have two different functions; by a modifier that can describe more than person, thing, or action; or by a pronoun that can refer to two different antecedents.

Vague sentences are unclear because pronoun antecedents or modifier referents are not sufficiently specific.

Strive for **variety in word choice and sentence structure**. Combine or revise sentences to minimize repetition and use synonyms wisely.

Finally, an engaging style uses fresh, original language, **avoiding clichés**.

Practice Answers and Explanations

Practice 1

Answers may vary. We offer two possible revisions for each sentence.

1. (a) Selena enjoys professors who are challenging.
   (b) Selena enjoys challenging her professors.
2. (a) What an amazing photograph!
   (b) What an amazing jump shot!
3. (a) Ride the bus from the corner to the end of Willow Street.
   (b) Move the bus from the corner to the end of Willow Street.
4. (a) You'll be lucky if he accepts your job offer.
   (b) You'll be lucky if he does any work for you.
5. (a) Twins Reuinted in Convenience Store after Fifteen Years
   (b) After Fifteen Years, Twins Reunited in Convenience Store

Practice 2

Answers will vary. We've underlined our changes to each sentence below.

1. Nadine hasn't been earning good grades lately.
2. The company launched a new ad campaign, believing it would boost sales and increase market share.
3. New York City is always loud, always crowded, always in motion. These features are what I love about it.
4. Beneath the painting, the curators found an original copy of the Declaration of Independence.
5. Colin is having difficulty making friends at school.

Practice 3

Answers will vary. We've underlined our changes to each sentence below.

1. My sister Eleanor is very price conscious. She never pays <u>retail</u> for anything. She will only buy something if it is at least <u>50% off</u>.

2. To live a healthy lifestyle, you must eat <u>nutritious</u> foods. Avoid unhealthy foods such as sodas and chips. Instead, opt for <u>beneficial</u> foods such as nuts and yogurt.

3. I've been <u>searching</u> for a new apartment for months now, but every time I look at one I'm disappointed. Nothing I've <u>seen</u> comes close to my current apartment.

Practice 4

Answers will vary. Here's our version.

Most Americans have heard of the Dalai Lama, but they don't know much about him beyond the fact that he is a holy man. Revered by people all over the world, the Dalai Lama is the spiritual and political leader of Tibet. The 14th Dalai Lama, Tenzin Gyatso lives in exile in India where he fled in 1959 after the Tibetan people rose up against Chinese rule. A Buddhist monk, the Dalai Lama advocates nonviolence, as did other Dalai Lamas before him. He has fought tirelessly for the freedom of his people and won the Nobel Peace Prize in 1989.

Practice 5

Answers will vary. We've underlined our changes to the sentences below.

1. I know you wanted the party to be a surpise, Josh, but the <u>secret's out</u>.

2. Oliver definitely <u>has a unique personality</u>.

3. I think it's time we had an <u>honest, intimate</u> talk.

4. Please don't be <u>indirect</u>, Adele. Get to the point.

5. [Deleted opening clause] I will wait to hear your proposal.

CHAPTER 13 TEST

Determine which answer choice is most effective. If the original is best, choose (A).

1. Carlos thinks we should wait, <u>but I say there's no time like the present</u>.

   (A) No change
   (B) but I say this point in time is the best time.
   (C) but I say we should do it now.
   (D) however, in my opinion, we should do it now.
   (E) but I think we should get the ball rolling now.

2. Please file those folders over there.

   (A) No change
   (B) Please file those folders in the cabinet over there.
   (C) Please take those folders and file them in the cabinet over there.
   (D) Please file those folders in that spot.
   (E) I beseech you to file those folders over there.

3. After falling asleep and missing his stop, the train pulled into an unfamiliar station.

   (A) No change
   (B) After falling asleep and missing his stop, Baruk's train pulled into an unfamiliar station.
   (C) The train pulled into an unfamiliar station. After Baruk fell asleep and missed his stop.
   (D) After falling asleep and missing his stop, Baruk awoke to see the train pull into an unfamiliar station.
   (E) Because of the fact that he fell asleep and missed his stop, Baruk found the train pulling into an unfamiliar station.

4. Because the presentation was bad, it was a bad meeting.
   - (A) No change
   - (B) Because the presentation was bad, the meeting went badly.
   - (C) Because the presentation was a problem, the meeting was a disaster.
   - (D) Because our presentation wasn't ready, the meeting was a disaster.
   - (E) Because our presentation was a failure. The meeting was a disaster.

5. Thanks for the advice, Cole. <u>It worked like a charm!</u>
   - (A) No change
   - (B) It was very effective!
   - (C) The impact was potent!
   - (D) It worked charmingly!
   - (E) It was like a charm in how it worked!

6. The artist said she uses strong colors and strong lines because she wants a strong reaction from her audience.
   - (A) No change
   - (B) The artist said she uses strong colors and lines because she wants a strong reaction from her audience.
   - (C) The artist said she uses bold colors and sharp lines because she wants a strong reaction from her audience.
   - (D) The reason the artist uses bold colors and lines is because she said she wants a strong reaction from her audience.
   - (E) Seeking a strong reaction from her audience, bold colors and lines is what the artist uses.

7. Walker got ten years for his role in the robbery.
   - (A) No change
   - (B) Walker was sentenced to ten years for his role in the robbery.
   - (C) For his role in the robbery, Walker got ten years.
   - (D) Ten years is what Walker was sentenced to for his role in the robbery.
   - (E) Having participated in the robbery, Walker was sentenced to ten years.

8. Uma wants the book and that bookshelf, but they belong to me.
   (A) No change
   (B) Uma wants the book and that bookshelf, but it belongs to me.
   (C) The book and that bookshelf are what Uma want, but it belongs to me.
   (D) Uma wants the book and that bookshelf, but they are possessions of mine.
   (E) Uma wants the book and bookshelf that belongs to me.

9. Kyle was in a wheelchair following the accident.
   (A) No change
   (B) Following the accident, Kyle was in a wheelchair.
   (C) Kyle, following the accident, was in a wheelchair.
   (D) Before the accident, Kyle was not in a wheelchair, but after it, he was.
   (E) After the accident, Kyle was in a wheelchair.

10. Oren takes the bus to work each morning. He takes bus number 52. It comes at 8:04.
    (A) No change
    (B) Oren takes the bus to work, it's number 52 which comes at 8:04 each morning.
    (C) At 8:04 each morning, Oren catches bus number 52 to work.
    (D) Each morning, Oren takes bus number 52 to work, which he catches at 8:04.
    (E) Catching bus number 52 at 8:04 each morning, Oren goes to work.

11. Bela spoke to the woman on the bus.
    (A) No change
    (B) Bela spoke to the woman next to him on the bus.
    (C) Bela spoke to the woman on the bus next to him.
    (D) Bela and the woman on the bus spoke to each other.
    (E) The woman on the bus was to whom Bela spoke.

12. The native wolf population is again on the rise and the deer population seems to have steadied, <u>which pleases the conservationists and animal activists alike</u>.
    (A) No change
    (B) which both the conservationists and animal activists are pleased about.
    (C) and both conservationists and animal activists are pleased by these trends.
    (D) and these trends make conservationists and animal activists pleased as punch.
    (E) and because of these trends, both conservationists and animal activists are pleased.

13. <u>You'll stick out like a sore thumb</u> if you wear that dress to the party.
    (A) No change
    (B) You shall be a garish and protrusive sight
    (C) You'll stand out like crazy
    (D) Everyone will notice you
    (E) You'll stand out like a camel in a hen house

14. Ignacio is a poor teacher.
    (A) No change
    (B) Poor Ignacio is a teacher.
    (C) Ignacio is not a good teacher.
    (D) Ignacio is poor and a teacher.
    (E) Ignacio is an ineffective teacher.

15. It's time to stop wasting time and start using your time wisely.
    (A) No change
    (B) It's time to manage your time more effectively.
    (C) The time has come to more effectively manage your time.
    (D) Start using your time wisely so you can stop wasting it.
    (E) Now is the moment to stop wasting time and manage it more effectively.

16. This copier isn't working right.
    (A) No change
    (B) This copier is having problems.
    (C) This copier is malfunctioning.
    (D) This copier keeps jamming.
    (E) This copier is broke.

17. <u>We're really under the gun to get this done</u> by our Saturday deadline.
    (A) No change
    (B) We're really under the gun to finish this
    (C) We're really under pressure to finish this
    (D) We're just going to get this done by the skin of our teeth
    (E) It will be a challenge to our productivity to achieve completion

18. Yoshi is my neighbor. He is 23. He is a medical student.
    (A) No change
    (B) Yoshi, my neighbor, is 23. He is a medical student.
    (C) At 23, my neighbor Yoshi is a medical student.
    (D) A medical student, Yoshi, my neighbor, is 23.
    (E) My 23-year-old neighbor Yoshi is a medical student.

19. My problem with Carl is that whenever there's a problem, he tries to blame it on someone else, even when the problem is his fault.
    (A) No change
    (B) My difficulty with Carl is that whenever there's a problem, he tries to blame it on someone else, even if it's his fault.
    (C) With Carl, I have difficulty with the fact that he always tries to blame a problem on someone else, even if it's his fault.
    (D) My issue with Carl is that he always tries to blame problems on others, even if he's at fault.
    (E) Even when he's the one at fault, Carl always tries to blame problems on others, and that's why I have a problem with him.

20. Samir said he didn't open the door because the solicitor was acting weird.

   (A) No change
   (B) According to what Samir said, he didn't open the door because the solicitor was acting weird.
   (C) Samir said he didn't open the door because the solicitor was making strange noises.
   (D) Samir said he didn't open the door because strange noises were being made by the solicitor.
   (E) Acting weirdly, the solicitor was denied entrance by Samir.

Answers and Explanations

1. C

The clause *there's no time like the present* is a cliché. (B) is wordy. (D) creates a fragment. (E) replaces one cliché with another. (C) effectively revises the cliché.

2. C

Should you file the folders *that are* over there or file those folders *over there*? (B) and (D) don't fix the ambiguity. Only (C) is clear.

3. D

The original has a dangling modifier; (D) tells you *who* fell asleep. (B) gives us the wrong subject; *Baruk's* is a modifier. (C) is a fragment. (E) is wordy.

4. D

(A)–(D) are grammatically correct; (D) is the most specific. (A)–(C) all carry the vague words *bad* and *problem*. (E) is a fragment.

5. B

(A) relies on the cliché *it worked like a charm*. (B) rephrases it in literal terms. (C) is pretentious, (D) uses an awkward adverb (*charmingly*), and (E) is wordy.

6. C

The word *strong* appears three times. (B) eliminates one. (C) effectively replaces the first two *strongs*. (D) uses *bold* but is wordy. (E) uses the passive voice.

7. B

The original uses the vague and ambiguous *got*. (B) is much clearer and more effective. (C) doesn't address the problem. (D) and (E) are wordy and indirect.

8. A

The original sentence is correct. There are two things Uma wants, the book and that bookshelf, so the pronoun and verb must be plural.

9. E

Did Kyle follow the accident in a wheelchair, or was he in a wheelchair after the accident? (E) makes it clear. (D) is wordy.

10. C

The original contains three short subject-verb sentences. (C) effectively combines them. (B) is a run-on.

11. B

Did Bela speak to a woman who was with him, or to a woman who was on the bus? (B) corrects the ambiguity. (C) is still ambiguous. (D) and (E) don't correct the error.

12. C

What exactly does *which* refer to? (B) repeats the error. (C) replaces the pronoun with a clear referent. (D) uses the cliché *pleased as punch*. (E) corrects the error, but it is not concise and direct.

13. E

The original uses a cliché, *stick out like a sore thumb*. (B) is pretentious and (C) is slangy. (D) is clear and straightforward, but (E) provides an original comparison.

14. E

Does Ignacio lack money, or does he lack teaching skills? (B) is still ambiguous; does it mean without money or pitiful? (C) uses a vague term (*good*). (D) changes the meaning. (E) is clear and effective.

15. B

(A) uses the word *time* three times. (B) eliminates one use and offers the most concise version of the sentence.

16. D

The original uses the vague *isn't working right*. (B)–(D) get increasingly more specific, with (D) the best. (E) incorrectly uses the past tense *broke* instead of the past participle *broken*.

17. C

Under the gun is a cliché. (B) repeats the error. (C) translates the cliché into plain English. (D) uses a different cliché and (E) is pretentious.

18. E

The original presents three short subject-verb sentences—and all three verbs are *is*! (E) effectively and concisely combines the sentences.

19. D.

(A) uses the word *problem* three times. (B)–(D) reduce that to once, but (B) and (C) are wordy. (D) is clear and concise. (E) is wordy.

20. C

The original uses the vague *acting weird*. (B) repeats the error and adds bulk to the sentence. (D) and (E) are passive.

CHAPTER 14

Commonly Confused Words

Start with this 10-question Building Block Quiz. The first few questions test material you've already seen.

BUILDING BLOCK QUIZ

Which underlined portion of each sentence contains an error? If there is no error, choose (E).

1. Though many believe <u>it</u> helps protect them <u>against</u> germs,
   (A)   (B)
   <u>using</u> antibacterial products actually <u>allow</u> bacteria to mutate
   (C)   (D)
   into more virulent strains. <u>No error</u>
                      (E)

2. <u>Mankind's</u> greatest achievement will not lie in <u>extending</u> its
   (A)   (B)
   reach into outer <u>space but</u> in <u>eradicating</u> poverty and disease
                (C)   (D)
   here on Earth. <u>No error</u>
               (E)

3. The Centers for Disease Control and Prevention (CDC) <u>is</u>
                                      (A)
   <u>responsible for</u> tracking and <u>monitoring</u> health problems
       (B)   (C)
   and <u>to inform</u> citizens about health matters. <u>No error</u>
        (D)   (E)

4. <u>There's</u> nothing better <u>then</u> hot chocolate <u>to warm</u> you up
     (A)   (C)   (D)
   after <u>being</u> outside in the cold. <u>No error</u>
       (D)   (E)

5. The <u>ingenious</u> study is designed to <u>measure</u> the <u>affects</u> of
    (A)   (B)   (C)
    food coloring on <u>children's</u> behavior. <u>No error</u>
                (D)   (E)

6. I can't see <u>any</u> difference <u>between</u> these three paintings
           (A)   (B)
    <u>except</u> that this one is lighter on <u>its</u> edges. <u>No error</u>
     (C)   (D)   (E)

7. A scientific experiment must be designed <u>so that</u> it can be
                                   (A)
    <u>reproduced</u> to <u>insure</u> that the results are <u>accurate</u>. <u>No error</u>
     (B)   (C)   (D)   (E)

8. <u>Its</u> highly <u>unlikely</u> that you'll find any <u>correlation</u> <u>between</u>
    (A)   (B)   (C)   (D)
    the consumption of chocolate and intelligence. <u>No error</u>
                                           (E)

9. We must <u>precede</u> <u>with caution</u> as we continue our <u>ascent</u> to
            (A)   (B)   (C)
    the <u>campsite</u> at the top <u>of the</u> mountain. <u>No error</u>
        (D)   (E)

10. Are you <u>inferring</u> that my <u>visions</u> of a <u>past</u> life are only an
            (A)   (B)   (C)
    <u>illusion</u>? <u>No error</u>
     (D)   (E)

Answers and Explanations

1. D

Though *products* is plural, the subject is the gerund phrase *using antibacterial products,* therefore singular.

2. A

Mankind refers only to one gender and is therefore sexist.

3. D

The sentence lacks parallel structure. *To inform* should be *informing*.

4. B

The words *than* and *then* are frequently confused. *Then* indicates when something happened; *than* is used for comparisons.

5. C

Affect is the verb meaning to have an impact on. *Effect* is the noun meaning result, impact, the correct word.

6. B

Between should only be used for *two* items. For more than two, the correct word is *among*.

7. C

Assure means to convince, *ensure* (the correct word) means to make certain, and *insure* means to guard against loss.

8. A

Its, a possessive pronoun, is frequently confused with *it's* (the correct word), the contraction for *it is*.

9. A

Precede means to come before. It is often confused with the correct word *proceed*, which means to go forward.

10. A

Infer means to draw a conclusion based on reasoning or evidence. *Imply* means to suggest or state indirectly.

Usage refers to the proper *use* of words, phrases, and expressions. Whether you say "I'm going *to the* hospital" or "I'm going *to* hospital" is a matter of usage. (*Going to hospital* is standard usage in British and Australian English, but not American.)

Usage includes idioms (specific word combinations and expressions such as *dream about* and *keep an eye on*) or colloquialisms (informal expressions). Our focus in this chapter, however, is commonly confused and misused words, 101 of which are arranged in manageable groups for your review.

HOMOPHONES

Homophones sound the same but mean different things. They are often, but not always, spelled differently.

accept (v.): to take or receive. *Camille <u>accepted</u> a job offer in Singapore.*

except (prep.): leave out. *I love everything about my job <u>except</u> the commute.*

> ### MEMORY TIP
> *Accept* is a verb, the action. Both *accept* and *action* begin with *a*.

affect (v.): to have an impact or influence on. *The amount of sleep you get directly <u>affects</u> your ability to concentrate.*

effect (n.): result, impact. *One <u>effect</u> of sleep deprivation is an inability to focus.* (v.): to cause, implement. *Irfan <u>effected</u> several changes in his sleep schedule.*

altar (n.): an elevated structure, typically intended for religious rituals. *Determined to get married despite the storm, the couple exchanged vows at a makeshift altar.*

alter (v.): to change. *If the ship does not alter its course, it will head straight into the hurricane.*

ascent (n.): climb, upward movement. *Vanessa's rapid ascent up the corporate ladder impressed us all.*

assent (v.): to agree; (n.): agreement. *Peter has given his assent to the plan.*

bazaar (n.): a market consisting of various shops; a fair selling miscellaneous items. *I found these fantastic bracelets at the school bazaar.*

bizarre (adj.): very strange, weird. *No one knew how to respond to the bizarre question.*

capital (n.): a seat of government; accumulated assets; (adj.) first rate; extremely serious; involving the death penalty. *It's near the state capital, Harrisburg.*

capitol (n.): the building(s) in which lawmakers meet. *Security at the state capitol is tight.*

cite (v.): to quote, to refer to. *The article cited our school's test scores.*

sight (n.): something seen or visible; the faculty of seeing. *Manolo's sight was restored after the operation.*

site (n.): location; (v.): to place or locate. *This is the perfect site for a picnic.*

coarse (adj.): rough to the touch, large grained; crude, vulgar; of low quality. *Lou's coarse language offended everyone.*

course (n.): path, route, direction; mode of action or behavior; series of classes on a subject; (v.): to move swiftly through or over. *You've chosen a wise course of action.*

Practice 1

Circle the correct word(s) within the parentheses.

1. Julio needs the client's (ascent / assent) to use this (coarse / course) fabric instead of the twill.

2. This is the most (bazaar / bizarre) (cite / sight / site) I have ever seen!

3. There will be a (bazaar / bizarre) on the steps of the state (capital / capitol) tomorrow.

4. I had to (altar / alter) my intended (coarse / course) to avoid traffic.

5. There's nothing we can do now (accept / except) wait to see how the medication (affects / effects) Kelly's condition.

Now back to our list of homophones:

complement (n.): something that completes; (v.): to go with or complete. *That shirt complements your eyes.*

compliment (v.): to flatter; (n.): a flattering remark. *I'm not sure that compliment was sincere.*

council (n.): a body called together for consultation or discussion; an assembly of officials or advisors. *The town council discussed the impact of the proposed landfill.*

counsel (v.): to advise or recommend; (n.): advice or guidance; a lawyer. *I try to keep my own counsel.*

elicit (v.): to call forth or draw out. *Raul was provocative to elicit a response from the apathetic audience.*

illicit (adj.): unlawful. *He accepted illicit contributions to his campaign.*

past (n.): time before the present; (adj.): pertaining to time before the present; (prep., adv.): going by or beyond. *In the past, phones couldn't be carried around easily.*

passed (v.): simple past or past participle of the verb *to pass*. *Thank goodness that time has passed!*

principal (n.): head of a school or organization, primary participant, main sum of money; (adj.): main, most important. *Joshua is one of the principals of the company.*

principle (n.): a basic truth or law. *I run my business based on the principle that honesty is the best policy.*

rein (n.): a means of restraint or guidance; (v.): to restrain, control. *You need to rein in your temper before it gets you in trouble.*

reign (v.): to exercise power; (n.): period in which a ruler exercised power. *Under the reign of Mrs. Walker, the students became studious and kind.*

stationary (adj.):   not moving; not capable of moving. *Jojo rides a stationary bike each morning.*

stationery (n.):   writing paper. *I've ordered stationery with my name and address on it.*

> ## MEMORY TIP
> Use another "a" memory trick: *stationary* with an *a* is the adjective.

weather (n.):   climatic conditions. *The bad weather will keep people away from our fundraiser.*

whether (conj.):   refers to a choice between alternatives. *I am not sure whether I will attend the fundraiser or not.*

Practice 2

Circle the correct word(s) within the parentheses.

1. I can't tell (weather / whether) these fabrics will (complement / compliment) the décor in my room.
2. The (council / counsel) (passed / past) the proposal to renovate the existing meetinghouse rather than build a new one.
3. If Hannah ever sought my (advice / advise), I'd (council / counsel) her to (reign / rein) in her jealousy.
4. We just (passed / past) the (weather / whether) station.
5. I must (complement / compliment) you on your beautiful selection of (stationary / stationery).

CONTRACTIONS AND OTHER TROUBLEMAKERS

This list includes frequently confused pairs such as *it's/its* and *lose/loose*.

One Word or Two?

In each set below, the meaning of the term depends upon whether it's one word or two.

> **MEMORY TIP**
>
> If you want to express <u>action</u>, you need a contr<u>action</u>, which includes both a subject and a verb.

a lot (adv.):	very many or much. *I have a lot of studying to do.*
allot (v.):	to give out or distribute, parcel out. *We were each allotted 15 minutes to defend our position.*
all ready (adj.):	completely prepared. *I am all ready for my interview.*
already (adv.):	prior to a specific time. *I have already read* Fahrenheit 451.
altogether (adv.):	all included or counted. *I am altogether lost; I've no idea where we are!*
all together (adj. or adv.):	everyone gathered; all members of a group acting collectively. *All together now: 1, 2, 3, pull!*
its (pn.):	third-person, singular, possessive pronoun. *This computer is on its last legs.*
it's (pn + v.):	contraction of *it + is*. *It's time to get a new one.*
your (pn.):	second-person, singular, possessive pronoun. *Your drawings are quite impressive.*
you're (pn + v):	contraction of *you + are*. *You're going to be a famous artist someday.*
their (pn.):	third-person, plural, possessive pronoun. *Is that their bag, or yours?*
there (adv.):	at or in that place; (n.): that place or point. *I'll meet you over there.*

they're (pn + v.): contraction of *they + are. They're going to meet us as well.*

whose (pn.): the possessive form of the pronoun *who. Whose car should we take?*

who's (pn + v.): contraction of *who + is. Who's going to drive?*

Practice 3
Choose the correct word(s) within the parentheses.

1. Since (your / you're) (already / all ready) here, let's go ahead and get started.
2. (Your / You're) car—if you can even call it that—is (altogether / all together) a lost cause.
3. I hope (your / you're) (already / all ready) to go, because we have (a lot / allot) of work to do today.
4. (Its / it's) a shame that (its / it's) too late for you to join the team this year.
5. I have (already / all ready) decided (whose / who's) going to get the award.

Other Troublemakers
Whether they're similar in sound or meaning, these pairs frequently cause writers trouble.

advice (n.): recommendation. *Ask Eton for advice about writing a good resume.*

advise (v.): to recommend what should be done. *He will be happy to advise you.* **Pronunciation note:** The *s* in *advise* is pronounced like a *z.*

> ### MEMORY TIP
> When you *advise* someone, you *say* your advice. *Advise* and *say* both have the letter *s.*

allusion (n.): an indirect reference. *The story makes an allusion to* Moby Dick.

illusion (n.): erroneous perception; false impression; misleading or deceptive image. *Captain Ahab's dream of catching the great white whale was an illusion.*

among (prep.): in the midst of. [**Usage note:** Use *among* for three or more items or entities.] *Anthropologist Margaret Mead lived among the Samoans for many years.*

between (prep.): in an intermediate position or interval. [**Usage note:** Use *between* for two items or entities.] *Many immigrants feel they must choose between their native culture and American culture.*

amount (n.): number or quantity; (v.): to add up in number or quantity. [**Usage note:** Use *amount* with quantities that *cannot* be counted.] *She has a great amount of courage.*

number (n.): symbol representing a mathematical unit; total, sum; quantity of units or individuals; (v.): to count; add up to. [**Usage note:** Use *number* with quantities that *can* be counted.] *She has auditioned for a number of plays.*

conscience (n.): awareness of moral principles, together with preference for right over wrong. *My conscience has been bothering me since I cheated on the exam.*

conscious (adj.): aware, alert; perceiving one's surroundings and existence. *I was very conscious of the fact that Colette kept staring at me.*

fewer (adj.): consisting of a smaller number. [**Usage note:** Use *fewer* with items that can be counted.] *We received fewer votes than I'd expected.*

less (adj.): not as great in quantity or amount; of lower rank or importance. [**Usage note:** Use *less* with general amounts.] *Voter turnout this year was less than last year.*

incidence (n):   instance of happening; frequency of occurrence. *There is a high incidence of accidents at this corner.*

incident (n):   an occurrence or event. *There have been several incidents involving disorderly fans.*

loose (adj.):   not securely fastened; not taut or rigid. *In the loose atmosphere of the writing workshop, April was able to be more creative.*

lose (v.):   to misplace; to fail to win or maintain. *Please be quiet so I don't lose my train of thought.*

personal (adj.):   private or pertaining to the individual. *My personal trainer is helping me.*

personnel (n.):   employees. *As a human resources intern, I help maintain the files on personnel.*

> ### MEMORY TIP
> The <u>a</u>djective *personal* is spelled with an *a*.

---

quotation (n.):   a passage cited from a person or text; a statement of a price or bid. *I have a great quotation by John Wayne in my essay about early Westerns.*

quote (v.):   to repeat a passage from; to state a price for services or goods. *I quote John Wayne in my essay about stereotypes in early Westerns.* [**Usage note**: Using *quote* as a short form of *quotation* is considered informal and should be avoided in formal writing.]

than (conj.):   used to compare. *I have more experience than Marie.*

then (adv.):   at that time, therefore. *I was very naïve back then.*

Practice 4

Circle the correct word(s) within the parentheses.

1. I would (advice / advise) you to take a (coarse / course) in statistics even if you aren't majoring in business.

2. If you don't tighten that (loose / lose) knot, (your / you're) going to (loose / lose) your balloon.

3. As Dakota wandered (among / between) the numerous displays, she wished (their / there / they're) were (fewer / less) choices.

4. Don't forget to use (quotation / quote) marks whenever you (quotation / quote) somebody.

5. Yesterday's shouting (incidence / incident) has been troubling my (conscience / conscious).

ADJECTIVE PAIRS AND VERB PAIRS

These can be particularly tricky since they share the same part of speech.

Adjectives

adverse (adj.): unfavorable. *Not doing your homework will have an adverse impact on your grades.*

averse (adj.): opposed or reluctant. *I am averse to doing homework.* [**Usage note**: *Averse* is almost always followed by the preposition *to*.]

amoral (adj.): without a sense of moral judgment. *Claire was upset with the amoral discussion of terrorist acts.*

immoral (adj.): morally wrong. *Claire said, "All terrorist acts are immoral."*

continual (adj.): repeated regularly and frequently. *Meditation should be a continual practice.*

continuous (adj.): extended or prolonged without interruption. *The continuous banging from the construction site gave me a severe headache.*

discreet (adj.):   modest, having discretion; not allowing others to notice. *I must be very discreet about looking for a new job.*

discrete (adj.):   separate, not connected. *They look connected, but are actually two discrete panels.*

disinterested (adj.):   impartial, objective. *We need a disinterested person to act as an arbitrator.*

uninterested (adj.):   not interested. *My nephew is uninterested in anything that doesn't have wheels.*

eminent (adj.):   outstanding, distinguished. *The eminent Judge Blackwell will teach a seminar.*

imminent (adj.):   about to happen, impending. *Warned of imminent layoffs, Loretta began looking for another job.*

explicit (adj.):   fully and clearly expressed or defined. *Please leave explicit instructions for your substitute.*

implicit (adj.):   implied or understood though not directly expressed. *Implicit in John's letter was the reason he wasn't coming home: He didn't want to see Nell.*

ingenious (adj.):   very clever; showing great inventiveness or skill. *It was ingenious of him to protect the window so effectively.*

ingenuous (adj.):   frank, candid; not cunning or deceitful; naive. *Her compliment was not entirely ingenuous.*

sensual (adj.):   sensory; gratifying to the physical and especially sexual appetites.

sensuous (adj.):   pleasing to or gratifying the senses. [**Usage note:** *Sensual* is used primarily to describe physical gratification while *sensuous* describes aesthetic enjoyment as of art and music.]

Practice 5

Circle the correct word(s) within the parentheses.

1. Don't ask Quinn for (advice / advise); he is not a (disinterested / uninterested) party.

2. What an (ingenious / ingenuous) idea, Erik. You're brilliant!

3. The (sensual / sensuous) sound of a Chopin sonata drifted down the hall to my apartment.

4. Our (continual / continuous) friendship is one of the most important things in my life.

5. You can't see the cell walls, but you can see two nuclei, which means these are two (discreet / discrete) cells, not one.

Verbs

adapt (v.): to change to suit a new purpose or conditions. *Hasaan has adapted well to his new country.*

adopt (v.): to legally take a child into one's family; to accept as if one's own; to accept formally and put into effect. *The English faculty voted to adopt a new grammar book.*

assure (v.): to convince or guarantee. *Cole assures me there's nothing wrong with this car.*

ensure (v.): to make certain. *Please ensure that there's nothing wrong with this car before I buy it.*

insure (v.): to guard against loss. *The "lemon law" helps insure the rights of used car buyers.*

censor (v.): to remove or suppress objectionable material. (n.): one who censors. *Parents protested when the principal censored Anthony's article.*

censure (v.): to criticize severely, rebuke formally. *The principal was later censured for his actions.*

emigrate (from) (v.):	to leave one country or region and settle in another. *My great-grandfather emigrated from Ireland in 1880.*
immigrate (to) (v.):	to enter another country or region and settle there. *He immigrated to Canada, then to the United States.*
imply (v.):	to suggest or state indirectly. *Are you implying that I can't handle the job?*
infer (v.):	to draw a conclusion based on reasoning or evidence. *Katrina inferred from Aaron's comments that he didn't think she could handle the job.*
precede (v.):	to come before. *In your book report, the summary should precede your analysis.*
proceed (v.):	to go forward. *The weather is not ideal, but we will proceed as planned.*

Practice 6

Circle the correct word(s) within the parentheses.

1. We cannot (precede / proceed) without your (ascent / assent).
2. I (assure / ensure / insure) you that I was not (implying / inferring) that you don't know what you're doing.
3. I would like to (adapt / adopt) a new policy that will (assure / ensure / insure) that our patient data is properly protected.
4. We plan to (emigrate / immigrate) to Australia to be closer to our families.
5. The senator was (censored / censured) for his sexist remarks.

SUMMARY

You've reviewed 101 commonly confused words—words that you can now use with confidence. Unless you use these words regularly, you should review them often.

Practice: On Your Own

After you complete the Chapter 14 Test, check your answers carefully. Make a list of the words you still confuse. Add a definition and sample sentence for each. As you work, try to think of mnemonic devices to help you remember their differences.

Practice Answers and Explanations

Practice 1
1. assent, coarse
2. bizarre, sight
3. bazaar, capitol
4. alter, course
5. except, affects

Practice 2
1. whether, complement
2. council, passed
3. advice, counsel, rein, past
4. passed
5. compliment, stationery

Practice 3
1. you're, already
2. Your, altogether
3. you're, all ready, a lot
4. It's, it's
5. already, who's

Practice 4
1. advise, course
2. loose, you're, lose
3. among, there, fewer
4. quotation, quote
5. incident

Practice 5
1. advice, disinterested
2. ingenious
3. sensuous
4. continuous
5. discrete

Practice 6
1. proceed, assent
2. assure, implying
3. adopt, ensure
4. immigrate
5. censured

CHAPTER 14 TEST

Part A. For questions 1–10, which word matches the definition?

1. frank, candid, not cunning or deceitful
   (A) adverse   (B) averse   (C) ingenious
   (D) ingenuous   (E) explicit

2. an indirect reference
   (A) allusion   (B) illusion   (C) counsel
   (D) quotation   (E) quote

3. to draw a conclusion based on reasoning, evidence, or circumstances
   (A) imply   (B) infer   (C) censor   (D) censure   (E) advise

4. impartial, objective
   (A) sensual   (B) sensuous   (C) discrete
   (D) discreet   (E) disinterested

5. opposed or reluctant
   (A) illicit   (B) stationary   (C) amoral
   (D) averse   (E) implicit

6. to go with or complete
   (A) compliment   (B) complement   (C) adapt
   (D) adopt   (E) proceed

7. to criticize severely, rebuke formally
   (A) infer   (B) imply   (C) elicit   (D) reign   (E) censure

8. prudent, modest, having discretion
   (A) discrete   (B) discreet   (C) disinterested
   (D) adverse   (E) averse

9. unlawful
   (A) illicit   (B) elicit   (C) eminent
   (D) ingenuous   (E) amoral

10. about to happen, impending
    (A) explicit   (B) implicit   (C) imminent
    (D) eminent   (E) continual

Part B. For questions 11–20, which set of words best fills in the blanks?

11. The __ you __ here __ that there's a direct correlation
    between this medication and obesity.
    (A) quotation, sight, infers
    (B) quote, cite, infers
    (C) quotation, cite, implies
    (D) quote, site, implies
    (E) quotation, cite, infers

12. __ is no evidence that dying __ hair during pregnancy will
    have any negative __ on the fetus.
    (A) Their, you're, affect
    (B) There, your, effect
    (C) They're, your, effect
    (D) There, your, affect
    (E) Their, your, effect

13. Please __ my apologies for my __ behavior in the __.
    (A) accept, bizarre, past
    (B) except, bizarre, passed
    (C) accept, bazaar, passed
    (D) except, bazaar, past
    (E) accept, bazaar, past

14. The __ has agreed to __ __ procedures for appointing new members.
    (A) counsel, altar, it's
    (B) counsel, alter, it's
    (C) council, altar, its
    (D) council, alter, it's
    (E) council, alter, its

15. __ __ were 250 __ from schools across the country at the conference.
    (A) All together, their, principles
    (B) Altogether, there, principals
    (C) Altogether, they're, principals
    (D) All together, there, principles
    (E) Altogether, their, principals

16. I wish you would spend __ time giving me __ and more time worrying about your own __ problems.
    (A) less, advice, personal
    (B) less, advise, personnel
    (C) fewer, advice, personnel
    (D) fewer, advise, personal
    (E) less, advise, personal

17. I __ you, an __ person cannot have a clear __.
    (A) ensure, amoral, conscience
    (B) assure, amoral, conscious
    (C) insure, immoral, conscience
    (D) assure, immoral, conscious
    (E) assure, immoral, conscience

18. The __ of __ involving __ language in the classroom has declined.
    (A) number, incidents, coarse
    (B) amount, incidents, course
    (C) amount, incidence, coarse
    (D) number, incidence, course
    (E) amount, incidence, course

19. In the __, the __ was __ more predictable.
    (A) past, whether, allot
    (B) passed, weather, a lot
    (C) past, weather, a lot
    (D) passed, whether, a lot
    (E) past, weather, allot

20. Once you provide __ instructions, __ we can __.
    (A) explicit, then, precede
    (B) explicit, then, proceed
    (C) implicit, than, proceed
    (D) implicit, then, precede
    (E) explicit, than, proceed

Answers

No explanations; when in doubt, check your dictionary.

1.	D	6.	B	11.	C	16.	A
2.	A	7.	E	12.	B	17.	E
3.	B	8.	B	13.	A	18.	A
4.	E	9.	A	14.	E	19.	C
5.	D	10.	C	15.	B	20.	B

SECTION III

Punctuation and Mechanics

CHAPTER 15

Commas

Start with this 10-question Building Block Quiz. The first few questions test material you've already seen.

BUILDING BLOCK QUIZ

Determine which underlined portion(s) of each sentence contains an error (a blank line may indicate missing punctuation). If there is no error, choose (E).

1. Time was up, however, Gail still had 20 questions left_ to answer.
   (A)   (B)   (C)

2. Such a small <u>amount</u> of caffeine_ shouldn't have any <u>affect</u> on
   (A)   (B)   (C)
   <u>your</u> ability to fall asleep tonight.
   (D)

3. Chuck <u>felt</u> really <u>bad</u> when Xu Mei started <u>to cry</u>, and he
   (A)   (B)   (C)
   decided never to tease her_ again.
   (D)

4. *Jade*_ Horace's favorite novel_ is being made into a movie_
   (A)   (B)   (C)
   starring his favorite actor.

5. By the time the dinner party was over_ it was well past
   (A)
   midnight, and_ everyone was exhausted
   (B) (C)

6. Ever so slowly, the turtle made its way across the road,
   (A)   (B)
   ducking into its shell_ every time a car drove by.
   (C)

7. The bright‚ blue sky showed no sign of rain‚ but the forecast
      (A)   (B)

   called for dangerous_ thunderstorms_ throughout the day.
                (C)   (D)

8. Did you know‚ that my cat will eat anything‚ including‚ peas?
         (A)   (B)   (C)

9. We should_ clean up_ Joe_ before your mom gets home.
       (A)   (B) (C)

10. The chief complaint of our patients‚ however_ continues to
                             (A)   (B)

   be_ the length of time they must wait_ before seeing a doctor.
   (C)   (D)

Answers and Explanations

1. A

This is a run-on; a comma is not strong enough to separate independent clauses without a coordinating conjunction (*however* is a conjunctive adverb; see chapter 1).

2. C

Affect is a verb; *effect* is a noun and is the correct word for this sentence.

3. B

Bad is an adjective; this sentence needs the adverb *badly* to modify *felt*.

4. A and B

That the novel is Horace's favorite is not essential to the sentence, so set it off with commas.

5. A

The clause *by the time the dinner party was over* introduces the main action of the sentence, so set it off with a comma.

6. E

There is no error.

7. A

A comma belongs between two consecutive adjectives when the adjectives modify the same word, but *bright* and *blue* do not; *bright* modifies *blue*.

8. E

The clause *that my cat will eat anything* is essential to the sentence, so it should not be set off by commas.

9. B and C

The speaker directly addresses *Joe*. Without commas around *Joe*, the sentence means *we* should clean up *Joe*.

10. B

The transition word *however* should be set off by commas.

Writing that is otherwise powerful and clear can be mangled by misplaced commas, misspelled words, and incorrect capitals—the subjects of this final section.

Many writers consider punctuation an instrument of torture, but it really *is* designed to help express ideas clearly:

> **a.** I know who did it, Winston.

> **b.** I know who did it: Winston.

Punctuation clarifies ideas and signals relationships between them. In **a**, the speaker tells Winston that she knows who did it; in **b**, the speaker says *Winston* did it. Effective punctuation can also add vigor, conveying emotion and tone:

> Don't do that!

> That tie is a little … colorful, don't you think?

We'll cover all of punctuation in the next three chapters; this chapter is devoted to the comma.

WHEN TO USE A COMMA

The comma is the most common punctuation mark; it gently separates sentence elements from each other or from the main clause. Here are its nine rules.

1. Between two independent clauses connected by a coordinating conjunction

Place the comma at the end of the first clause *before* the coordinating conjunction. If both clauses are short and there's no chance for confusion, you can omit the comma. On the other hand, you may want to keep that comma for effect.

Anuj always loved animals, <u>so</u> I'm not surprised that he is a veterinarian.

I love you and you love me.

I love you, <u>but</u> you don't love me.

> ### FLASHBACK
>
> A comma alone isn't strong enough to stand between two independent clauses; it must be paired with a coordinating conjunction (*and, or, nor, for, so, but* and *yet*).

2. After an introductory word, phrase, or clause

Introductory words, phrases, and clauses are typically adverbs that tell us the when, where, why, how or under what conditions the action of the sentence took place. They should always be followed by a comma.

<u>Unfortunately,</u> the roster is already full.

<u>Without a cup of coffee,</u> I'm useless in the morning.

<u>Because she was so quiet,</u> everyone forgot that little Ellen was there.

In the last example, a subordinate clause introduces the main clause. But be careful: a subordinate clause at the beginning of a sentence does not always serve that function:

> **Incorrect:** <u>Whoever ate my lunch,</u> is going to pay!

This subordinate clause is the subject of the main clause, so the comma is wrong.

Practice 1

Insert any necessary commas in the following sentences.

1. I wanted to call you right away but I didn't want to wake you so I decided to wait until the morning.
2. Whatever you decide I will support you for you are my best friend.

3. Early Monday morning a main transformer was hit by lightning and city residents spent the next 32 hours without power.

4. Much to my dismay you're right and I'm wrong.

3. Between items in a series

Three or more items in a series should be separated by commas. This includes a comma between the last two items (but *not* a comma after the last item). Some consider this penultimate comma optional, but it's best to play it safe and use the comma to clearly separate the two items.

The <u>sandhill crane, American alligator,</u> and West Indian manatee are all endangered Florida wetland species.

When one or more items in the series itself has a comma, use semicolons to separate the items in the list (see chapter 16).

4. Between adjectives that modify the same word

Coordinate adjectives modify the same noun or pronoun; they must be separated by commas:

The <u>dark, dingy room</u> could use a coat of bright paint.

> ### MEMORY TIP
> If you can logically insert the word *and* between two consecutive adjectives, there should be a comma between them.

Cumulative adjectives build up to one modifying phrase and do not take commas:

The <u>light blue paint</u> really brightens the room.

Cumulative: The <u>fierce north wind</u> threatened to knock over the old barn.

Coordinate: The <u>fierce, steady wind</u> threatened to knock over the old barn.

Practice 2

Insert any necessary commas in the following sentences.

1. Neither rain nor sleet nor hail nor a plague of grasshoppers will keep me from Miller's one-day sale.

2. The only thing we had to eat was watery vegetable soup.

3. Rescue workers were ecstatic to find that the frightened shivering child was unharmed by the blast.

4. Bekah's constant, unequivocal support gave me the strength to overcome my depression.

5. To set off nonessential modifiers

Appositives and adjective phrases or clauses should be set off with commas if they are not essential to the meaning of the sentence.

An **appositive** is a modifier that defines or renames another noun (much like a subject complement defines or renames the subject).

Adjective phrase:	Henry Ford, openly challenging his own role as a history maker, once said, "History is bunk."
Adjective clause:	Henry Ford, who is one of the most important figures in American history, once said, "History is bunk."
Appositive:	Henry Ford, one of the most important figures in American history, once said, "History is bunk."

Essential elements are not set off by commas. Without the information in the phrase, clause, or appositive, the sentence loses its specific meaning.

The documents <u>signed by Henry Ford</u> fetched $2,000 each at the auction. ←

The dusty pile of papers <u>that I found in the corner of the attic</u> turned out to be original blueprints signed by Henry Ford.

> ### REMEMBER THIS!
> Any information that is essential (that limits the meaning of the sentence) should **not** be set off by commas.

Practice 3

Insert any necessary commas in the following sentences.

1. My cousin Mikala who has been suffering from back pain for years swears that acupuncture has cured her.
2. The package that I needed for the meeting had been delivered to the wrong address.
3. Jasmine my best friend since grade school is moving to Montana.
4. Remember the book that you're borrowing is very special and I want it back as soon as possible.

6. To set off transitional and parenthetical expressions, question tags, affirmatives and negatives, and mild interjections

Transitions

Transitional words and phrases link sentences or parts of sentences, showing the relationship between them (e.g., comparison or cause and effect).

Wolhee's grandfather, for example, was a master potter in Korea.

Similarly, the newt's diet also consists primarily of worms and insects.

Parenthetical expressions

A parenthetical expression offers ancillary information or acts as an afterthought that interrupts or concludes the sentence.

The wipers need to be replaced, you know.

Sometimes you just have a run of bad luck, I guess.

Question tags

Question tags are exactly that: questions we tack on to the end of a sentence.

You're coming with us, aren't you?

This is a perfect gift for Mojca, don't you think?

Affirmatives and negatives

Words or phrases indicating acceptance or rejection should also be set off from the main sentence.

> On second thought, no, Haily and Jules would not make good lab partners.

> Sure, you can come along.

Mild interjections and other interrupters

Strong interjections stand alone as short sentences ending in an exclamation point (e.g., *Back off!*); but mild interjections are usually part of a sentence and are separated by a comma. Mild or casual interrupters such as *um, like,* and *well* follow the same rule.

> Hey, isn't that Old Man Morrison's dog running down the street?

> We were, like, totally exhausted.

7. To set off a direct address or direct quotation

Direct address

In a direct address, the specific person being addressed should be set off by commas.

> We should grill Huang since it's such a nice day outside.

> We should grill, Huang, since it's such a nice day outside.

This is essential for clarity; without the commas, we might grill Huang.

Direct quotation

When you quote someone else's words, set them off with commas as well as quotation marks (see chapter 16). *Indirect* quotes should have neither commas nor quotation marks:

> **Direct:** Omar said, "Ted, I really need your help."
> **Indirect:** Omar told Ted he really needs his help.

Quotations consisting of more than four lines are usually introduced by colons instead of commas (see chapter 16).

> ### REMEMBER THIS!
> Direct address and direct quotations get commas; indirect quotations do not.

Practice 4
Insert any necessary commas in the following sentences.

1. We have lots of time to kill Eddie so what should we do?

2. "Please excuse me" Joel said and then he raced out of the room.

3. No it doesn't sound like a very good idea does it?

4. "Wow that really is great news" said Victor.

8. To separate parts of dates, numbers, addresses, and titles

Dates
Place commas around the year, unless the date is inverted or only the month and year are stated:

On February 11, 1998, Lukas was born.

April 2000 was the rainiest month in this town's history.

Applications are due 1 May 2006.

Numbers
Numbers with more than four digits are separated into groups of three, except in street addresses, telephone numbers, zip codes, and dates.

Hasaan bought his house for $26,000, renovated it, and sold it for $274,000.

Addresses
Use commas to separate the street from the town, the town from the state or province, and the state or province from the country.

His mailing address is 2234 Vine Street, Oak Ridge, PA 19042.

Titles
When a title follows a noun, set it off with commas.

Katarina Nagy, Ph.D., has agreed to chair the committee.

9. As needed to prevent confusion

Occasionally a comma is needed to clarify meaning or prevent confusion, such as when a word or phrase is repeated or omitted.

Sometimes what you believe is <u>true, is</u>.

Practice 5

Insert any necessary commas in the following sentences.

1. I met my husband at Waterloo Lounge in Watertown New York in January 2001.
2. I was very very disappointed by that movie.
3. Noam Feighter AIA was the chief architect for the building at 3305 Main Street in Red Rock Arkansas.
4. For lunch we ordered lobster ravioli and for dinner glazed duck.

WHEN *NOT* TO USE A COMMA

Here are some reminders to help you avoid superfluous commas.

1. Between a subject and its verb, a verb and its object, or a linking verb and subject complement

Incorrect: The cotton <u>crops, were</u> destroyed by boll rot.

Incorrect: Grandpa gave <u>Wiley, a lecture</u> about respecting one's elders.

2. Between parts of a compound predicate

Predicates can have compound verbs or other compound parts. Do not put a comma between these compound elements.

Incorrect: The water <u>overflowed, and quickly covered</u> the bathroom floor.

Incorrect: I always believed that you <u>were innocent, and would be acquitted</u>.

Practice 6

Cross out any unnecessary commas in the sentences below.

1. Cyan, is a color between green and blue on the spectrum.
2. Standing before a crowded courtroom, the defendant stated, his name, and swore to tell the truth.
3. I'm sorry, but the map is missing the page, that we need.
4. Indigo, an intense shade of blue, has always been, my favorite color.

3. After a coordinating or subordinating conjunction

Commas may be necessary *before* a coordinating or subordinating conjunction, but not after them.

> Incorrect: Dr. Chan tried for years, <u>but, he</u> never succeeded in recording his dreams.

4. Before the first item in a series or after the last

Commas belong *between* items in a series but not *around* them.

> Incorrect: The children <u>collected, feathers,</u> pine cones, and <u>pebbles, during</u> their nature walk.

5. Between a modifier and what it modifies

Do not put commas between modifiers and their referents.

> Incorrect: The <u>red, door</u> needs another coat of paint.

Practice 7

Cross out any unnecessary commas in the sentences below.

1. My nightmares have subsided, but, I still have trouble, falling asleep at night.
2. I'd rather stay home tonight because, I have an important meeting early tomorrow, remember?
3. The fans cheered wildly as the Olympians passed by in a long, slow, procession.
4. You're an obnoxious, overbearing, boss, and, I refuse to work here any longer.

6. Before parentheses

Parentheses themselves are enough to set off information; adding a comma is overkill.

> **Incorrect:** Your computer is short on RAM, (Random Access Memory).

7. After *such as*, *like*, or *including*

These words should not be separated from the examples and lists that they introduce.

> **Incorrect:** My favorite restaurants, including, Sushi Roku and Balboa, are in Los Angeles.

8. With an exclamation point or question mark

The exclamation point and question mark are endmarks and do not need to be followed by a comma in dialogue.

> **Incorrect:** "Did you try the quiche?", Annette asked.

Practice 8

Cross out any unnecessary commas in the sentences below.

1. "It felt like, I would never get out of there!", Rachel complained.
2. *ER*, (which is my favorite television series, by the way), first aired in September, 1994.
3. Well, Harold told me, I'm supposed to be in charge, while he's gone.
4. "Are you ready yet?", Piotr asked, impatiently.

SUMMARY

DO use a comma:

1. between two independent clauses connected by a coordinating conjunction
2. after an introductory word, phrase, or clause
3. between items in a series
4. between adjectives that modify the same word
5. to set off nonessential modifiers

6. to set off transitional and parenthetical expressions, question tags, affirmatives and negatives, and mild interjections
7. to set off a direct address or direct quotation
8. to separate parts of dates, numbers, addresses, and titles
9. as needed to prevent confusion.

DO NOT use a comma:

1. between a subject and verb, a verb and object, or verb and complement
2. between parts of a compound predicate
3. after a coordinating or subordinating conjunction
4. before the first item in a series or after the last
5. between a modifier and what it modifies
6. before parentheses
7. after *such as, like,* or *including*
8. with an exclamation point or question mark.

Practice: On Your Own

Choose a magazine or book and look for examples of each comma rule. You can also search for examples of superfluous commas. Check samples of your own writing, letters you receive, or websites such as blogs.

Practice Answers and Explanations

Practice 1

1. I wanted to call you right away, but I didn't want to wake you, so I decided to wait until the morning. [Comma between independent clauses; it would be acceptable to omit the first comma as both clauses are short.]
2. Whatever you decide, I will support you, for you are my best friend. [Comma after the introductory clause and between the two independent clauses]
3. Early Monday morning, a main transformer was hit by lightning, and city residents spent the next 32 hours without power. [Comma after the introductory phrase and between the two independent clauses]

4. Much to my dismay, you're right and I'm wrong. [Comma after introductory phrase; no comma is needed between the independent clauses since both are short]

Practice 2

1. Neither rain, nor sleet, nor hail, nor a plague of grasshoppers will keep me from Miller's one-day sale. [Comma between items in the series]
2. The only thing we had to eat was watery vegetable soup. [No comma between cumulative adjectives; vegetable describes soup]
3. Rescue workers were ecstatic to find that the frightened, shivering child was unharmed by the blast. [Comma between two coordinate adjectives]
4. Bekah's constant, unequivocal support gave me the strength to overcome my depression. [No additional comma; the comma between constant and unequivocal is correct as both adjectives modify support]

Practice 3

1. My cousin Mikala, who has been suffering from back pain for years, swears that acupuncture has cured her. [Commas around nonessential clause]
2. The package that I needed for the meeting had been delivered to the wrong address. [No comma; the clause is essential]
3. Jasmine, my best friend since grade school, is moving to Montana. [Commas around nonessential phrase]
4. Remember, the book that you're borrowing is very special, and I want it back as soon as possible. [Comma after introductory word and between independent clauses; no commas around an essential clause]

Practice 4

1. We have lots of time to kill, Eddie, so what should we do? [Commas around direct address and between independent clauses]
2. "Please excuse me," Joel said, and then he raced out of the room. [Comma after direct quotation and between independent clauses]
3. No, it doesn't sound like a very good idea, does it? [Comma after negation and before question tag]
4. "Wow, that really is great news," said Victor. [Comma after mild interjection and after direct quotation]

Practice 5

1. I met my husband at Waterloo Lounge in Watertown, New York, in January 2001. [Commas around the state; no comma between month and year when no day is included]
2. I was very, very disappointed by that movie. [Comma to avoid confusion]
3. Noam Feighter, AIA, was the chief architect for the building at 3305 Main Street in Red Rock, Arkansas. [Commas around title and between town and state]
4. For lunch we ordered lobster ravioli and for dinner, glazed duck. [Comma to prevent confusion]

Practice 6

1. Cyan is a color between green and blue on the spectrum. [No comma between subject and verb]
2. Standing before a crowded courtroom, the defendant stated his name and swore to tell the truth. [No comma between the verb and object; no comma before the second verb in compound predicate; the first comma sets off introductory phrase]
3. I'm sorry, but the map is missing the page that we need. [No comma sets off essential information. The first comma is between independent clauses connected by a coordinating conjunction. (Though the first clause is very short, the length of the second makes it unwise to omit the comma.)]

4. Indigo, an intense shade of blue, has always been my favorite color. [No comma between verb and complement; the first two commas set off an appositive]

Practice 7
Commas that should be deleted are enclosed in brackets.

1. My nightmares have subsided, but[,] I still have trouble[,] falling asleep at night.
2. I'd rather stay home tonight because[,] I have an important meeting early tomorrow, remember?
3. The fans cheered wildly as the Olympians passed by in a long, slow[,] procession.
4. You're an obnoxious, overbearing[,] boss, and[,] I refuse to work here any longer.

Practice 8
Commas that should be deleted are enclosed in brackets.

1. "It felt like[,] I would never get out of there!"[,] Rachel complained.
2. ER[,] (which is my favorite television series, by the way)[,] first aired in September[,] 1994.
3. Well, Harold told me[,] I'm supposed to be in charge[,] while he's gone.
4. "Are you ready yet?"[,] Piotr asked[,] impatiently.

CHAPTER 15 TEST

For questions 1–10, determine where in the sentence a comma(s) needs to be placed.

1. A kiss can be_ a comma_ a question mark_ or an
        (A)   (B)   (C)
exclamation point. —*Mistinguett*

2. That_ must be fine_ for_ I don't understand a word.
   (A)   (B) (C)
—*Molière*

3. All meanings_ we know_ depend_ on the key of
      (A)   (B)   (C)
interpretation. —*George Eliot*

4. The first rule for a good style is_ to have something to say;
                 (A)
in fact_ this in itself_ is almost enough. —*Schopenhauer*
  (B)   (C)

5. In good writing_ words_ become one_ with things.
        (A)   (B)   (C)
—*Ralph Waldo Emerson*

6. Everything_ that is written_ merely to please the author_
     (A)   (B)   (C)
is worthless. —*Pascal*

7. Sticks and stones_ may break my bones_ and_ words
        (A)   (B) (C)
can sting_ like anything. —*Anonymous*
  (D)

8. George Santayana_ once said_ "Words_ are weapons."
       (A)   (B)   (C)

9. After many_ long_ challenging years_ I am finally
  (A) (B)   (C)
Alyssa Jones_ M.D.
    (D)

10. Congratulations_ Alyssa_ on your remarkable_ achievement.
      (A)   (B)   (C)

For questions 11–20, determine which commas, if any, are superfluous.

11. Is it possible for contestants on a reality show, to be
                                              (A)
    themselves, or are they always acting?", Joachim asked.
        (B)   (C)

12. With tears in his eyes, the defendant told the jurors, he was
                      (A)   (B)
    deeply sorry, for what he'd done.
              (C)

13. The course, that I most wanted to take, Civilizing Society,
              (A)   (B)   (C)
    is already full.

14. Though, advice about which foods we should eat may vary,
           (A)   (B)
    experts always agree, that exercise is an essential part of
                          (C)
    a healthy lifestyle.

15. The house at 310 Riley Lane needs several, major repairs,
                                          (A)   (B)
    including, a new roof.
            (C)

16. After ripping up the carpet, Elian sanded the floor, and
                              (A)   (B)
    stained it a dark, cherry color.
                    (C)

17. We agreed that, we will meet at 1,700 Wilson Avenue on July, 14.
                  (A)   (B)   (C)

18. The cake is ready, but, I'm still working on the cookies, that
                    (A) (B)   (C)
    you added to the order.

19. "Yes, you *are* crazy, Maurice!", Stefan yelled.
        (A)   (B)   (C)

20. Wow, you really *do* love, me, don't you?
        (A)   (B) (C)

Answers and Explanations

1.   B and C

Items in a series should be set off by commas.

2.   B

Insert a comma between independent clauses connected by a coordinating conjunction.

3.   A and B

The parenthetical expression *we know* interrupts the sentence and should be set off by commas.

4.   B

The transitional phrase *in fact* should be set off by commas.

5.   A

The introductory phrase *in good writing* should be set off by commas.

6.   E

No commas are needed.

7.   B

Use a comma between independent clauses connected by a coordinating conjunction.

8.   B

Use a comma before a direct quotation.

9.   B, C, and D

Two adjectives modifying the same word should be separated by a comma (B). The introductory phrase should also be set off by a comma (C), and titles that follow a name should be set off by a comma (D).

10.   A and B

Direct address should be set off by a comma.

11.   A and C

(A) has a superfluous comma between a subject and verb. (C) is an unnecessary comma after a question mark. The second comma correctly separates independent clauses connected by a coordinating conjunction.

12. B and C

The clause *he was deeply sorry* should not be set off by commas; it serves as the object (B). The comma between *sorry* and *for* (C) unnecessarily sets off the prepositional phrase. The first comma sets off an introductory phrase.

13. A

The clause *that I … to take* is essential. The comma after the clause sets off non-essential information (the course name).

14. B and C

Do not use commas after subordinating conjunctions (A). The clause *that excercise … lifestyle* is essential (C). The second comma sets off an introductory clause.

15. A and C

Do not put a comma between a modifier and the word it modifies (A). Do not use a comma after *including* (C). The second comma sets off non-essential information.

16. B and C

Do not use a comma to separate compound parts of a predicate (B). A comma only belongs between two consecutive adjectives if they modify the same word. *Dark* modifies *cherry*. The first comma sets off an introductory phrase.

17. A, B, and C

All of these commas are superfluous. The first sets off essential information; the second breaks up a long number in an address; and the third separates a month from a day (the comma belongs between the day and the year).

18. B and C

Do not use commas after coordinating conjunctions (B). (C) sets off essential information. The first comma sets off an independent clause.

19. C

Do not use a comma after an exclamation point. The first comma sets off an affirmative; the second marks direct address.

20. B

Do not insert a comma between a verb and its object. The first comma sets off a mild interjection; the third sets off a question tag.

CHAPTER 16

Semicolon, Colon, Dash, and Quotation Marks

Start with this 10-question Building Block Quiz. The first few questions test material you've already seen.

BUILDING BLOCK QUIZ

Choose the best version of each sentence. If the original is best, choose (A).

1. Judge a man by his questions rather than considering his answers. —*Voltaire*

   (A) No change
   (B) Judge a man by his questions rather than his answers.
   (C) A man should be judged by his questions rather than being judged by his answers.
   (D) Judge a man by his questions, his answers are less important.
   (E) Questions are what a man should be judged by, not his answers.

2. Keep your mouth shut and one's eyes open. —*Samuel Palmer*

   (A) No change
   (B) One's mouth should be kept shut and one's eyes should be kept open.
   (C) Keep your mouth shut and your eyes open.
   (D) Keep your mouth, shut, and your eyes, open.
   (E) Keep one's mouth shut and your eyes open.

3. Opinions, that are well rooted, should grow and change like a healthy tree —*Irving Batcheller*

   (A) No change
   (B) Opinions, that are well rooted, should experience growth and change in the manner of a healthy tree.
   (C) Opinions that are well rooted should grow and change like a healthy tree.
   (D) Opinions that are well rooted, like a healthy tree, should grow and change.
   (E) Opinions, like a healthy tree, that are well rooted, should grow and change.

4. If you wish to please people; you must begin by understanding them. —*Charles Reade*

   (A) No change
   (B) If you wish to please people, you must begin by understanding them.
   (C) If you wish to please people: You must begin by understanding them.
   (D) If you wish to please people you must begin by understanding them.
   (E) Wishing to please people, you must begin by understanding them.

5. Anne announced that "she was going to resign."

   (A) No change
   (B) Anne announced that, "she was going to resign."
   (C) Anne announced that "she was going to resign".
   (D) Anne announced that she was going to resign.
   (E) Anne announced that, she was going to resign.

6. Safe popular freedom consists of four things, the diffusion of liberty, of intelligence, of property, and of conscientiousness. —*Joseph Cook*

   (A) No change

   (B) Safe popular freedom consists of four things, the diffusion of: liberty, intelligence, property, and conscientiousness.

   (C) Safe popular freedom consists of four things: the diffusion of liberty, of intelligence, of property, and of conscientiousness.

   (D) Safe popular freedom consists of four things: the diffusion of liberty; of intelligence; of property; and of conscientiousness.

   (E) Safe popular freedom consists of four things; the diffusion of liberty, of intelligence, of property, and of conscientiousness.

7. Frank Scully said, "Why not go out on a limb? Isn't that where the fruit is"?

   (A) No change

   (B) Frank Scully said: "Why not go out on a limb? Isn't that where the fruit is"?

   (C) Frank Scully said; "Why not go out on a limb? Isn't that where the fruit is?"

   (D) Frank Scully said, "Why not go out on a limb? Isn't that where the fruit is?"

   (E) Frank Scully said, Why not go out on a limb? Isn't that where the fruit is?

8. Either I will find a way: or I will make one. —*Sir Philip Sidney*

   (A) No change

   (B) Either I will find a way—or I will make one.

   (C) Either I will find a way, or I will make one.

   (D) Either I will find a way; or I will make one.

   (E) Either I will find a "way," or I will make one.

9. Now is the watchword of the wise. —*Charles H. Spurgeon*
   (A) No change
   (B) Now, is the watchword of the wise.
   (C) Now is: the watchword of the wise.
   (D) "Now" is the watchword of the wise.
   (E) "Now", is the watchword of the wise.

10. There is only one success: to be able to spend your life in your own way. —*Christopher Morley*
    (A) No change
    (B) There is only one success, to be able to spend your life in your own way.
    (C) There is only one success; to be able to spend your life, in your own way.
    (D) There is only one "success", to be able to spend your life—in your own way.
    (E) There is only, one success: the ability to spend your life in the manner in which you choose.

Answers and Explanations

1.   B

(B) is the most concise, with effective parallel structure.

2.   C

The original has inconsistent pronouns. (B) uses the passive voice, so it's wordy. (D) uses superfluous commas; no commas are needed.

3.   C

The clause *that are well rooted* is essential, so it should not be set off by commas. (B) is wordy. (D) and (E) misplace the modifier.

4.   B

The introductory subordinate clause should be followed by a comma, not a semicolon (A) or colon (C). The comma is missing in (D). (E) is wordy and indirect.

5. D

(A), (B), and (C) put quotation marks around an indirect quotation. (B) also puts the period outside the quotation marks. (B) and (E) incorrectly set off the indirect quotation.

6. C

Because the list follows a complete thought, it should be introduced by a colon, not a comma, (A) and (B), or a semicolon (E). There is no comma in any of the items in the list, so the items should not be separated by semicolons (D).

7. D

Quotations introduced by *said* should usually be preceded by a comma, not a colon, (A) and (B), or semicolon (C). (A) and (B) also incorrectly put the question mark outside the quotation marks. (E) omits the quotation marks.

8. B

A colon introduces lists, quotations, and explanations; it should not separate independent clauses (A). (B) and (C) are both correct; either a comma or a dash effectively separate independent clauses with a coordinating conjunction. Given the nature of the quotation, however, (B) is more emphatic and therefore more effective. A semicolon is incorrect when two clauses are connected by a coordinating conjunction. (E) incorrectly puts quotation marks around *way*.

9. D

The word *now* is being discussed—used specially—and should therefore be set off by quotation marks. (D) and (E) make this correction, but (E) incorrectly uses a comma to separate subject from verb. (B) makes this mistake as well.

10. A

The original is correct. The phrase *to be able to spend your life in your own way* explains the opening clause *there is only one success,* so the correct punctuation is a colon. (E) incorrectly has a comma between the cumulative modifiers.

If you felt a bit overwhelmed by the number of comma rules, take heart: the other punctuation marks have far fewer.

SEMICOLON

The semicolon's form actually reflects its function. Like a period, the semicolon separates two independent clauses; like a comma, it keeps them connected.

Between Two Independent Clauses

Two closely related independent clauses can be joined by a semicolon (with or without conjunctive adverb or other transitional word or phrase):

> *You* tell Sidney; he's less likely to be angry if he hears it from you.

> The polls suggest we are losing ground with young voters; however, our level of support from all other demographic groups remains strong.

FLASHBACK

Common conjunctive adverbs include *however, therefore, furthermore, similarly, still,* and *thus* (see chapter 1).

If one clause is independent and the other subordinate, a semicolon will create a sentence fragment. If the clauses are not closely related, they should not be connected:

> **Incorrect:** The first Oscars were awarded in 1927; this year, the nominees for best picture include three historical films.

In this case, even a coordinating conjunction isn't wise; the best punctuation between these two sentences is a period.

Practice 1

Determine whether the semicolon is correct and appropriate in each of the following sentences.

1. You don't get ulcers from what you eat; you get ulcers from what's eating you. —*Anonymous*

2. Without risk; faith is an impossibility. —*Søren Kierkegaard*

3. A failure is not always a mistake; it may simply be the best one can do under the circumstances. —*B.F. Skinner*

4. When we know how to understand our own hearts; we acquire wisdom of the hearts of others. —*Denis Diderot*

REMEMBER THIS!

Note that the key to correct use of the semicolon is twofold: (1) *both* clauses must be independent and (2) the sentences must be closely related.

Between Items in a Series

Generally, items in a series should be separated by commas, but if one or more items in a list contain a comma, use semicolons to separate each item:

> Bela's list of favorite bands includes Coldplay; Ween; and Crosby, Stills, Nash and Young.

When Not to Use a Semicolon

Semicolons are easy to misuse. **Do not** use a semicolon:

1. Between independent clauses joined by a coordinating conjunction. Use a comma (see chapter 15) or change the coordinating conjunction to a conjunctive adverb.

   Incorrect: I usually drink coffee; but today I'm drinking tea.

2. Between a subordinate and independent clause. Semicolons join grammatically equivalent parts. A subordinate clause and independent clause are not grammatically equal. Use a comma or make both clauses independent.

   Incorrect: Although I usually drink coffee; today I'm drinking tea.

3. To introduce a list. If there's any punctuation at all, it should be a colon (see the next section).

   Incorrect: Bela's list of favorite bands includes; Coldplay; Ween; and Crosby, Stills, Nash and Young.

Practice 2

Determine whether each space should be filled by a comma or a semicolon, or left blank.

1. Never be haughty to the humble_ never be humble to the haughty. —*Jefferson Davis*

2. It's great to be great_ but it's greater to be human. —*Will Rogers*

3. Truth must be preached again and again_ because error is constantly being preached round about. —*Johann Wolfgang von Goethe*

4. If it is not seemly_ do it not_ if it is not true_ speak it not. —*Marcus Aurelius Antoninus*

COLON

The colon's main function is to introduce quotations, lists, summaries, or explanations.

Introducing Quotations

Quotations introduced by an independent clause should be preceded by a colon.

> According to Maria Tatar, the power of fairy tales lies in their ability to help us cope: "Fairy tales register an effort to develop maps for coping with personal anxieties."

If the quotation is introduced by a phrase or subordinate clause, use a comma if necessary; otherwise, no punctuation is needed.

> According to Maria Tatar, "[f]airy tales register an effort to develop maps for coping with personal anxieties."

> Maria Tatar states that "[f]airy tales register an effort to develop maps for coping with personal anxieties."

If the quotation is introduced with *said* or other words of dialogue, use a comma, not a colon, even if the introduction is a full sentence.

> **Incorrect:** Professor Grimes said: "Pay particular attention to word choice in this poem."

Introducing Lists

If a list is introduced by an independent clause, separate the clause and list with a colon:

> Be sure to pack the following items: a sleeping bag, a flashlight, bug spray, and a canteen.

However, do not use a colon to introduce (1) a series of objects or complements following a verb, (2) a series of objects following a preposition, or (3) a list introduced by *such as, including,* or *for example* (these words already introduce, so a colon is redundant).

Incorrect:	Be sure to <u>pack: a sleeping bag</u>, a flashlight, bug spray, and a canteen. [The colon incorrectly separates the verb from its objects.]
Incorrect:	You will find that I <u>am: outgoing</u>, intelligent, kind, and modest. [The colon incorrectly separates the linking verb from its complement.]

Practice 3

Determine whether the colons in the following sentences are correct.

1. Henry L. Doherty said: "It is the studying that you do after your school days that really counts."

2. I like what Henry L. Doherty has to say about education: "It is the studying that you do after your school days that really counts."

3. According to Henry L. Doherty: "It is the studying that you do after your school days that really counts."

4. If you think education ends when you graduate, consider this thought by Henry L. Doherty: "It is the studying that you do after your school days that really counts."

5. According to Henry L. Doherty, our formal education is the least important part of our learning: "It is the studying that you do after your school days that really counts."

Introducing Summaries or Explanations

Use a colon to introduce a word, phrase, or clause that summarizes or explains the preceding sentence. When what follows a colon is a complete clause, the first letter should be capitalized.

> The Allies' mission was twofold: to halt the advance of German troops near the capital and to open up a safe supply route to the city.

> If you smoke, I have but one word of advice: Quit.

Don't insert a colon before a summary or explanation that is a subject complement.

> Incorrect: Luck is: an accident that happens to the competent. —*Albert M. Greenfield*

Minor Uses of the Colon

1. To separate salutation from body in a formal or business letter: Dear Eleanor:
2. To separate hours and minutes: We'll meet at 2:45.
3. To show ratios or proportions: The chances of winning the lottery are 1:10,000,000.
4. To separate titles from subtitles: The most-taught novel in college campuses continues to be Mary Shelley's masterpiece *Frankenstein; or, The Modern Prometheus.*
5. To separate city and publisher in a bibliography: Shelley, Mary. *Frankenstein; or, The Modern Prometheus.* New York: Penguin Putnam, 1994.

Practice 4

Correct any colon, semicolon, or comma errors in the following sentences.

1. The tongue is: more to be feared than the sword.
   —*Japanese proverb*
2. Life is like a game of poker: If you don't put any in the pot; there won't be any to take out. —*Moms Mabley*
3. Experience is the worst teacher, it gives the test before presenting the lesson. —*Vernon Law*
4. Complacency is: the enemy of progress. —*Dave Stutman*

DASH

A favorite punctuation mark of many writers, the dash is often used in places where a comma, semicolon, colon, or parenthesis would also be correct. Writers choose the dash instead because it's dramatic.

> We were alone—all alone at last—and I was too nervous to tell her how I feel.

> We were alone, all alone at last, and I was too nervous to tell her how I feel.

The dashes emphasize the writer's emotions; the commas are correct, but deflating.

Don't overuse the dash: that defeats its purpose and makes your writing choppy. Unless you have a specific reason for using it, stick to the more conventional punctuation marks.

To Set off Appositives with Commas

Appositives—nouns or noun phrases that rename nearby nouns—should generally be set off by commas. But if an appositive contains commas, use dashes.

> Everything that I'd packed—my suitcases, my golf clubs, and a box of presents—was lost by the airline.

Practice 5

Correct any inappropriate uses of the dash in the following sentences.

1. You do not lead by hitting people over the head—that's assault, not leadership. —*Dwight D. Eisenhower*

2. Delegating work works—providing the one delegating works, too. —*Robert Half*

3. Conscience is the inner voice that warns us—that someone may be looking. —*H.L. Mencken*

4. The three parts of the mind—the id, the ego, and the superego—are often in conflict; it is our task to manage them properly.

QUOTATION MARKS

Quotation marks have three main functions:

To Set Off Direct Quotations

Any **direct** quotation—of a person, book, article, song, etc.—should be enclosed in quotation marks.

> Eric Hoffer said, "We lie loudest when we lie to ourselves."

Direct vs. Indirect Quotations

Be sure to distinguish between direct and indirect quotations. Indirect quotations *are not* enclosed in quotation marks.

Direct:	Ivy said, "Did you know a ten-minute shower uses 50 gallons of water?"
Indirect:	According to Ivy, a ten-minute shower uses 50 gallons of water.

Long Quotations

When quoting poetry or prose and the quotation is more than four full lines of text or more than three lines of poetry, omit the quotation marks. Instead, indent the quotation.

> In Anne Sexton's version of "Little Red Riding Hood," deception itself, not the wolf, is the true villain:

> The wolf, they decided, was too mean
> to be simply shot so they filled his belly
> with large stones and sewed him up.
> He was as heavy as a cemetery
> and when he woke up and tried to run off
> he fell over dead. Killed by his own weight.
> Many a deception ends on such a note.

Quotations within Quotations

A quotation that appears within a quotation is set off using single quotes.

> In his August 2003 article in *The Nation*, Joe Conason explains the term "compassionate conservative": "'Compassionate' softens 'conservative,' a word that tends to be associated with smug stinginess."

Practice 6

Correct any quotation mark errors in the following sentences.

1. According to Juanita Lawes, "Frankenstein's greatest error was not in creating the creature but in abandoning him, leaving him a "miserable wretch" forever."

2. Piu said "his favorite novel is *Frankenstein*."

3. Piu said, "My favorite novel is *Frankenstein*."

4. There is no failure, "said Elbert Hubbard," except in no longer trying.

Around Titles

Titles of short works or portions of long works should appear in quotation marks (see chapter 17 for longer titles). Short works include: newspaper and magazine articles, short stories, poems, chapters or sections of books, songs, episodes of television or radio programs.

Thus, the title of Bob Dylan's song "Tangled Up in Blue" should be in quotation marks while the album title, *Blood on the Tracks*, belongs in italics.

Words Used In Special Ways

On those occasions when you want to discuss a particular word (e.g., what it means, how it is used, etc.), enclose it in quotation marks.

The word "fiction" comes from the Latin verb "fingere," which means to make or shape.

Italics may also be used for this purpose (as we've done throughout this book). Either option is acceptable, as long as you are consistent.

When a word is being used sarcastically or ironically, however, only quotation marks will do:

My "free" vacation ended up costing me over $2,000.

Only put slang or common expressions in quotation marks to call attention to those words.

Incorrect: Hendrix tries too hard to "play it cool."

Quotation Marks and Other Punctuation Marks

One common area of confusion is where to place other punctuation marks when you have a quotation. Fortunately, there are only two rules:

1. In American usage, periods and commas always go **inside** the quotation marks.

   "I need a new job," Juno said. "This one is driving me crazy."

2. Colons, semicolons, dashes, question marks and exclamation marks go **inside** if they are part of the quotation and **outside** if they apply to the whole sentence.

   Colin said excitedly, "There it is!"—and there it was, barely visible: the Statue of Liberty.

   Harrison wrote, "Dear Jane: I cannot tell you how deeply you hurt me"; then he tore up the paper and threw it away, deciding it was best to speak to Jane in person.

Practice 7

Insert quotation marks where needed in the following sentences.

1. Do not say illicit when you mean elicit.
2. Read Chapter 3: Invertebrates for next class.
3. The Love Song of J. Alfred Prufrock is one of T. S. Eliot's most famous poems.
4. The 1951 film *The Day the Earth Stood Still* is based on the short story Farewell to the Master by Harry Bates.
5. Charlotte's big secret was something we all already knew.

SUMMARY

Semicolons are used primarily to separate independent clauses that are closely related. They can be connected with or without a transitional word or phrase. Semicolons should also be used to separate items in a series if one or more of those items contains a comma.

Colons have three major functions: to introduce quotations, lists, and summaries or explanations that are introduced by an independent clause. If the quotation is introduced by *said*, use a comma. Never use a colon between a verb and its objects or complement, between a preposition and its object, or after *such as, including*, and *for example*.

Minor functions of the colon include separating a salutation from the body of the letter, separating hours and minutes, showing ratios or proportions, separating titles and subtitles, and separating city and publisher in a bibliography.

The **dash** sets off words, phrases or clauses for emphasis. It should be used sparingly, only when an idea really deserves to be set off.

Finally, **quotation marks** set off direct quotations, titles of short works, and words being used in a special way within sentences. Long quotations should be indented and quotation marks omitted. If you have a quotation within a quotation, use single quotation marks (') for the internal quotation. Periods and commas always go inside quotation marks; semicolons, colons, dashes, question marks, and exclamation points go inside the quotation marks only if they are part of the quotation.

Practice: On Your Own

Imitation is the best form of flattery. Look through some of your favorite novels or stories, or your favorite magazine or newspaper for sample sentences using the punctuation marks discussed in this chapter. Try to find examples of all the different uses (e.g., the three different functions of the colon). Using those sentences as models, craft your own sentences following a similar sentence structure.

Practice Answers and Explanations

Practice 1

1. Yes. Both clauses are independent and directly related.
2. No. The semicolon incorrectly separates a phrase (*without risk*) from an independent clause.
3. Yes. Both clauses are independent and directly related.
4. No. The first clause is subordinate, so the semicolon should be a comma.

Practice 2

1. Semicolon. Both clauses are independent and there is no coordinating conjunction, so a comma would create a sentence fragment.
2. Comma. The independent clauses are connected by a coordinating conjunction, so a comma is the correct punctuation mark.
3. No punctuation is necessary. If the subordinate clause preceded the independent clause, a comma would be required, but the sentence as it stands is correct.
4. The correct punctuation is as follows: *If it is not seemly, do it not; if it is not true, speak it not.* The subordinate *if* clauses should be set off by commas and the two *if...do* complex sentence pairs connected by a semicolon.

Practice 3

1. No. Use a comma with the *he said* construction.
2. Yes. The quotation is introduced by a full sentence.
3. No. The introduction is only a phrase, so the punctuation mark should be a comma.
4. Yes. The introduction is a complete sentence.
5. Yes. The introduction is a complete sentence.

Practice 4

1. Delete the colon; do not use a colon to introduce an explanation that is a subject complement.
2. The colon correctly introduces an explanation, but the semicolon should be a comma (*if...pot* is a subordinate clause, not an independent clause).
3. The comma creates a sentence fragment because it stands alone between two independent clauses. A semicolon would be correct since the clauses are closely related. A colon is even more correct as the second clause explains the first (telling us *why* experience is the worst teacher).
4. Delete the colon; it incorrectly separates the linking verb *is* from its complement *the enemy of progress*.

Practice 5

1. The dash is appropriate.
2. The dash is appropriate.
3. The dash is unnecessary. Why separate the subordinate clause? It is especially awkward because the clause is essential to the sentence.
4. The dashes appropriately set off the appositive which contains commas.

Practice 6

1. The quotation marks around *miserable wretch* and *become linked to the chain of existence* should be single quotation marks (') since they are quotations within a quotation.
2. This is an indirect quotation, so there shouldn't be any quotation marks.
3. Correct.
4. The quotation marks are around the speaker tag (*said Elbert Hubbard*), not around what Hubbard said. The correct placement is as follows: "There is no failure," said Elbert Hubbard, "except in no longer trying."

Practice 7

1. Do not say "illicit" when you mean "elicit." [Period goes inside quotation mark.]
2. Read "Chapter 3: Invertebrates" for next class.
3. "The Love Song of J. Alfred Prufrock" is one of T. S. Eliot's most famous poems.
4. The 1951 film *The Day the Earth Stood Still* is based on the short story "Farewell to the Master" by Harry Bates.
5. Charlotte's "big secret" was something we all already knew.

CHAPTER 16 TEST

Is the punctuation correct in each of the following? How might you improve it?

1. If we are ever to enjoy life, now is the time; not tomorrow, nor next year, nor in some future life after we have died. —*Thomas Dreier*
2. The Jester Brothers' new song Ice Cold is getting a lot of radio play lately.
3. Love is blind; friendship closes its eyes. —*Anonymous*
4. Life is the greatest bargain, we get it for nothing. —*Yiddish proverb*
5. Doing what you like is freedom, liking what you do is happiness. —*Frank Tyger*
6. Some people grow under responsibility: others merely swell. —*Carl Hubbell*
7. Never mind your happiness, do your duty.—-*Will Durant*
8. Thinking well is wise, planning well, wiser, doing well, wisest and best of all. —*Persian proverb*
9. No is always a door-closing word: Yes is a door-opening word. —*Thomas Dreier*
10. According to Desiderius Erasmus: "Every definition is dangerous".

11. My grandfather once told me that there are two kinds of people: those who do the work and those who take the credit. —*Indira Gandhi*

12. Amateurs hope, professionals work. —*Garson Kanin*

13. What did Lindsay mean when she said "We need to take a break?"

14. The editorial Justice for Mall is worth reading.

15. Never to have changed—what a pitiable thing of which to boast! —*Johann Wolfgang von Goethe*

16. If you look closely, you will see, that the numbers increase at a ratio of 1–3.

17. A friend is a person who knows all about you: and still likes you. —*Elbert Hubbard*

18. My favorite episode of *Seinfeld* is The Parking Garage, when Kramer spends the whole day trying to find his car.

19. Hey guys listen to this, Dear Miss Manners, How can I get my husband to stop barking when he's hungry?

20. Happiness is not a reward, it is a consequence. —*Robert G. Ingersoll*

Answers and Explanations

1. The punctuation is not wrong, but the dash would set off the list for emphasis. *If we are ever to enjoy life, now is the time—not tomorrow, nor next year, nor in some future life after we have died.*

2. Song titles are enclosed in quotation marks, and because the title is not essential, it should be set off by commas. *The Jester Brothers' new song, "Ice Cold," is getting a lot of radio play lately.*

3. No correction needed.

4. The colon correctly sets off the explanation for why life "is the greatest bargain." *Life is the greatest bargain: we get it for nothing.*

5. The two independent clauses are closely related and should be connected by a semicolon. *Doing what you like is freedom; liking what you do is happiness.*

6. These two independent clauses are also closely related and should be separated by a semicolon. *Some people grow under responsibility; others merely swell.*

7. Again, the two independent clauses are closely related and should be connected by a semicolon. A pair of dashes would make the quotation choppy. *Never mind your happiness; do your duty.*

8. The items in the series contain commas, so they should be separated by semicolons. *Thinking well is wise; planning well, wiser; doing well, wisest and best of all.*

9. The two words are being discussed, so they should be enclosed in quotation marks. The two clauses are closely related and should be connected by a semicolon. *"No" is always a door-closing word; "yes" is a door-opening word.*

10. The quotation is introduced by a phrase, so a comma and quotation marks are correct. The period belongs inside the quotation marks. *According to Desiderius Erasmus, "Every definition is dangerous."*

11. No correction needed. The colon correctly introduces the explanation of the two kinds of people. It is an indirect quotation.

12. The two independent clauses are closely related, so they should be separated by a semicolon. Dashes would make the sentence choppy. *Amateurs hope; professionals work.*

13. The direct quotation should be introduced by a comma and enclosed in quotation marks. The question mark is part of the whole sentence and should be outside the quotation marks. *What did Lindsay mean when she said, "We need to take a break"?*

14. The title of the editorial should be enclosed in quotation marks. The title is essential to the meaning of the sentence so it should not be set off by commas. *The editorial "Justice for Mall" is worth reading.*

15. No correction needed. The dash effectively sets off the introduction from the main clause. The exclamation point suggests that the dash is ideal, indicating emotion.

16. The introductory clause needs to be set off by a comma, but the comma after *see* and the object (the *that* clause) is incorrect. The ratio is correctly expressed by a colon between the numbers. *If you look closely, you will see that the numbers increase at a ratio of 1:3.*

17. The dash effectively sets off the phrase *and still likes you*, highlighting the implied idea that there are things about each of us that are not necessarily likeable. Colons should never be inserted between the parts of a compound verb. *A friend is a person who knows all about you—and still likes you.*

18. The title of the episode needs to be enclosed in quotation marks, and the comma belongs inside the marks. *My favorite episode of* Seinfeld *is "The Parking Garage," when Kramer spends the whole day trying to find his car.*

19. Direct address (*guys*) should be set off by commas, and the quotation from the letter introduced by a colon. The quotation needs to be enclosed in quotation marks with the question mark inside the quotation marks. The salutation *Dear Miss Manners* needs to be separated from the letter by a colon. *Hey, guys, listen to this: "Dear Miss Manners: How can I get my husband to stop barking when he's hungry?"*

20. The best choice for punctuation between these independent clauses is the dash, which highlights the idea that happiness is the result of our actions. *Happiness is not a reward—it is a consequence.*

CHAPTER 17

End Marks, Apostrophes, and the Rest

Start with this 10-question Building Block Quiz. The first few questions test material you've already seen.

BUILDING BLOCK QUIZ

Identify which underlined portion (if any) contains an error. If there is no error, choose (E)

1. Despite her discomfort, in the weeks following her surgery,
   (A)   (B)
   Amelia enjoyed rereading some of her favorite novels,
                                                         (C)
   including: *Emma* and *The Shipping News*. <u>No error</u>
   (D)   (E)

2. Ever since I've <u>known</u> him, Sameer <u>hasn't never</u> varied his
                     (A)   (B)   (C)
   morning routine; each day he gets up at 5:00, runs five miles,
                    (D)
   showers, and goes to work. <u>No error</u>
                              (E)

3. The problem <u>I think</u> is that the boards are too wide; they
                (A)   (B)(C)
   don't quite match the rest of the fence, do they? <u>No error</u>
                                                      (D) (E)

4. Did you <u>know that</u> the ballpoint pen was invented by two
            (A)
   Hungarian brothers, Ladislas and Georg Biro, in <u>1935. No error</u>
                       (B)   (C) (D)   (E)

5. Yes, every <u>boy/girl</u> in the school <u>(including kindergarteners)</u>
    (A)   (B)   (C)

   will take the test, and the results will be used to <u>assess</u>
                                              (D)

   achievement of state standards. <u>No error</u>
                             (E)

6. I <u>have read</u> <u>Fatimas</u> play, and I think she is a remarkable
    (A)   (B)

   writer—the play is <u>simply phenomenal</u>. <u>No error</u>
                  (C)   (D)

7. In a strange coincidence, everyone in the <u>doctor's</u> waiting
                                      (A)

   room, including the pharmaceutical sales representative,
    (B)

   <u>had graduated</u> in the late <u>1980's</u>. <u>No error</u>
    (C)   (D)   (E)

8. <u>Ferguson's</u> allegations, which shocked the entire community,
    (A)   (B)

   are <u>being</u> investigated by the <u>F.B.I.</u>. <u>No error</u>
    (C)   (D)   (E)

9. Well, if I have to choose right now, I guess <u>I'll</u> pick...that one
    (A)   (B)   (C)

   over <u>there</u>. <u>No error</u>
      (D)   (E)

10. The pitcher <u>threw</u> a curve ball. Quintero swung with all his
             (A)   (B)

   might! It was a grand slam! <u>No error</u>
    (C)   (D) (E)

Answers and Explanations

1. D

Do not use a colon after *including*.

2. C

Hasn't never is a double negative.

3. A

The parenthetical expression *I think* should be set off by commas.

4. D

This is a direct question, so the sentence should end in a question mark, not a period.

5. B

The *boy/girl* paired construction is awkward, informal, and unnecessary. The writer should use *boy and girl* or *student*.

6. B

Fatimas needs an apostrophe to show possession.

7. D

Do not use apostrophes to make plural numbers, especially dates; simply add *s*.

8. D

Abbreviations for organizations do not take periods: *FBI*, not *F.B.I.* Also, if a sentence ends in an abbreviation with a period, do not add an additional period.

9. E

There is no error. The ellipsis (…) is correctly used to show hesitation in speech.

10. C

The exclamation point is overused. It is effective after the last sentence.

This chapter answers some of those burning questions you've had about punctuation: When can you use an exclamation point? How do you use an ellipsis? And just what are brackets for?

END MARKS

Few of us need much help with the period, question mark, or exclamation point.

The Period

All sentences except direct questions and exclamations should end in a period.

Statement: It's getting late.

Statement   Géza wants to know if you're ready to go.
(indirect question):

The Question Mark

A direct question should be followed by a question mark. If you have a series of questions, each question can be followed by a question mark, even if each question is not a complete sentence.

Indirect: Cameron asked who is in charge around here.

Direct: "Who is in charge around here?" Cameron asked.

Series: Did you pack your pajamas? Your toothbrush? Your medication?

If a sentence ends in a question mark, do not add a period. A question mark *is* an end mark, so no other punctuation is necessary. (The same is true for the exclamation point, below.)

Incorrect: What time is it?.

Correct: What time is it?

> ### REMEMBER THIS!
> Only use question marks for direct questions.

The Exclamation Point

Genuine exclamations—words, phrases, or clauses that express strong emotions or forceful commands—take the exclamation point as their end mark.

This is the most exciting day of my life!

"Duck!" Melinda yelled as Chet threw an icy snowball toward my head.

In the second example, the quotation gets the exclamation point, not the entire sentence—and the exclamation point is inside the quotation marks.

Don't overuse the exclamation point. It is generally considered informal (commonly used in comic strips, for example), and overuse will reduce the impact of true exclamations.

Practice 1

Correct any errors in end mark punctuation in the sentences below.

1. The results are in! We won!
2. You don't know where you're going, do you.
3. Juanita asked me whether I thought it was a good idea?
4. Are you absolutely certain you turned off and unplugged the iron.
5. "Hey. It's my turn" Genevieve wailed!

FLASHBACK

Remember, end marks go inside quotation marks.

Periods in Abbreviations

The period is also used in many abbreviations. Generally, abbreviations for social, professional, and academic titles, time references, and common Latin terms have periods; abbreviations for names of states and organizations do not.

There are no spaces after the periods in abbreviations. When in doubt about an abbreviation, consult a dictionary or style guide. Here are some notes on using abbreviations correctly:

1. If a sentence ends in an abbreviation that uses a period, do not add another period.

> **Incorrect:** Someday, I will be Bakhtan Balarasan, <u>Ph.D.</u>

Period(s)	No Period(s)
Social titles: **Mr., Mrs., Ms., Jr., Sr.** Professional titles or rank: **Dr., R.N., D.D.S., Sgt.**	State names: **PA, CA, TX** Organization names: **UN, FTC, NASA, NAACP, CIA, YMCA**

Academic titles:
B.A., M.A., Ph.D.
Time references:
B.C., B.C.E., A.D.; a.m.
Latin abbreviations:
i.e., e.g., vs., et al., etc.
Quantities or measurements:
lb., in., oz., no.

2. Do not abbreviate titles *unless* they appear with a name.

 Incorrect: My <u>dr.</u> said I should stay in bed for about a week.

 Correct: <u>My doctor</u> said I should stay in bed for about a week.

3. To use an abbreviation that isn't familiar to your readers, write out the full word(s) followed by the abbreviation in parentheses; thereafter you may use the abbreviation.

 Incorrect: The <u>AFWA</u> reports an unusual weather pattern over the North Pole.

 Correct: The <u>Air Force Weather Agency (AFWA)</u> reports an unusual weather pattern over the North Pole.

4. Use time and number abbreviations only with specific numbers.

 Incorrect: Kobe wakes early every <u>A.M.</u>

 Correct: Kobe wakes at <u>6 A.M.</u> every morning.

5. Avoid informal abbreviations of days of the week, months, measurements, names, states, company names, and academic subjects.

 Incorrect: Ty <u>Bros. Co.</u> has a big <u>Xmas</u> sale each <u>Dec.</u>

 Correct: Ty <u>Brothers Company</u> has a big <u>Christmas</u> sale each <u>December</u>.

Practice 2

Correct any errors in abbreviations in the following sentences.

1. Tamar earned her BS degree in just three yrs.
2. The rev. roused the sleepy congregation with a soaring homily.
3. Maj Wrubleski has a reputation for being especially tough on new recruits.
4. Representatives of the local S.P.C.A. will be soliciting donations outside the store tomorrow.
5. The SLCS (submarine laser communication system) is still under development.

THE APOSTROPHE

The apostrophe has two uses you know well: to show possession and omission.

Possessives

Most nouns and indefinite pronouns (e.g., *someone, anybody*) show possession by adding the apostrophe and –*s*.

<u>Uncle Ming's</u> homemade dumplings were the hit of the party.

Nouns ending in –s

For singular nouns ending in –*s*, add both the apostrophe and –*s* unless the pronunciation will be awkward.

The <u>witness's</u> statement sounded forced.

For plural nouns ending in –*s*, only add the apostrophe.

The <u>witnesses'</u> statements corroborated the defendant's story.

Joint possession and compound nouns

When two or more nouns share possession of an item, add the apostrophe only to the last noun. However, if each individual possesses the item, show possession for each noun.

Individual: <u>Roxanne's</u> and *Ravi's* dogs won prizes in the dog show. [Roxanne and Ravi each own dogs.]

Joint: <u>Roxanne and Ravi's</u> dogs won prizes in the dog show. [Roxanne and Ravi jointly own the dogs.]

To Show Omission

Use the apostrophe when you omit one or more letters from a word or numbers from a date.

I <u>can't</u> believe <u>you're</u> going without me.

Say what you like about disco; I still love the music of the <u>'70s</u>.

"<u>Ain't</u> gonna do <u>nothin'</u> <u>'bout</u> it," Seth said.

> ### REMEMBER THIS!
> In writing, if you take something away, you must leave something in its place.

Incorrect Uses

Avoid the following common misuses of the apostrophe.

1. **To form plurals.** Plurals are formed *only* with *-s* (or *-es*)—not with an apostrophe.

   Incorrect: The <u>dog's</u> chased the cat up the tree.

2. **With possessive pronouns.** The possessive pronouns (*mine, yours, his, whose,* etc.) already show possession; to add an apostrophe is both incorrect and redundant (see chapters 1 and 14).

   Incorrect: Is this jacket <u>your's</u> or <u>her's</u>?

3. **With plural numbers and letters.** Don't use the apostrophe to make plural numbers and letters. Use only the plural *-s* or *-es* for numbers. To make a letter plural, italicize or capitalize the letter and add *-s* or *-es* unless the result is a word. In that case, use the apostrophe to prevent confusion.

   Incorrect: There are two <u>10's</u> missing from this deck of cards.

   Correct: There are two <u>10s</u> missing from this deck of cards.

   Incorrect: Both of the <u>M's</u> had faded, so the sign read "Toy's" instead of "Tommy's."

   Correct: Both of the <u>*M*s</u> had faded, so the sign read "Toy's" instead of "Tommy's."

   Correct: There are four <u>*i*'s</u> and four <u>*s*'s</u> in *Mississippi*. [Without the apostrophe, readers might mistake *is* for *is;* use the apostrophe for both letters for consistency.]

4. **With plural abbreviations and words used specially.**
   Abbreviations and words used specially don't need an apostrophe for the plural (unless the word is in quotation marks).

Incorrect:	There are no <u>ATM's</u> around here.
Incorrect:	You can bury me in <u>*please's*</u>, but I still won't let you go to that party.
Correct:	You can bury me in <u>*pleases*</u>, but I still won't let you go to that party.
Correct:	You can bury me in "<u>please's</u>," but I still won't let you go to that party.

Practice 3

Correct any apostrophe errors in the following sentences.

1. Alanas résumé is very impressive, isnt it?
2. The past three winters' have been colder than normal.
3. The 1980's is known as the "me" decade.
4. Who's keys are these—your's or their's?
5. My mother keeps complaining that people in their 20's are so impatient.

ALL THE REST

Parentheses

Parentheses set off information that is supplemental or tangential—a minor example, a digression, an afterthought. In that sense, they are the opposite of the dash, which sets off ideas for emphasis. Parentheses are also used for numbering items in a list as well as for citation material.

My brother has many nicknames (including Bullfrog, Tadpole, and T-Man, to name a few), but he only ever answers to the name Eugene.

Which would you rather have: (a) $1,000,000 in one lump sum or (b) $100,000 a year for life?

The fiscal crisis that ensued was due "solely to the greed of a few top managers" (Jacobs 113).

Do not use a period at the end of a statement inside of parentheses unless the parenthetical statement is a complete sentence *and* the final parenthesis comes after a full stop.

> **Incorrect:** My favorite versions of the Grimm fairy tales are in Roald Dahl's collection *Revolting Rhymes* (his baby bear, for example, eats up the bratty Goldilocks.).
>
> **Correct:** My favorite versions of the Grimm fairy tales are in Roald Dahl's collection *Revolting Rhymes*. (His baby bear, for example, eats up the bratty Goldilocks.

Formal writing should contain few parenthetical thoughts. As you revise, see how many of your parenthetical ideas can be worked into the text or omitted.

FLASHBACK

Parenthetical remarks that are not enclosed in parentheses should be set off by commas (see chapter 15).

Brackets ([])

Brackets indicate that you have added words to, or changed words in, a quotation.

> In his memoir, Carlson confessed that he "never knew just how devoted [his] mother was to her music until after she died." [The original text was in the first person, so the author changed *my* to *his* for clarity.]

Brackets indicate stage directions in a play. (These lines are from Henrik Ibsen's 1879 play *A Doll's House*.)

> NORA [*looking incredulously at her*] But Kristine, how could that be?
>
> MRS. LINDE [*smiling wearily and smoothing her hair*] Oh, sometimes it happens, Nora.

As you've seen over and over in this text, brackets can also set off special instructions or explanations.

Practice 4

Correct any errors in the use of parentheses or brackets in the following sentences.

1. Do you want to 1. go to the movies, 2. go out to dinner, or 3. both?

2. Charles meets Lulu [his sister] at the grocery store (but he doesn't find out she's his sister until the end of the play.).

3. In the final scene, Joy [crying softly] confesses to Hitch (her dying son), "Dylan (Hitch's coach) is your real father, and he's loved you more than you'll ever know."

4. The committee meets bi-weekly (twice a month) in the library conference room.

Ellipsis (...)

Ellipsis has two uses: (1) to indicate that you have deleted one or more words from a quotation and (2) to indicate hesitation, interruption, or unfinished thought in speech. (If you delete a full sentence or more from a quotation, use an additional period after the ellipsis.)

> In his memoir *Factory of Facts*, Luc Sante acknowledges that the theme of loss is a constant for exiles... My parents lost friends, lost family ties and patterns of mutual assistance, lost rituals and habits and favorite foods, lost any link to an ongoing social milieu....We lost connection to a thing larger than ourselves, and as a family failed to make any significant new connection in exchange.

The first ellipsis indicates that only part of a sentence was omitted. The second—four periods—indicates that a full sentence or more was omitted.

In MLA (Modern Language Association) format, put brackets around any ellipsis you use in a quotation to make it clear that *you* omitted text and that the ellipsis did not appear in the original quotation.

If you omit a full line or more of a poem that you are quoting, use a full line of ellipses:

> In John Donne's "Holy Sonnet 10," the speaker attempts to "dethrone" death:

> Death, be not proud, though some have called thee
> Mighty and dreadful, for thou art not so;
> ....
> Thou art slave to fate, chance, kings and desperate men,
> And dost with poison, war, and sickness dwell.

Do not use ellipsis at the beginning or end of a quotation, even if you are only quoting part of a sentence.

> **Incorrect:** Sante writes that "…the theme of loss is a constant for exiles…"
>
> **Correct:** Sante writes that "the theme of loss is a constant for exiles."

Slash (/)

Finally, the slash has two main uses: (1) to separate lines of poetry (with a space before and after the slash) and (2) to separate words that are paired (in which case, there is **no** space before or after the slash).

> Donne's poem addresses Death directly: "Death, be not proud, though some have called thee / Mighty and dreadful, for thou art not so."

> I decided to register for this course pass/fail rather than simply audit it.

Another use of the slash is generally considered informal and should be used sparingly, if at all. Instead, use *and* or *or* and write out the word pair if possible:

> **Incorrect:** Every student must cast <u>his/her</u> vote by noon.
>
> **Correct:** Every student must cast <u>his or her</u> vote by noon.

Practice 5

Here is a paragraph from the introduction to Ralph Waldo Emerson's essay "Nature."

> All science has one aim, namely, to find a theory of nature. We have theories of races and of functions, but scarcely yet a remote approach to an idea of creation. We are now so far from the road to truth, that religious teachers dispute and hate each other, and speculative men are esteemed unsound and frivolous. But to a sound judgment, the most abstract truth is the most practical. Whenever a true theory appears, it will be its own evidence. Its test is, that it will explain all phenomena.

> 1. How would you punctuate the following, which omits part of one sentence.
>
>   But the most abstract truth is the most practical.

2. How would you punctuate the following, which omits the second, third, and fourth sentences?

> All science has one aim, namely, to find a theory of nature. Whenever a true theory appears, it will be its own evidence. Its test is, that it will explain all phenomena.

SUMMARY

Most sentences should end in a **period**. A sentence that asks a direct question should end in a **question mark**. Sentences that express strong emotion (e.g., interjections) or forceful commands should end in an **exclamation point**.

Periods are used in many **abbreviations**. In general, abbreviations of social, professional, and academic titles; time references; Latin abbreviations; and quantities or measurements should have periods. Sentences ending in an abbreviation with a period do not take another period. Titles should only be abbreviated if used with names. Unfamiliar abbreviations should be written out first, with the abbreviation in parentheses. Time and number abbreviations should only be used with specific numbers, and informal abbreviations (e.g., *Mon.* or *phys. ed.*) should be avoided.

Apostrophes show possession and omission. To show possession, add an apostrophe and *–s* (if the noun is plural and ends in *–s*, or if adding *–s* to a singular noun ending in *–s* makes an awkward pronunciation, add only the apostrophe). To show joint possession, add the apostrophe only to the last noun. Do not use the apostrophe to make plurals or with possessive pronouns, except to prevent confusion.

Parentheses set off supplemental or tangential information. **Brackets** indicate added words or changed words in a quotation, and set off stage directions in a play.

Ellipsis indicates omitted words in a quotation, or hesitation or interruption in speech. A **slash** separates lines of poetry and paired words such as *either/or*.

Practice Answers and Explanations

Practice 1

1. The results are in. We won! [The exclamation point is overused in both sentences; it is much more effective if left only on the second sentence.]

2. You don't know where you're going, do you? [This is a direct question and should end in a question mark. (Note the comma setting off the question tag.)]
3. Juanita asked me whether I thought it was a good idea. [This is a statement, not a question, so it should end in a period.]
4. Are you absolutely certain you turned off and unplugged the iron? [This is a direct question and should end in a question mark.]
5. "Hey! It's my turn!" Genevieve wailed. [The wailing merits exclamation points, so set the exclamation points after the exclamations in the quotation marks. The sentence itself should end in a period.]

Practice 2

1. Tamar earned her <u>B.S.</u> degree in just three <u>years</u>. [Use periods in academia degrees and avoid informal abbreviations.]
2. The <u>reverend</u> roused the sleepy congregation with a soaring homily. [Only abbreviate titles if they appear with names.]
3. <u>Maj.</u> Wrubleski has a reputation for being especially tough on new recruits. [Use periods for title abbreviations.]
4. Representatives of the local <u>SPCA</u> will be soliciting donations outside the store tomorrow. [Do not use periods in abbreviations for organizations.]
5. The <u>submarine laser communication system (SLCS)</u> is still under development. [State the full name of an unfamiliar organization or item first, then its abbreviation in parentheses.]

Practice 3

1. <u>Alana's</u> resume is very impressive, <u>isn't</u> it? [*Alana's* is possessive, not plural; *isn't* is a contraction needing an apostrophe.]
2. The past three <u>winters</u> have been colder than normal. [*Winters* is plural, not possessive.]
3. The <u>1980s</u> is known as the "me" decade. [No apostrophes for decades or other numbers.]

4. <u>Whose</u> keys are these—<u>yours</u> or <u>theirs</u>? [No apostrophes in possessive pronouns.]

5. My mother keeps complaining that people in their <u>20s</u> are so impatient. [No apostrophe with plural numbers.]

Practice 4

1. Do you want to (1) go to the movies, (2) go out to dinner, or (3) both? [Put parentheses around the numbers; the periods create confusion.]

2. Charles meets Lulu (his sister) at the grocery store, but he doesn't find out she's his sister until the end of the play. [Brackets aren't used to set off supplemental information; the parentheses in the original version set off important information that should be incorporated into the sentence.]

3. In the final scene, Joy, crying softly, confesses to Hitch, her dying son, "Dylan [Hitch's teacher] is your real father, and he's loved you more than you'll ever know." [The brackets are incorrect; though the sentence discusses a play, these are not stage directions. The first parentheses can be replaced by commas for an appositive. The parentheses in the quotation should be brackets.]

4. The committee meets bi-weekly in the library conference room. [The parenthetical information is unnecessary (redundant) and can be eliminated.]

Practice 5

1. To omit part of a sentence, use a single ellipsis: "But … the most abstract truth is the most practical." If using MLA format, the ellipsis should be in brackets: "But […] the most abstract truth is the most practical." Do not start or end the quotation with ellipsis.

2. To omit a full sentence or more, use the ellipsis plus a period for a total of four periods: "All science has one aim, namely, to find a theory of nature…. Whenever a true theory appears, it will be its own evidence. Its test is, that it will explain all phenomena."

CHAPTER 17 TEST

Identify which change, if any, is needed to correct each sentence.

1. Today's "smart home" technologies enable home owners to remotely access and control audio, video, telephone, and/or computer networks from anywhere in the home.

   (A) Delete the apostrophe in *today's*.

   (B) Change *and/or* to *and*.

   (C) Change commas to semicolons.

   (D) Add an apostrophe before the *s* in *owners*.

   (E) No change

2. The looting of archeological treasures is a serious problem worldwide, not just in war-torn region's, although countries at war are particularly at risk for losing their cultural and historical treasures.

   (A) Delete the apostrophe in *region's*.

   (B) Add an apostrophe before the *s* in both *treasures*.

   (C) Change the second comma to a semicolon.

   (D) Change the period to an exclamation point.

   (E) No change

3. Is it ethical to release a drug that could help hundreds of thousands of people if a small enough percentage of users risk serious side effects. What percentage is "small enough"?

   (A) Add an apostrophe before the *s* in *users*.

   (B) Change the period to a question mark.

   (C) Change the question mark to a period.

   (D) Put the question mark inside the quotation marks.

   (E) No change

4. The question you need to answer is whether or not the attorney has a conflict of interest in accepting this case?
   (A) Delete *or not*.
   (B) Set *of interest* off with commas.
   (C) Insert a colon after *is*.
   (D) Change the question mark to a period.
   (E) No change

5. As Picasso puts it, art "…is a lie that makes us realize the truth…"
   (A) Change the comma to a colon.
   (B) Delete the quotation marks.
   (C) Delete the ellipses before and after the quote.
   (D) Delete only the ellipsis after the quote.
   (E) No change

6. In James Finn Garner's number one best-seller (*Politically Correct Bedtime Stories*), "Cinderella" ends with all the men at the ball killing each other in a "macho dance of destruction."
   (A) Move the period outside the quotation marks.
   (B) Delete the parentheses.
   (C) Move the parentheses to around *number one best-seller*.
   (D) Change the period to an exclamation point.
   (E) No change

7. The women (spelled *womyn* throughout the text to avoid having *men* in the word) live happily ever after after "set[ting] up a clothing co-op that produce[s] only comfortable, practical clothes for womyn."
   (A) Delete the parentheses.
   (B) Delete the first brackets.
   (C) Delete both sets of brackets.
   (D) Insert ellipsis before *set[ting]*.
   (E) No change

8. The class of 96 will present a special gift to the university at its ten-year reunion in April.

    (A) Change *April* to *Apr.*

    (B) Insert an apostrophe before *96*.

    (C) Change *its* to *it's*.

    (D) Put parentheses around *to the university*.

    (E) No change

9. Our cat UFO (short for Unique Feline Organism) licked it's paws and curled up on the pillow, purring contentedly.

    (A) Put *UFO* in the parentheses.

    (B) Change *it's* to *its*.

    (C) Change *paws* to *paw's*.

    (D) Insert periods in *UFO*.

    (E) No change

10. Dear Mr. Holmes: Enclosed please find a copy of my invoice from Sept. Please remit ASAP as the invoice is now several months past due. Thx.

    (A) Write out *Sept.*, *ASAP*, and *Thx*.

    (B) Write out only *ASAP*.

    (C) Insert periods between letters in *ASAP*.

    (D) Change *Thx* to *thank you*.

    (E) No change

11. Carlito tried to open the door, but it was locked! So was the other one! How was he going to get out?

    (A) Change the question mark to an exclamation mark.

    (B) Change the first exclamation point to a period.

    (C) Change both exclamation points to periods.

    (D) Change both exclamation points to question marks.

    (E) No change

12. After Shaban's and Beti's house sold for 25% more than their asking price, several other families in the neighborhood decided to put their houses up for sale, too.

    (A) Delete the *'s* in *Shaban's*.

    (B) Delete the apostrophe in both *Shaban's* and *Beti's*.

    (C) Change *their* to *they're*.

    (D) Change *families* to *family's*.

    (E) No change

13. Javan still writes his b's and d's backwards, but otherwise he has mastered the alphabet much more quickly than I'd expected.

    (A) Change the comma to a semicolon.

    (B) Change *b's and d's* to *B's and D's*.

    (C) Change *b's and d's* to *Bs and Ds*.

    (D) Change *he* to *he's*.

    (E) No change

14. In the opening lines to "Blessing for the Liver," David Keplinger writes that "the heart with its lies, is a lesser thing."

    (A) Insert ellipses before and after the quotation, inside the quotation marks.

    (B) Change the comma to a slash.

    (C) Insert slashes at the beginning and end of the quotation.

    (D) Insert brackets around the quotation.

    (E) No change

15. It doesn't really matter what you decide, because I am going with/without you—Celeste needs me!

    (A) Change the exclamation point to a period.

    (B) Change the dash to a colon.

    (C) Change *with/without* to *with or without*.

    (D) Change *with/without* to *with...or without*.

    (E) No change

16. I just have one question for you, Irving: How much are you willing to sacrifice to make this dream a reality.

    (A) Change the colon to a semicolon.

    (B) Put *How…reality* in quotation marks.

    (C) Change the colon to a question mark.

    (D) Change the period to a question mark.

    (E) No change

17. I want a car that gets at least 18 m.p.g. and that I can finance at a reasonable APR.

    (A) Change *APR* to *A.P.R.*

    (B) Change *m.p.g.* to *mpg.*

    (C) Change *APR* to *A.P.R.* and add a period at the end of the sentence.

    (D) Change *m.p.g.* to *miles per gallon* and *APR* to *rate.*

    (E) No change

18. After surveying both crime scenes, Det. Mombasa had no doubt that the two robberies were the work of the same thief.

    (A) Change *Det.* to *det.*

    (B) Change *Det.* to *detective.*

    (C) Change *scenes* to *scene's.*

    (D) Change *were* to *we're.*

    (E) No change

19. "We're goin fishin," Bubba said "Do you wanna come?"

    (A) Move the comma outside the quotation mark.

    (B) Add apostrophes to the end of *goin* and *fishin.*

    (C) Delete the apostrophe in *we're.*

    (D) Move the question mark outside the quotation mark.

    (E) No change

20. "Giles needs to take his P.M. medicine," Patricia told the R.N. on duty.

 (A) Change *P.M.* to *evening* and *R.N.* to *nurse*.

 (B) Change *P.M.* to *pm* and *R.N.* to *RN*.

 (C) Change *P.M.* to *P.M.*

 (D) Move the comma outside of the quotation mark.

 (E) No change

Answers and Explanations

1. B

Avoid informal uses of the slash.

2. A

Regions should be plural, not possessive, so the apostrophe must be deleted.

3. B

Both sentences are direct questions, so both should end in question marks.

4. D

This sentence is an indirect question and should end in a period.

5. C

Do not use ellipses at the beginning or end of a quotation, even if the quotation is only part of a sentence.

6. B

The title of the book is not supplementary information and should not be enclosed in parentheses.

7. E

This sentence is correct.

8. B

The year 1996 is abbreviated to *96*; an apostrophe should show the omission of the *19*.

9. B

The cat's name *is* UFO—it's not an abbreviation. The error in this sentence is *it's*, the contraction for *it is* (see chapter 14).

10. A

All three of these informal abbreviations should be written out.

11. C

None of these sentences are strong enough to warrant an exclamation point. The question mark at the end of the third sentence, a direct question, is correct.

12. A

Shaban and Beti own the house together, so add the apostrophe and –'s to *Beti* only.

13. C

Do not use the apostrophe to make plurals of letters except to prevent confusion. Here, the best correction is to capitalize the letters or italicize them.

14. B

Use a slash to separate lines of poetry.

15. C

Avoid informal uses of the slash.

16. D

What follows the colon is a direct question and should end in a question mark.

17. D

Both of these informal abbreviations should be written out.

18. E

This sentence is correct.

19. B

Both *goin* and *fishin* are missing the final *g;* mark this omission with an apostrophe.

20. A

Don't use *P.M.* except with a specific time. Don't abbreviate titles unless used with a name.

CHAPTER 18

Spelling, Capitalization, and Italics

Start with this 10-question Building Block Quiz. The first few questions test material you've already seen.

BUILDING BLOCK QUIZ

Determine which underlined portion, if any, contains an error in grammar, mechanics, or style. If there is no error, choose E.

1. I think <u>it's</u> an <u>ingenuous</u> idea, Shashi; <u>however,</u> I don't think
      (A)   (B)   (C)   (D)
   it's very practical. <u>No error</u>
              (E)

2. <u>Here's</u> an interesting fact for <u>you:</u> more deer are killed by
    (A)   (B)
   drivers each year <u>than</u> by <u>hunter's</u>. <u>No error</u>
            (C)   (D)   (E)

3. If you think <u>Americans</u> are not wasteful, think again: <u>We</u> use
            (A)   (B)
   more than 67 million tons of paper each year—that's 580 <u>lbs.</u>
                                                   (C)
   per person! <u>No error</u>
            (D)

4. The highest point in Ohio is said to be <u>mount rumpke,</u>
                                      (A)
   a "<u>mountain</u>" that is really a giant landfill owned by Rumpke,
       (B)
   one of the <u>largest</u> waste and recycling <u>companies</u> in the
            (C)   (D)
   nation. <u>No error</u>
         (E)

5. Steven <u>Siegel's</u> massive sculpture <u>Scale</u> appears at first to be a giant
(A)   (B)

    block of stone, but it is really <u>composed</u> of 20,000 pounds of
(C)

    <u>recycled</u> newspaper that will eventually begin to degrade. <u>No error</u>
(D)   (E)

6. Siegel's sculpture is on <u>permanent</u> display at the
(A)

    <u>Sculpture Garden</u> of the Abington <u>art center</u> in Jenkintown,
(B)   (C)   (D)

    Pennsylvania <u>No error</u>
(E)

7. <u>Neither</u> option is <u>desireable</u>, but if we have no other choice,
(A)   (B)

    <u>then</u> we should take Johnson's <u>advice</u> and reallocate our
(C)   (D)

    funds. <u>No error</u>
(E)

8. While many <u>over the counter</u> cold <u>remedies</u> are safe during
(A)   (B)

    pregnancy, pregnant women should always consult <u>their</u>
(C)

    <u>doctor</u> before taking any medication. <u>No error</u>
(D)   (E)

9. Elise is bidding on a <u>coop</u> in the new <u>Myer Building</u>
(A)   (B)

    <u>downtown</u>, but she is <u>worried</u> that she will end up in
(C)   (D)

    a bidding war. <u>No error</u>
(E)

10. The <u>secretarys</u> in the office have filed a joint complaint <u>alleging</u>
(A)   (B)

    sexual <u>harassment</u> by several top <u>managers</u> at the firm. <u>No error</u>
(C)   (D)   (E)

Answers and Explanations

1. B

Ingenious is the correct word in this context, not *ingenuous*.

2. D

Hunters should be plural, not possessive; delete the apostrophe.

3. D

The informal abbreviation *lbs.* is inappropriate and should be written out.

4. A

The proper noun *Mount Rumpke* should be capitalized.

5. B

The title of the sculpture *Scale* should be italicized.

6. C

The name of a specific place should be capitalized: *Abington Art Center*.

7. B

The *e* in *desire* should be dropped when adding a suffix beginning with a vowel.

8. A

The words *over the counter* work together to form one modifier for *cold remedies*, so they should be hyphenated: *over-the-counter*.

9. A

Coop should be hyphenated—*co-op*—to differentiate it from *coop*.

10. A

When forming the plural of words ending in –*y*, if the *y* is preceded by a consonant, change the *y* to *ie* before adding –*s*.

Mark Twain hated spelling "merely for the reason that when I was a boy there was not a thing I could do creditably except spell according to the book. It was a poor and mean distinction, and I early learned to disenjoy it."

That said, there remain the practical matters of communicating clearly in the workplace and personal correspondence, or of hurdles like graded essays and exams.

SPELLING

English spelling may seem illogical or haphazard, but there are a few powerful rules.

General Rules

Rule 1: *I* before *e* except after *c*, unless the sound is *a* or *i*.

I **before e:** relief, achieve, believe, lien, field, chief, mischief, friend, thief

Except after c: deceive, conceive, receive

Unless the sound is *a* or *i*: eight, veil, height, weight, neighbor

There are numerous exceptions, including *either and neither* (for those who pronounce those words with a long e sound instead of an *i* sound), *counterfeit, caffeine, weird, foreign, seize, protein, skein, leisure, science,* and *conscience.*

Rule 2: Form plurals of most words by adding –*s*.

Add –*s* to nouns ending in –*s, -sh, -ch,* and –*x*. For most nouns ending in *f*, change the *f* to a *v* before adding –*es*.

letters	foxes	wishes	thieves

Rule 3: Form plurals of hyphenated words by adding the –*s* to the main word.

editors-in-chief	forget-me-nots

Rule 4: Form plurals of most words derived from foreign languages as they would in their original language.

-um → -a	medi<u>um</u> → medi<u>a</u>
-us → -i	alumn<u>us</u> → alumn<u>i</u>
-a → -ae	vertebr<u>a</u> → vertebr<u>ae</u>
-sis → -ses	hypothe<u>sis</u> → hypothe<u>ses</u>
-on → -a	criteri<u>on</u> → criteri<u>a</u>

Rule 5: If a word ends in a silent –*e*, drop the e if adding a suffix that begins with a vowel. Keep the e if the suffix begins with a consonant.

live → li<u>ving</u>, lively	erase → eras<u>ed</u>, era<u>sure</u>

Exceptions include *argument, truly,* and *changeable.*

Rule 6: If a word ends in *–y* that is preceded by a consonant, change the *y* to *ie* when adding *–s* or *–d*. If the *y* is preceded by a vowel, keep the *y*.

chutney → chutneys   lily → lilies

Exceptions include proper names ending in *–y* (e.g., *Mahonys*).

Rule 7: If the stress falls on the final syllable and the final vowel is short, double the consonant when adding a suffix beginning with a vowel.

If the consonant is a *c*, use *ck* instead of doubling the *c*.

Double	Don't Double
hop → hopped	hope → hoped
fat → fatten	fate → fated
occur → occurrence	label → labeled
panic → panicked	reveal→ revealing

> ### REMEMBER THIS!
> Double the final consonant when adding a suffix if the preceding vowel needs to be kept short.

The main exception is words with two vowels that sound short. For example, *ea* usually produces the long *e* sound (as in *plead*), but in *head*, the vowel sound is short. Since there's an extra vowel (the *a*) between the first vowel and the consonant to keep the vowel short, there's no need to double the consonant.

head → heading

Practice 1

Circle the correct spelling of the word in parentheses in each sentence.

1. These (merry-go-rounds / merries-go-round) were built in the late 1800s.
2. The most important (criteria / criterions) for the award are originality and effectiveness of design.
3. We must remain in the shelter while the flood waters are (recedeing / receding).

4. I am simply (dreadding / dreading) my physics exam.

5. The (O'Mallys / O'Mallies) are heading to the Grand Canyon for a month-long vacation.

6. I am (transferring / transfering) money from my savings to my checking account to make a down payment on a new car.

Hyphenation

Here are the half-dozen rules for proper hyphen use.

Rule 1: Use hyphens to connect some compound nouns.

Some compound nouns are hyphenated, others are not; some are combined into one word, others stay as two separate words. When in doubt, consult a dictionary.

compound, hyphenated: mother-in-law, cross-examination

compound, one word: roommate, pigtail, sunlight

compound, separate words: test tube, right of way

Rule 2: Use hyphens to connect words functioning together as a modifier.

When two or more words work together to create one modifier for a noun or pronoun that follows them, hyphenate them. Do not use hyphens when they *follow* the noun.

Correct: Charlise is a <u>well-known</u> photographer.

Incorrect: Charlise's photographs are <u>well known</u>.

Rule 3: Hyphenate the prefixes *all-*, *ex-* (when *ex-* means *former*) and *self-*.

Practicing meditation has made me more <u>self-confident</u>.

The team's <u>all-out</u> effort game after game led it to the state championships.

Chloe's <u>ex-boyfriend</u> is still devastated by their breakup.

Most other words formed with prefixes do not have hyphens, except if the second element is capitalized or a number (*anti-Semitic, pre-1800s, mid-May*).

Rule 4: Hyphenate fractions and compound numbers from twenty-one to ninety-nine.

My grandmother turned <u>ninety-five</u> yesterday.

The tank is <u>three-quarters</u> full.

Rule 5: Use hyphens to divide words between syllables at the end of a line.

Divide words *only* between syllables. Don't separate the final syllable unless it is more than two letters.

Rule 6: Use hyphens as needed to avoid ambiguity or separate awkward doubling or tripling of letters.

The <u>re-creation</u> of the accident made it clear who was at fault.

This is a <u>non-negotiable</u> offer.

Practice 2
Insert any necessary hyphens.

1. I made a list of my short and long term goals.
2. Make sure your records are up to date before you register for the fall semester.
3. The movie tells the story of an excon who falls in love with his parole officer.
4. I thought it was an all expense paid vacation, but I had to pay for my airfare.
5. Please resort these beads by size, not color.

Practice 3
Indicate with a slash where each word could be divided at the end of a line.

1. egregious
2. microphone
3. stadium
4. blatantly
5. renovation

Top 100 Homophones

Homophones—unrelated words that sound alike—bedevil us all. They're one of the main reasons you need to proofread carefully.

*An asterisk indicates a mnemonic device in the Memory Tips that accompany each list.

MEMORY TIPS

* An *arc* is curved like a *c*.

* A *censor* *c*uts; a *sensor* *s*ees.

* You *hear* with your *ear*.

* All three words in the phrase *whole wide world* begin with *w*.

* The *inn* is crowded because there are two *n*s.

* You *peer* with your two *eyes*.

* You add –*s* to form the plural: It's nice to get lots of *presents* on your birthday.

* When you were learning to read, you were *taught* that the *gh* in words like *taught, caught,* and *bought* is silent.

ad, add
aide, aid
air, ere, err, heir
arc, ark*
bail, bale
bare, bear
beat, beet
berth, birth
boar, bore
board, bored
bough, bow
brake, break
bread, bred
bridal, bridle
broach, brooch
buy, by, bye
cede, seed
censor, sensor*
cent, scent, sent
cereal, serial
creak, creek
dear, deer
die, dye
fair, fare
flair, flare
flew, flu, flue
flour, flower
for, fore, four
foreword, forward
foul, fowl
gait, gate
grate, great
grisly, grizzly
hail, hale

hall, haul
heal, heel
hear, here*
hoard, horde
hoarse, horse
hole, whole*
in, inn*
lead, led
lean, lien
loan, lone
main, mane
mall, maul
marshal, martial
meat, meet, mete
medal, meddle
moose, mousse
morning, mourning
muscle, mussel
oar, or, ore
pail, pale
pain, pane
pair, pare, pear
peace, piece
peak, peek, pique
peal, peel
pedal, peddle
peer, pier*
plain, plane
pole, poll
poor, pore, pour
pray, prey
presence, presents*
profit, prophet
raise, rays, raze

read, reed
real, reel
reek, wreak
role, roll
root, route
sail, sale
scene, seen
seam, seem
seas, sees, seize
sew, so, sow
shear, sheer
slay, sleigh
soar, sore
sole, soul
some, sum
stair, stare
stake, steak
steal, steel
tail, tale
taught, taut*
tea, tee
threw, through
to, too, two
troop, troupe
vain, vane
vial, vile
waist, waste
wait, weight
ware, wear, where
way, weigh, whey
weak, week
yoke, yolk

Top 100 Frequently Misspelled Words

absence
accommodate*
acknowledge
acquaintance
acquire
amateur
apparently
appearance
arithmetic
arrangement
ascend
attendance*
basically
bureau
calendar
campaign
cannot
cemetery
column
congratulations
conqueror
conscience*
conscientious
conscious
correspondence
definite*
descend, descendant
development
dictionary*
disastrous
eighth
eligible
embarrass
environment

especially
exaggerate
exercise
exhaust
existence
extraordinary
extremely
fascinate
grammar
grateful
harass
humorous
incident, incidentally
incredible
independence,
   independent*
indispensable
irrelevant
irresistible
knowledge
license
loneliness
maintenance
maneuver
marriage
mathematics
mischievous
necessary
noticeable
occasion*
pamphlet
parallel
particularly
pastime

permissible
perseverance
phenomenon
physically
playwright
practically
precede
preference, preferred
prejudice
prevalent
privilege*
proceed
professor, profession
pronunciation
questionnaire
responsible
restaurant
rhythm
roommate
schedule
separate*
sergeant
sincerely
sophomore
subtle, subtly
succeed
surprise
thorough
unanimous
unnecessarily
vacuum
vengeance
villain

MEMORY TIPS

* *Accommodate* has four pairs: two *a*'s, two *c*'s, two *m*'s, and two *o*'s.
* *Attendance*: You attend a dance.
* *Conscience* contains the word *science*.
* *Definite*: We definitely have two eyes; *definite* has two *i*'s.
* A *dictionary* starts with the letter A.
* *Independence* and *independent* depend upon *e*'s.
* *Occasion*: There was a lot to see (two *c*) on the occasion.
* *Privilege*: The vowels in this word are privileged to be in pairs (two *i*'s, then two *e*'s).
* *Separate*: The *e*'s are separated by the *a*'s.

Practice 4

Choose the correct homophone(s) within parentheses.

1. This design is stunning, but I don't think the bridge will be able to (bare / bear) (wait / weight) in the center.
2. If you come over (hear / here) you can (hear / here) the noise clearly.
3. I (kneed / need) to (buy / by / bye) a car by the weekend so I can get to my (knew / new) job on Monday.
4. Julianne and Brad parked (their / there / they're) car over (their / there / they're), but you can pull into the driveway.
5. The storyteller was annoyed by the children who talked all (threw / through) the (tail / tale).

A Note About Spell Checkers

If spelling is not your forte, spell checkers in word processing programs can be a tremendous help. But they do *not* eliminate the need for proofreading. Both *fair* and *fare* are spelled correctly, but only one will be correct in context.

Capitalization

Even minor capitalization errors can be disconcerting for readers, so it's important to master these dozen rules.

Rule 1: Capitalize proper nouns.

Proper nouns are the *specific* names of people, places, and things.

Woodrow Wilson	Parker Avenue
Bright Eyes Coffee Company	La Jolla Public Library

Family titles such as *mom* and *dad* should be capitalized only when used as a proper name (as when you directly address that person):

Correct: My <u>mom</u> is going back to college to finish her degree.

Correct: Hey, <u>Mom</u>, are you really going back to college to finish your degree?

Rule 2: Capitalize the first word in a sentence.

This applies to email and other online communications, too.

Rule 3: Capitalize the first word of a quoted sentence but not a quoted word or phrase.

Capitalize: To Divjani, "The intensity with which we worship celebrities is profoundly disturbing."

Don't capitalize: Divjani is "profoundly disturb[ed]" by the "intensity with which we worship celebrities."

Rule 4: You *may* capitalize the first word after a colon if it begins an independent clause.

But you don't have to. As always, be consistent; capitalize all independent clauses after colons or don't capitalize any.

With capital: Here's my advice: Be honest, but don't share everything.

Without capital: Here's my advice: be honest, but don't share everything.

Rule 5: Capitalize abbreviations for organizations, corporations, departments and agencies, and radio and television stations.

The FBI was founded in 1908; the CIA was created 40 years later in 1947.

The program *Kids Korner* is on WXPN every night at 7:00.

We bought stock in UJB back when the company first started.

Rule 6: Capitalize the first word and all important words in the titles of publications, movies, songs, and works of art.

Do not capitalize prepositions (e.g., *of, for, in*) or articles (*a, the*) except at the beginning of the title.

Hemingway's novel *For Whom the Bell Tolls* takes its title from John Donne's poem "Meditation XVII: No Man Is an Island."

My favorite Auguste Rodin sculpture is *The Kiss*.

Rule 7: Capitalize titles when they precede a name.

Capitalize: Captain Sirico plans to retire at the end of the year.

Don't capitalize: Sirico has been a captain for 20 years.

Rule 8: Capitalize the days of the week and months of the year.

The semester ends May 18; I start my internship on the first Tuesday in June.

Rule 9: Capitalize names of specific places and nouns and adjectives derived from them.

I'm a New Yorker through and through.

The Toledo Cathedral in Spain is the most amazing building I've ever seen.

Rule 10: Capitalize the names of special events and historical periods, but not centuries.

The Industrial Revolution began in the late eighteenth century in Great Britain.

The Academy Awards are held in February or March of each year.

Rule 11: Capitalize the names of countries, specific regions, languages, and religions, and adjectives derived from them.

According to the latest census, ninety-five percent of <u>Italians</u> are <u>Roman Catholic</u>.

Rule 12: Capitalize the names of the planets, stars, and other celestial structures.

The <u>Crab Nebula</u>, which is 6000 light years away, is the remnant of a supernova explosion that was visible from <u>Earth</u> in 1054.

What Not to Capitalize

- **Words used for emphasis.** Use italics instead: *never* rather than NEVER.
- The names of **academic subjects** (except languages, specific regions, and specific courses or departments).

  Incorrect: I am majoring in <u>Political Science</u>.

  Correct: My <u>Contemporary Political Science</u> class is fascinating.

- **Seasons:** Tomorrow is the first day of <u>spring</u>.
- The first word of an indirect quotation.

  Incorrect: Hedy told me that <u>She's</u> interested in joining our book group.

  Correct: Hedy told me that <u>she's</u> interested in joining our book group.

Practice 5

Correct any errors in capitalization in the following sentences.

1. Construction on the new Middle School begins next Month.
2. Connor is participating in the re-enactment of the battle of Germantown.
3. The new magic club is meeting Today at 3:00.
4. Take your forms to the financial aid office on the Third Floor in the Meyer building.
5. The MacAdoo annual flower and art show is coming up in april.
6. The dry earth was cracked and barren.
7. The Officer said, "there's an accident ahead; you'll have to turn around."

ITALICS

Italics—*slanted typeface*—and <u>underlining</u> serve the same functions in writing. Whichever you choose, be consistent. If you can't italicize or underline (e.g., in an email program), enclose the text in asterisks or underscore (e.g., *Looking Ahead* is a fine novel). Here are five rules:

Rule 1: Italicize or underline titles of long or major works.

This includes books, newspapers, magazines, plays, long poems, films, television and radio programs, musical compositions, works of visual or performance art, comic strips, software, and web sites.

This month's *Home Style* magazine has some excellent recipes.

The author of *American Mania* was recently interviewed on WHYY's *Radio Times*.

> **Exceptions:** Do not italicize or underline the Bible or books of the Bible, titles of legal documents, or the title of your own paper when writing an essay.

FLASHBACK

Titles of short works or portions of long works (e.g., a poem or chapter in a book) should be enclosed in quotation marks.

Rule 2: Italicize or underline foreign words.

DeeDee's *joie de vivre* is infectious.

Rule 3: Italicize or underline words used specially or (as you've seen in this chapter) letters used as letters.

The right word here is *allusion*, not *illusion*.

Rule 4: Italicize or underline names of ships, trains, aircraft, and spacecraft.

The *Queen Mary II* is the largest cruise ship in the world.

The *Sputnik II* carried the first living creature—a dog—into orbit.

Rule 5: Use italics or underlining to emphasize words or ideas.

As with exclamation points, excessive use of italics or underlining will detract from the emphasis and be distracting.

Ok, but this is the *last time*—I mean it!

Practice 6

Circle any words or phrases that should be italicized or underlined.

1. The Italian word for beautiful is bella.
2. The movie Apollo 13 is the true story of the spacecraft Apollo 13.
3. Oh, Anna, I'm so sorry!
4. Only the contraction they're gets an apostrophe, not their or there.
5. We have orchestra seats for tonight's performance of Handel's Messiah.

SUMMARY

General rules for correct **spelling** include:

1. *I* before *e*, except after *c*, unless the sound is *a* or *i*
2. Form the plural of most words by adding –*s*.
3. Form the plural of hyphenated words by adding –*s* to the main word.
4. Form the plural of most words derived from foreign languages as they would in their original language.
5. If a word ends in a silent –*e*, drop the *e* if adding a suffix that begins with a vowel. Keep the *e* if the suffix begins with a consonant.
6. If a word ends in a –*y* preceded by a consonant, change the *y* to *ie* when adding –*s* or –*d*.
7. If the stress falls on the final syllable and the final vowel is short, double a final consonant when adding a suffix beginning with a vowel.

Use a **hyphen:**

1. to connect some compound nouns (check a dictionary)
2. to connect words functioning together as a modifier
3. after the prefixes *all-, ex-* (when it means *former*), and *self-*
4. for fractions and compound numbers up to ninety-nine
5. to divide words between syllables at the end of a line
6. as needed to avoid ambiguity or awkwardness

Be alert for **homophones.**

Most people forget to **capitalize:**

1. the first and all important words in the titles of publications, movies, songs, and artworks
2. titles when they precede a name, but not if they follow a name or stand on their own
3. days of the week and months of the year, but not seasons
4. names of special events and historical periods, but not centuries
5. names of the planets, stars, and other celestial bodies and structures

Use **italics** or **underlining** for:

1. titles of long or major works (e.g., novels, movies, or newspapers)
2. foreign words
3. words used specially or letters used as letters
4. the names of ships, trains, aircraft, and spacecraft
5. to emphasize words or ideas (but only sparingly)

Answers and Explanations

Practice 1

1. merry-go-rounds
2. criteria
3. receding
4. dreading
5. O'Mallys
6. transferring
7. riches

Practice 2

1. short- , long-term [*short* and *long* both modify *term*]
2. No hyphens. *Up to date* follows the noun it modifies, so it isn't hyphenated.
3. ex-con
4. all-expense-paid
5. re-sort

Practice 3

1. e/gre/gious
2. mi/cro/phone
3. sta/dium [don't break the 2-letter ending]
4. bla/tantly [don't break the 2-letter ending]
5. re/no/va/tion

Practice 4

1. bear, weight
2. here, hear
3. need, buy, new
4. their, there
5. through, tale

Practice 5

1. Construction on the new <u>m</u>iddle <u>s</u>chool begins next <u>m</u>onth.
2. Connor is participating in the re-enactment of the <u>B</u>attle of Germantown.
3. The new <u>M</u>agic <u>C</u>lub is meeting <u>t</u>oday at 3:00.
4. Take your forms to the <u>F</u>inancial <u>A</u>id <u>O</u>ffice on the <u>t</u>hird <u>f</u>loor in the Ostermeyer <u>B</u>uilding.
5. The MacAdoo <u>A</u>nnual <u>F</u>lower and <u>A</u>rt <u>S</u>how is coming up in <u>A</u>pril.

6. The dry earth was cracked and barren. [Here *earth* refers to dirt, not the planet, so it is not capitalized.]

7. The <u>o</u>fficer said, "<u>T</u>here's an accident ahead; you'll have to turn around."

Practice 6

1. The Italian word for <u>beautiful</u> is <u>bella</u>.

2. The movie <u>Apollo 13</u> is the true story of the spacecraft <u>Apollo 13</u>.

3. Oh, Anna, I'm <u>so</u> sorry! [*So* could be italicized for emphasis.]

4. Only the contraction <u>they're</u> gets an apostrophe, not <u>their</u> or <u>there</u>.

5. We have orchestra seats for tonight's performance of Handel's <u>Messiah</u>.

CHAPTER 18 TEST

Determine which correction, if any, would most improve each sentence. If the sentence is correct, choose (E).

1. According to Scientists, the typical raindrop falls at the speed of 17 miles per hour.

    (A) Change the capital *s* in *Scientists* to a lower case *s*.

    (B) Change the comma to a colon.

    (C) Change *raindrop* to *rain-drop*.

    (D) Change *miles per hour* to *miles-per-hour*.

    (E) No change

2. Mothers to be crave nachos more than any other food, including ice cream and pickles.

    (A) Change mothers to be to mothers-to-be.

    (B) Capitalize nachos.

    (C) Change nachos to nachoes.

    (D) Change ice cream to ice-cream.

    (E) No change

3. It is officially against the law to burp or sneeze in a Church in Omaha, Nebraska.
   (A) Change against the law to against-the-law.
   (B) Change the capital c in Church to a lower case c.
   (C) Change the capital o in Omaha to a lower case o.
   (D) Change Nebraska to its abbreviation, NE.
   (E) No change

4. The eight year old child has already composed two symphonies that have been critically acclaimed and are being performed by orchestras around the world.
   (A) Change eight year old to eight-year-old.
   (B) Change symphonies to symphonys.
   (C) Change critically acclaimed to critically-acclaimed.
   (D) Change orchestras to orchestra's.
   (E) No change

5. The beauty of the California coastline, especially Big Sur, is unparallelled.
   (A) Capitalize *coastline*.
   (B) Italicize *Big Sur*.
   (C) Capitalize *unparallelled*.
   (D) Change *unparallelled* to *unparalleled*.
   (E) No change

6. Though you doubt my dedication, I am fully committed to seeing this project through.
   (A) Capitalize *dedication*.
   (B) Change *fully committed* to *fully-committed*.
   (C) Change *committed* to *commited*.
   (D) Change *through* to *threw*.
   (E) No change

7. Dancing is the raison d'etre for Zelda, who has been studying ballet since she was three years old.

    (A) Change dancing to danceing.

    (B) Italicize raison d'etre.

    (C) Italicize ballet.

    (D) Change three years old to three-years-old.

    (E) No change

8. According to *www.hookedonfacts.com*, "there are more nutrients in the Cornflakes package than there are in the Cornflakes."

    (A) Remove the italics from *www.hookedonfacts.com*.

    (B) Capitalize *there*.

    (C) Change *nutrients* to *nutreints*.

    (D) Change *there* to *their*.

    (E) No change

9. After school, we will meet at Zoey's pizza shop to work on our American History project.

    (A) Capitalize *we*.

    (B) Capitalize *pizza shop*.

    (C) Change the capital *H* in *History* to a lower case *h*.

    (D) Capitalize *project*.

    (E) No change

10. I always seem to spell foreign wrong; either I switch the *i* and *e* or forget the *g*.

    (A) Change *foreign* to *foriegn*.

    (B) Italicize *foreign*.

    (C) Capitalize *foreign*.

    (D) Capitalize *i*, *e*, and *g*.

    (E) No change

11. Tim O'Brien's novel *In The Lake Of The Woods* won the James Fenimore Cooper Prize for historical fiction.
    (A) Capitalize *novel*.
    (B) Remove italics from *In The Lake Of The Woods*.
    (C) Change *In The Lake Of The Woods* to *In the Lake of the Woods*.
    (D) Italicize *James Fenimore Cooper Prize*.
    (E) No change

12. A magician's job is to deceive the members of the audience with slieght of hand.
    (A) Capitalize *magician*.
    (B) Change *deceive* to *decieve*.
    (C) Change *audience* to *audeince*.
    (D) Change *slieght* to *sleight*.
    (E) No change

13. We are two thirds of the way to our goal of $450,000 for the new Greenlawn Children's Library.
    (A) Change two thirds to two-thirds.
    (B) Italicize $450,000.
    (C) Italicize Greenlawn Children's Library.
    (D) Change Children's Library to children's library.
    (E) No change

14. Monica firmly believes her son (who just turned two) will become President of the United States one day.
    (A) Change believes to beleives.
    (B) Change son to sun.
    (C) Change the capital p in President to a lower case p.
    (D) Italicize United States.
    (E) No change

15. Even though Iain is an assistant professor, he is openly antiintellectual and has alienated many of his colleagues.

    (A) Capitalize assistant professor.

    (B) Change assistant professor to assistant-professor.

    (C) Change antiintellectual to anti-intellectual.

    (D) Capitalize colleagues.

    (E) No change

16. Prasaad's play Unamerican has caused quite a stir and has reportedly caught the attention of several major movie studios.

    (A) Italicize *Unamerican*.

    (B) Change *major movie* to *major-movie*.

    (C) Capitalize *movie studios*.

    (D) Change *studios* to *studioes*.

    (E) No change

17. In Guy de Maupassant's short story "The Necklace," Madame Loisel borrows and loses what she believes to be a very valueable necklace.

    (A) Italicize *The Necklace*.

    (B) Change *loses* to *looses*.

    (C) Change *believes* to *beleives*.

    (D) Change *valueable* to *valuable*.

    (E) No change

18. All leaders should remember this quotation by Epicurus: "a man who causes fear cannot be free from fear."

    (A) Change *leaders* to *leader's*.

    (B) Capitalize *leaders*.

    (C) Capitalize *a*.

    (D) Italicize *Epicurus*.

    (E) No change

19. Oliver was extremly disappointed by the reviews of his first novel, but that didn't stop him from writing a second, and third, and fourth...

    (A) Change extremly to extremely.

    (B) Change reviews to reveiws.

    (C) Capitalize novel.

    (D) Change writing to writeing.

    (E) No change

20. "*You* are the *only* person in the *whole world* that I can trust!" Xavier exclaimed.

    (A) Delete italics from *you* and *only*.

    (B) Delete all italics.

    (C) Italicize *trust*.

    (D) Put the exclamation point outside the quotation mark.

    (E) No change

Answers and Explanations

1. A

The general noun *scientists* should not be capitalized.

2. A

Mothers-to-be should be hyphenated.

3. B

The general noun *church* should not be capitalized.

4. A

Eight-year-old is a compound modifier.

5. D

The final *l* shouldn't be doubled; the stress isn't on the final syllable.

6. E

The sentence is correct.

7. B

Foreign words should be italicized.

8. B

The first word of a full-sentence quotation should be capitalized.

9. B

Pizza shop is part of the title of the company and should be capitalized.

10. B

Words used specially should be italicized.

11. C

Except as the first word, prepositions and articles in a title shouldn't be capitalized.

12. D

Sleight is an exception to the *i* before *e* rule.

13. A

Fractions like *two-thirds* should be hyphenated.

14. C

Titles should only be capitalized if they precede a name.

15. C

Hyphenate *anti-intellectual* to prevent the awkward doubling of the letter *i*.

16. A

Titles of major works such as plays should be italicized.

17. D

The silent *e* at the end of *value* should be dropped when adding a suffix beginning with a vowel.

18. C

Since the quotation is a full sentence, its first word should be capitalized.

19. A

The silent *e* at the end of *extreme* should not be dropped when adding a suffix beginning with a consonant.

20. B

Use italics for emphasis sparingly; here, the exclamation point is sufficient, though you might italicize *only*.

CHAPTER 19

Grammar Source Cumulative Test

Congratulations! You've completed all 18 lessons. Now challenge yourself to pull together everything you've learned. Work carefully and read the answers and explanations thoroughly. If you miss a question, review the chapters that deal with the relevant topics.

Part A. Questions 1–5 refer to the following sentence:

> Love is what's left of a relationship after all the selfishness has been removed. —*Cullen Hightower*

1. In this sentence, *is* is a/an:
   (A) helping verb   (B) linking verb   (C) action verb
   (D) infinitive   (E) adverb

2. In this sentence, *love* is a/an:
   (A) noun (B) verb (C) adjective (D) adverb   (E) preposition

3. Which of the following excerpts from the sentence is a prepositional phrase?
   (A) love is   (B) of a relationship   (C) all the selfishness
   (D) has been removed   (E) none of the above

4. Which of the following excerpts is the subject complement?
   (A) what's left
   (B) of a relationship
   (C) after all the selfishness has been removed
   (D) what's left of a relationship after all the selfishness has been removed
   (E) none of the above

5. Which of the following excerpts is a subordinate clause?
   (A) love is what's left
   (B) of a relationship
   (C) after all the selfishness has been removed
   (D) has been removed
   (E) none of the above

Part B. For questions 6–20, identify the best version of each sentence based on grammar, mechanics, and style. If the original is best, choose (A).

6. Esperanza, like many children, want to be a fireman when she grows up.
   (A) No change
   (B) Esperanza, like many children, wants to be a fireman when she grows up.
   (C) Like many children, Esperanza wants to be a fireman when she grows up.
   (D) Like many children, Esperanza wants to be a firefighter when she grows up.
   (E) Wanting to be a firefighter when she grows up, Esperanza is like many children.

7. The word fetus means offspring in latin.
   (A) No change
   (B) The word *fetus* means *offspring* in Latin.
   (C) The word "fetus" means "offspring" in latin.
   (D) The word Fetus means Offspring in Latin.
   (E) The word fetus has the meaning of offspring in the language of Latin.

8. Did you know that a flag flying upside-down is a signal of distress.
   (A) No change
   (B) Did you know that a flag, flying upside-down, is a signal of distress?
   (C) Did you know, that a flag flying upside-down is: a signal of distress.
   (D) Did you know that if a flag is flying upside-down, that flag is a signal of distress?
   (E) Did you know that a flag flying upside-down is a signal of distress?

9. Refusing to compromise her artistic freedom, Yelena decided to produce the CD on her own.
   (A) No change
   (B) Refusing to compromise her artistic freedom, it was decided by Yelena to produce the CD on her own.
   (C) Refusing to compromise her artistic freedom, on her own, Yelena decided to produce the CD.
   (D) Refusing to compromise her artistic freedom, Yelena did decided to produce the cd on her own.
   (E) In an effort to avoid the compromising of her artistic freedom, Yelena adjudged that it behooved her to produce the cd on her own.

10. Each new member must serve on two committees in there first year.
    (A) No change
    (B) Each new member must serve, on two committees, in their first year.
    (C) Each new member must serve on two committees in his or her first year.
    (D) All new members must serve on two committees in their first year.
    (E) All members who are new must serve on two committees in the first year of their membership.

11. Name tags and school uniforms should be worn by all children to insure that they are easily identified while in the museum.
    (A) No change
    (B) While in the museum, name tags and school uniforms should be worn by all children to insure that they are easily identified.
    (C) Name tags and school uniforms should be worn to ensure that all children are easily identified while in the museum.
    (D) The wearing of name tags and school uniforms is required for all children while they are in the museum for the purpose that they be easily identified.
    (E) To assure that they are easily identified, name tags and school uniforms should be worn by all children in the museum.

12. Between you and I, the whole thing totally stinks.
    (A) No change
    (B) Between you and me, the whole thing stinks like a rotten egg.
    (C) Between you and me, the proposed changes are appalling.
    (D) Between you and I; the whole thing has a very foul odor.
    (E) Between you and me, the whole thing with the proposed changes is very upsetting.

13. In Pieter Bruegels painting Landscape With The Fall Of Icarus no one notices as Icarus falls into the sea.

   (A) No change

   (B) In Pieter Bruegel's painting *Landscape with the Fall of Icarus*, no one notices as Icarus falls into the sea.

   (C) In Pieter Bruegels painting, "Landscape with the Fall of Icarus," no one notices, as Icarus falls into the sea.

   (D) In Pieter Bruegel's painting Landscape With The Fall Of Icarus. No one notices as Icarus falls into the sea.

   (E) In the painting by Pieter Bruegel called Landscape with the fall of Icarus, the Death of Icarus is not noticed by anyone.

14. On my vacation I will go snorkeling, visit the rain forest, and attending local festivals.

   (A) No change

   (B) Snorkeling, visiting the rain forest, and attending local festivals are all things that I plan to do while on vacation.

   (C) On my vacation, I will do many things, including: go snorkeling, visit the rain forest, and attend local festivals.

   (D) On my vacation I will go snorkeling and visit the rain forest, I will also attend local festivals.

   (E) On my vacation, I will go snorkeling, visit the rain forest, and attend local festivals.

15. I have to lay down because I have a really bad headache.

   (A) No change

   (B) I have to lay down because I have a nasty headache.

   (C) I have to lie down because I have a monstrous headache.

   (D) I have to lie down because my head hurts a lot.

   (E) Because I have a really awful headache. I have to lie down.

16. I ordered stationary a month ago, it still has not arrived!
    (A) No change
    (B) The stationary I ordered—a month ago—has still not arrived.
    (C) I ordered stationery a month ago, however it still hasn't arrived!
    (D) I ordered stationery a month ago—and it still hasn't arrived.
    (E) I ordered stationary a month ago; and it STILL hasn't arrived.

17. If I were as talented as Arvina, I'd be on Broadway by now.
    (A) No change
    (B) If I was as talented as Arvina, I'd be "on Broadway" by now.
    (C) If I was as talented as Arvina. I'd be on Broadway by now.
    (D) If I were as talented as Arvina, Broadway is where I'd be by now.
    (E) If I was as talented as Arvina, I would have been on Broadway by now.

18. In my judgement, the best profs. are those who teach you how to think, not just tell us the facts.
    (A) No change
    (B) In my judgement, the best Professors are those who teach you how to think, not just tell you the facts.
    (C) In my judgement, the best profs. teach you how to think not just tell you the facts.
    (D) In my judgment, the best profesors teach us how to think, not just tell you the facts.
    (E) In my judgment, the best professors teach students how to think, not just tell them the facts.

19. I've always done really good in math but have lots of trouble with science.

(A) No change

(B) I've always done really well in Math but have lots of trouble with Science.

(C) I've always done really well in math but struggled with science.

(D) I've always done really good in math, but struggling with science.

(E) I've always did really well in math, but with science I've always struggled.

20. After a bazaar series of coincidences, Sev and Lucinda decide they must be meant for each other and got married.

(A) No change

(B) After a bazaar series of coincidences Sev and Lucinda decided they must be meant for each other and got married.

(C) After a bizarre series of coincidences; Sev and Lucinda decide they must be meant for each other and get married.

(D) After a bizarre series of coincidences, Sev and Lucinda decided they must be meant for each other and got married.

(E) After a series of coincidences that were bizarre—Sev and Lucinda decided they must be meant for each other— and got married.

Part C. The following paragraphs contain numerous errors in grammar, mechanics, and style. Identify as many as possible. How would you correct them?

The first living creature in Space was a small dog named, Laika, she was sent into orbit on the Sputnik II. In 1957. Laika completed seven orbits. Then the oxygen supply on the spacecraft ran out. Laika died. But not before she proved: that living creatures could survive in space.

Three and a half years later the first man went into orbit. That man was Yuri Gagarin. He was from the Soviet Union. He spent two-hours in space. Before he came back down. Less than a month later, was the first American astronaut, Alan Shepard Jr.. It was the shortest space flight in history. His spacecraft didn't go into orbit. It simply rose to an altitude of 115 miles and then returned to earth. The american John Glenn Jr. was the first American to orbit the earth a year later in 1962. He was also the oldest astronaut ever to go into space, thirty six years later when he was 77 he went back into orbit.

Answers and Explanations

Part A

1. B

A linking verb connects a subject to its complement—the part of the predicate that renames or defines the subject.

2. A

A noun is a person, place, or thing. While *love* can function as a verb (an action), in this sentence, *love* is a thing being defined in the sentence.

3. B

Of is a preposition, and *of a relationship* is a prepositional phrase.

4. D

The subject complement renames or defines the subject. Here, the entire predicate minus the linking verb is the subject complement.

5. C

A subordinate clause contains a subject and verb but cannot stand on its own. It often begins with a subordinating conjunction such as *after*.

Part B

6. D

There are two errors: the verb *want* does not agree with the singular subject *Esperanza* and *fireman* is sexist. (D) corrects both. The modifying phrase *like many children* is still next to the word it modifies (Esperanza) and now does not interrupt the subject-verb pattern. (E) changes the meaning of the sentence.

7. B

When words are used in special ways, they should be italicized. *Latin* should be capitalized. (E) is wordy.

8. E

The original asks a direct question; it needs a question mark. This is corrected in (E). (B) sets off the essential phrase *flying upside-down* in commas. (C) separates the essential clause *that…upside-down* from the verb *know*, and misuses a colon. (D) is wordy.

9. A

The original is best. (B) changes from active to passive, and, in the process, creates a vague antecedent problem: what does *it* refer to? (C) creates awkward word order and slightly changes the meaning. (D) mixes the past-tense *did* with the past-tense *decided*; if the helping verb *do* is in the past tense, the main verb should be in its simple form (*did decide*). It also does not capitalize *CD*. (E) is wordy and pretentious, and neglects to capitalize *CD*.

10. D

The original has an error in pronoun agreement: *each new member* is singular, but *there* (or more correctly *their*) is plural. (B) incorrectly sets off *on two committees* with commas. (C) is correct—*his or her* agrees with the antecedent—but (D) is less bulky. (E) is wordy.

11. C

The original contains an ambiguous pronoun (*they* could refer to the tags and uniforms or to the children) and uses the incorrect homophone *insure*. (C) is the best revision. The passive voice is useful here. (B) misplaces the modifier *while in the museum*. (D) is wordy. (E) also misplaces a modifier and uses a different but still incorrect homophone.

12. C

The original uses the subjective *I* instead of the objective *me* for the object of the preposition *between*. In addition, word choice is imprecise and slangy. (B) adds a cliché. (C) corrects the pronoun error and adds precise, appropriate language: *the proposed changes are appalling*. (D) incorrectly places a semicolon after the introductory prepositional phrase. (E) addresses the slang, replacing it with *is very upsetting*, but *appalling* is more powerful.

13. B

The original is missing the possessive apostrophe in *Brueghel's,* the title of the painting should be italicized, and the introductory phrase should be followed by a comma after *Icarus*. Furthermore, the words *with, the,* and *of* in the title should not be capitalized. (B) corrects these errors. (C) sets the title of the painting off in commas, but the title is essential. It also places the second comma outside of the quotation marks and incorrectly places a comma after the verb *notices*. (D) does not italicize the title and creates a sentence fragment. (E) makes the second half of the sentence passive and is wordy.

14. E

The original lacks parallel structure; *attending* should be *attend*. (B) reverses word order, adding unnecessary words and creating an awkward structure. (C) incorrectly places a colon after *including*. (D) is a run-on sentence and unnecessarily repeats *I will*.

15. C

(A) incorrectly uses *lay* instead of *lie* and uses imprecise language (*really bad*). (B) does improve the language, changing *really bad* to *nasty*, but (C) is better, using *monstrous*. (D) is less precise and effective than (C). (E) creates an imprecise sentence fragment.

16. D

The original uses the incorrect homophone *stationary* instead of *stationery*. More importantly, it is a run-on sentence and would be better off without the exclamation point. (B) incorrectly uses dashes, which should set off words or ideas for emphasis. (C) retains the run-on error (*however* is a conjunctive adverb and should be used with a semicolon). (D) correctly uses a dash to set off the second clause and italicizes *still* (instead of an exclamation point) to emphasize the speaker's frustration. (E) misuses a semicolon and incorrectly uses capitals for emphasis.

17. A

The original is the most clear and correct. The verb must be in the subjunctive (*were*) to express something contrary to fact. (B) incorrectly changes the verb to the simple past and incorrectly puts quotation marks around *on Broadway*. (C) creates a sentence fragment. (D) adds unnecessary words. (E) incorrectly changes the conditional *would* to the past progressive *would have been*.

18. E

The original has three errors: (1) it misspells *judgment* (which drops the *–e* in *judge*); (2) it abbreviates *professors*; and (3) its pronouns shift from the second-person to the third-person plural. (B) incorrectly capitalizes *professors* and retains the misspelling. Only (E) corrects all three original errors. It also eliminates the phrase *are those who* (not incorrect, but unnecessary) and changes the pronouns to the third person to make a more inclusive statement.

19. C

(A) uses *good* when it needs the adverb *well* to modify the verb *done*. (B) incorrectly capitalizes the subject areas *math* and *science*. (D) uses the participle *struggling* instead of the simple past-tense. (E) incorrectly uses the past-tense *did*; the past participle *done* should be used with the helping verb *have*. (C) correctly uses *well* and streamlines the sentence by using a more precise verb, *struggled*, instead of *have lots of trouble*.

20. D

(A) uses *bazaar* instead of *bizarre* and is inconsistent in verb tense. (B) incorrectly removes the comma after the introductory phrase. (C) incorrectly puts a semicolon after the introductory phrase (semicolons belong only between independent clauses or in a list with internal commas). (E) incorrectly uses dashes to set off the part of the main clause. The *second* dash alone might be fitting in this sentence, but the first should definitely be eliminated. Only (D) corrects the errors of the original without introducing another error.

Part C

The 20 errors in these paragraphs are marked with numbers in brackets; explanations follow. There are of course numerous errors in style as well, primarily in sentence structure. Thus after the explanations we offer a revision that includes variety in sentence structure and combines sentences as needed to reduce wordiness.

The first living creature in Space[1] was a small dog named,[2] Laika,[3] she was sent into orbit on the Sputnik II [4]. In 1957. [5] Laika completed seven orbits. Then the oxygen supply on the spacecraft ran out. Laika died. But not before she proved: [6]that living creatures could survive in space.

Three and a half years later[7] the first man[8] went into orbit. That man was Yuri Gagarin. He was from the Soviet Union. He spent two-hours[9] in space. Before he came back down.[10] Less than a month later, was the first American astronaut, Alan Shepard[11] Jr..[12, 13] It was the shortest space flight in history. His spacecraft didn't go into orbit. It simply rose to an altitude of 115 miles and then returned to earth[14]. The american[15] John Glenn[16] Jr. was the first American to orbit the earth[17] a year later in 1962. He was also the oldest astronaut ever to go into space,[18] thirty six[19] years later[20] when he was 77[20] he went back into orbit.

1. *Space* should not be capitalized.
2. The name of the dog should not be set off by commas.
3. This comma creates a run-on sentence (comma splice) as it stands alone between two independent clauses.
4. The name of the spacecraft *Sputnik II* should be italicized.
5. The prepositional phrase *in 1957* is not a sentence (it is not even a clause) and therefore cannot stand alone; it is a fragment.
6. The colon is incorrect; it does not belong between a verb and its object (here, the clause explaining what Laika proved).
7. A comma should follow most introductory phrases.
8. A gender-free term (*human*) should be used to avoid sexist language (*man*).
9. *Two hours* should not be hyphenated; these two words do not work together as a compound noun or adjective.
10. *Before he came back down* is a subordinate clause and cannot stand alone; it is a sentence fragment.
11. Use a comma between a name and a title that follows (*Alan Shepard, Jr.*).
12. If a sentence ends in an abbreviation that uses a period, do not add another period.
13. The whole sentence (*Less than..Shepard, Jr.*) is a fragment.
14. *Earth* should be capitalized when it refers to the planet.
15. *American* should also be capitalized.
16. Again, use a comma between a name and a title that follows (*John Glenn, Jr.*).
17. Again, capitalize *Earth* when it refers to the planet.
18. The comma here creates another run-on sentence.
19. Compound numbers between 20–100 should be hyphenated (*thirty-six*).
20. This non-essential clause (*when he was 77*) should be set off by commas.

Revision: These paragraphs can be revised in many ways. Notice how the sentences have been combined in this version to create variety and reduce wordiness.

The first living creature in space was a small dog named Laika who was sent into orbit on the *Sputnik II* in 1957. Laika completed seven orbits before the oxygen supply on the spacecraft ran out. Laika died, but not before she proved that living creatures could survive in space.

Three and a half years later, the first human went into orbit. Yuri Gagarin of the Soviet Union spent two hours in space before he came back down. Less than a month later, the first American astronaut, Alan Shepard, Jr., followed with the shortest space flight in history. His spacecraft didn't go into orbit; it simply rose to an altitude of 115 miles and then returned to Earth. John Glenn, Jr. was the first American to orbit the Earth a year later in 1962. He was also the oldest astronaut ever to go into space: thirty-six years later, when he was 77, he went back into orbit.